# Adam Ferguson

## Selected Philosophical Writings

### Edited and Introduced
### by Eugene Heath

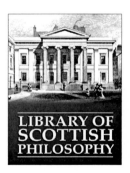

LIBRARY OF
SCOTTISH
PHILOSOPHY

*ia*

## IMPRINT ACADEMIC

Published in the UK by Imprint Academic
PO Box 200, Exeter EX5 5YX, UK

Published in the USA by Imprint Academic
Philosophy Documentation Center
PO Box 7147, Charlottesville, VA 22906-7147, USA

ISBN 978 184540 0569

A CIP catalogue record for this book is available from the
British Library and US Library of Congress

# Contents

# Series Editor's Note

The principal purpose of volumes in this series is not to provide scholars with accurate editions, but to make the writings of Scottish philosophers accessible to a new generation of modern readers in an attractively produced and competitively priced format. In accordance with this purpose, certain changes have been made to the original texts:

- Spelling and punctuation have been modernized.
- In some cases, the selected passages have been given new titles.
- Some original footnotes and references have not been included.
- Some extracts have been shortened from their original length.
- Quotations from Greek have been transliterated, and passages in foreign languages translated, or omitted altogether.

Care has been taken to ensure that in no instance do these amendments truncate the argument or alter the meaning intended by the original author. For readers who want to consult the original texts, full bibliographical details are provided for each extract.

**The Library of Scottish Philosophy** was originally an initiative of the Centre for the Study of Scottish Philosophy at the University of Aberdeen. The first six volumes, published in 2004, were commissioned with financial support from the Carnegie Trust for the Universities of Scotland, and the texts prepared for publication by Mr Jon Cameron, administrative and editorial assistant to the Centre. In 2006 the CSSP moved to Princeton where it became one of three research centers within the Special Collections of Princeton Theological Seminary. The next four volumes were prepared for publication by the new administrative and editorial assistant, Ms Elaine James.

## Acknowledgements

The CSSP gratefully acknowledges the support of the Carnegie Trust, the first class work of both Mr Cameron and Ms James, the enthusiasm and excellent service of the publisher Imprint Academic, and the permission of the University of Aberdeen Special Collections and Libraries to use the engraving of the *Faculty of Advocates* (1829) as the logo for the series.

*Gordon Graham,*
*Princeton, May 2007*

# *Editor's Note*

In the closing paragraph of his introductory remarks to the *Principles*, Ferguson states that "a work of this sort, to be properly executed, ought to be calculated, not for any particular class of readers, but for mankind." That, I take it, is also a purpose of this Library. In this instance, the editorial corrections to the original texts include some updated spellings and alterations of punctuation (where helpful), as well as some unification of paragraphs (in the *Institutes*). Italicizations are original. All omissions—excepting the omissions of some of Ferguson's very few footnotes—are indicated by ellipses. All inserted remarks are indicated by the use of brackets: [ ].

# Acknowledgements

I thank Gordon Graham, the Director of the Centre for the Study of Scottish Philosophy, for his leadership in publishing this and other volumes in this series. At Aberdeen, Jon Cameron performed, most expeditiously, the original scanning of these works. And Anthony Freeman at Imprint Academic has proven both kind and patient.

# *Introduction*

A philosopher and historian, Adam Ferguson occupies a unique place within eighteenth-century Scottish thought. A man of energy and verve, he made important contributions to social and moral theory, political philosophy, and to the study of history. Reared in the highlands of Scotland, he lived most of his life in the enlightenment world of Edinburgh, participating in the city's social clubs and in the broader public and intellectual life of his nation. Renown for *An Essay on the History of Civil Society* (1767), he also penned pamphlets on political issues, published works of moral and political philosophy, wrote a multi-volume history of the Roman Republic, and composed numerous manuscript essays. Distinguished by a moral and historical bent, his work is framed within a teleological outlook that upholds the importance of action and virtue in the emerging commercial society of the eighteenth century.

## I

Born in 1723, in Logierait, Perthshire, the young Adam was the last and ninth child of Mary Gordon and Adam Ferguson, a minister in the Church of Scotland. After graduating from St. Andrews in 1742, he began Divinity Studies there but soon moved to the University of Edinburgh, where he became friends with other divinity students, including William Robertson, Alexander Carlyle, and Hugh Blair. These individuals, who would be among the moderates within the Church of Scotland, would remain Ferguson's friends, and would be joined by such significant thinkers as David Hume and Adam Smith.

Ferguson had been born just over fifteen years after the Union of Parliaments (1707) ended the independence of Scotland. Not all were happy with the union, and in 1745 Ferguson witnesses the last major Jacobite uprising (to restore the exiled Stuart kings). A Gaelic speaker, he is appointed deputy-chaplain to a Highlander regiment, the Black Watch, having received an early ordination from the Church of Scotland. After eight years, Ferguson leaves the army, and by 1756 he is again in Edinburgh. There he publishes a defense of a citizens' militia, *Reflections previous to the Establishment of a Militia,* arguing that a militia—not permitted in Scotland since the uprising of 1745—is an important instrument for maintaining a vigorous public spirit among the citizenry. The alternative, an inactive citizenry and a standing professional army, would increase the risk of despotism.

In 1756, Ferguson marries Katherine Burnet, the niece of his friend, the chemist Joseph Black. The Fergusons have nine children, seven of whom survive infancy. Having left the ministry, in 1759 Ferguson secures a professorship, the Chair of Natural Philosophy at Edinburgh. In five years, he is able to shift to the more appropriate Chair of Pneumatics (philosophy of mind) and Moral Philosophy.

Ferguson's greatest work, *An Essay on the History of Civil Society*, appears in 1767, with six editions to follow. The book achieved a notable success: Excepting the estimation of his friend Hume, the *Essay* is highly regarded, and by the end of the eighteenth century the work has been translated into several European languages. Two years later Ferguson publishes *Institutes of Moral Philosophy for the use of Students in the College of Edinburgh*. Two editions follow, as well as translations into the major European languages.

A few years later, as the colonists in America call for independence. Ferguson and other Edinburgh moderates voice their opposition. In 1776, he pens a pamphlet against Richard Price's defense of the American Revolution. In another two years, Ferguson journeys to America with the Carlisle Commission to negotiate the loyalty of the colonies. The Commission's efforts bring nothing but controversy and rejection, and Ferguson returns to England by December. In 1779 he is back in Edinburgh.

At the age of 57 Ferguson suffers what may have been a mild stroke; he gradually recovers, perhaps as a result of dietary recommendations from Joseph Black. In 1783, his three-volume work, *The History of the Progress and Termination of the Roman Republic* is published. Later translated into French, German, and Italian, this may have been Ferguson's favorite work, even though it did not garner the favorable notice lavished on the *Essay*.

Citing ill health, he resigns his professorship in 1785, but the remainder of his long life is quite productive. In 1792 he publishes his *Principles of Moral and Political Science*, an elaboration of his university lectures. Not so well acclaimed as his earlier works, the two volumes nonetheless receive both German and French translations. Into the first decade of the nineteenth century, Ferguson continues to write, composing drafts of essays—ranging across political, historical, moral, and aesthetic topics—that seek to resolve and elaborate on themes undertaken in earlier works. By the fall of 1809, having outlived his wife and many friends, he moves to St. Andrews. In February of 1816, a few months from his ninety-third birthday, he succumbs to fever and dies. He is buried in the seaside cemetery adjoining the cathedral ruins of St. Andrews. In one draft of his epitaph, Ferguson included these words: "We whose Bones are buried here have trod like you this Stage of Earth And seen these works of God from Earth to Heaven. The Sight is Glorious[;] it is now your Turn[.] Enjoy it and be glad."

## II

In all of Ferguson's work, there reigns an overarching moral point, that the individual should bring to completion the qualities of human nature productive of virtue and happiness. Towards the close of a dialogue written late in life, and included in this collection, he affirms that, "the important and genuine question of moral philosophy [is] *de finibus*, or what is the end." The idea of a proper end resonates throughout his works and helps lift Ferguson's voice to a unique place in eighteenth-century Scottish philosophy. His focus on history, his emphasis on action and circumstance, his contention that virtue and happiness are the same, and his prescient understanding of how one's concerns may become so narrow, so focused on idle pleasure, that one is alienated from self and society, are themes that engage us today.

Ferguson's thought reflects a variety of influences. Acquainted with Highland clans and Edinburgh elites, he was the child of a minister, a student of divinity, and a chaplain. His religious training, not to mention his own reading of natural law theorists, inclines Ferguson to the acceptance of the clear evidence of basic moral propositions. Yet his outlook is also preeminently historical and imbued with a sense of contingency. Though he holds the human being, individually and socially, to be capable of development and improvement, he does not argue for inevitable progress or for some politics of perfection, to be wrought at the expense of liberty or in blindness to circumstance. The progress of society is achieved less by lawgivers than by the unintended accumulation of the actions of agents engaged in specific situations. In tracing the emergence of polished society, enriched by the goods of commerce, Ferguson inclines towards classical liberalism. But he also counsels caution in the face of modern pressure to retreat from public ends and embrace only private tasks and pleasures.

It is not unreasonable to understand Ferguson's outlook as expressing, in significant part, a unity of Christianity and Stoicism. Ferguson had read widely in the texts of ancient Greece and Rome and was, by his own admission, heavily influenced by Stoic thought, referring frequently to Roman thinkers. The Stoic emphasis on the reasoned order of the universe, the sufficiency of virtue to happiness, and the way in which virtues, like skills, might be honed and progressively developed, are doctrines easily unified with the providential design of God. Thus, virtue and self-interest do not conflict, for it is in one's interest to acquire non-material qualities of excellence, including a concern for the well-being of others.

Having begun his professorial career teaching natural philosophy, Ferguson, like most Scots of his circle, was acquainted with currents of modern science, with its appeals to experiment and law, including Francis Bacon's charge to observe, describe, classify, and systematize the regularities of nature. Ferguson nonetheless recognizes that if one is to develop a moral science, then one must study human nature and society. He is one of several eighteenth-century thinkers who seek a natural history of the human species as the basis of further progress in knowledge. The appeal to natural history also reflects the natural law jurisprudence of such seventeenth-century thinkers as Hugo Grotius and Samuel Pufendorf, each of whom (like Lord Shaftesbury and Frances Hutcheson) recognized an innate human sociability — a sociability rejected by the most famous of contract theorists, Thomas Hobbes. Ferguson was also acquainted with Jean-Jacques Rousseau's account — in his *Discourse on the Origins and Foundations of Inequality,* 1755 — of man's development from a primitive state of nature into a corrupt social state, but Ferguson regards Rousseau's account as too speculative. A more signal influence on Ferguson is Montesquieu. In Part I of his *Essay,* Ferguson admits, "When I recollect what the President Montesquieu has written, I am at a loss to tell, why I should treat of human affairs." Montesquieu's *Considerations on the Causes of the Romans' Greatness and Decline* (1734) and *The Spirit of the Laws* (1748) contain explanations — of law and the emergence of modern European states — that appeal to the interaction of human nature with circumstance. Enamored of the liberty enjoyed by the English, and of the virtuous love of country manifest in ancient Greece and Rome, Montesequieu, like Ferguson, worried that citizens might pursue private rather than public good, allowing thereby a decline into despotism.

## III

This collection includes selections from all six parts of Ferguson's richest work, *An Essay on the History of Civil Society.* The "civil society" to which the title refers is a whole society governed by political institutions, at least of the sort that are not despotic. The history that the title promises is not a factual narrative of specific events but a reconstruction of the gradual emergence of civil society from rude or less polished states. This sort of history, also found in the work of other eighteenth-century Scots (such as Lord Kames and Adam Smith), is what Dugald Stewart, a student of both Ferguson and Smith, would later describe as "theoretical or conjectural history."

Ferguson's natural or conjectural history begins with an account of human nature and the basic circumstances of society, emphasizing what is typical about human beings and their interactions. The features of human nature, like the facts of society, are drawn from experience and observation, with examples elicited from Asia and from the reports of travelers and missionaries to North America. The narrative does not commence in some primordial state of nature from which a society emerges via social contract. For Ferguson, we are forever in a state of nature: We are always found in groups and it is only within these groups that we may realize our natural qualities. The propensities of human nature, not reducible to some single motivation, include inclinations to self-preservation, to affiliate and identify with a larger whole, and to communicate to others one's passions and sentiments. Ferguson also notes a complementary disposition to distinguish oneself in opposition to others, a tendency instrumental in the development of civil society and the maintenance of liberty. As Ferguson will confess, "he who has never struggled with his fellow-creatures, is a stranger to half the sentiments of mankind." We also manifest a natural desire to improve and excel—a "principle of progression" or ambition—the proper object of which is the realization of moral qualities.

Others in the eighteenth-century, such as Adam Smith, describe how society develops through stages (typically, four). Ferguson offers a summary account of three stages—the savage, the barbaric, and the polished—each of which manifests a particular economic, social, and moral character. However, he does not relate the causes that move us from one state to another, nor does he specify any mechanism of change. Features present in polished commercial societies may not appear in earlier societies, and elements of conduct that flourish in earlier states may not survive in a modern state. Within the savage state, for example, individuals are distinguished by natural ability, age or sex, but otherwise this stage manifests no inequality, no government, and no property, the latter institution emerging only in the barbaric stage.

Ferguson rejects the idea that government could have been designed from a plan or that it requires some great lawgiver of uncanny foresight. In general, he refers to social structures and regularities as emerging gradually or by degrees: Complex and orderly outcomes arise as the cumulative and unintended effect of the interaction of individuals who are motivated more by felt instincts and discrete beliefs than systematic plans and ideas. As he explains, "Mankind, in following the present sense of their minds, in striving to remove inconveniences, or to gain apparent and contiguous advantages, arrive at ends which even their imagination could not anticipate...." Among the outcomes described as unintended are language, property, laws, traits and dispositions, as well as the very ethos of a social order. For example, the disposition to industry, or industriousness, is acquired by "many and by slow degrees", just as commerce also brings about the virtues of punctuality, enterprise, and liberality. (The idea of the spontaneous emergence of institutions and complex regularities is also incorporated into the theories of other eighteenth-century thinkers, such as Bernard Mandeville, and Hume. Adam Smith's reference to the "invisible hand" metaphorically summarizes the process of spontaneous emergence.)

Even if beneficent improvements result spontaneously, it is possible nonetheless that a society becomes corrupt and declines into despotism. Having adumbrated how the law is a response to the emergence of property, and having argued that liberty is preserved by opposition and pluralism, Ferguson proceeds, in the latter parts of the *Essay*, to consider how a decline may occur. Thus, he remains aware that within the freedom of commercial society, perfection is not possible. Not only may the very specialization of labor lead to fragmentation and the loss of a common perspective, but property and wealth may be confused with virtue or mistaken for happiness itself. Although the division of labor improves the quality and quantity of goods, some increasingly specialized vocations require little of the mind or heart, only repetitious physical acts. To Ferguson's chagrin, governing itself becomes a specialized occupation, rather than an obligation of all citizens.

Some scholars suggest that Ferguson believes there to be some inherent conflict between commercial life and virtue. Yet it is not clear that this is Ferguson's position. In his discussion of luxury, for example, Ferguson rejects the view that the mere existence of luxury goods is corrupting or that vice is proportioned to luxury. He does suggest, as has been noted, that the citizenry should be not only involved in the defense of the nation (a militia) but also engaged in social and political concerns that extend beyond the particularities of trade or vocation. However, when the enjoyment of luxury leads to a neglect of the "political spirit", corruption results.

The good life, therefore, is found not simply in trade but in activities embedded within a moral framework. The true good is virtue — this is what perfects us. If we lose this moral perspective or the will to defend it, then we are corrupted from our true ends. A degeneration into despotism may proceed slowly and insensibly. What is required is the spirit to resist:

> Liberty is a right which every individual must be ready to vindicate for himself, and which he who pretends to bestow as a favor has by that very act in reality denied. Even political establishments, though they appear to be independent of the will and arbitration of men, cannot be relied on for the preservation of freedom; they may nourish, but should not supersede that firm and resolute spirit, with which the liberal mind is always prepared to resist indignities, and to refer its safety to itself.[1]

## IV

Ferguson's pedagogical practice involved speaking from notes rather than reading lectures. In 1769 he published a finished outline of these notes, *The Institutes of Moral Philosophy*. Along with the introductory remarks, included here, the *Institutes* includes five parts, the first delineating the natural history of humankind, the second an account of mind (to include the understanding, will, and passions). The remaining three sections focus on God, moral laws, and jurisprudence. In the introduction, one glimpses Ferguson's empiricist outlook, with its Baconion inductivism and its Newtonian appeal to law. The objects of knowledge are either facts or rules, whether empirical or normative. A general rule

---

[1]   *Essay*, VI.V, "Of Corruption, as it tends to Political Slavery".

or natural law either explains some particular fact (empirical science) or serves to guide conduct (morals). Ferguson challenges the Cartesian notion—carried forth by John Locke and Hume—that knowledge and thought are to be explained by such notions as "idea, image, or picture." These, Ferguson suggests, are metaphorical and "cannot explain human knowledge or thought", conclusions redolent of the common sense realism of Thomas Reid. As to facts not secured within some natural or moral law, these are the province of history. Since the general laws of morality rest on ultimate facts about human beings and society, history is the very foundation of our knowledge of mind and morals. In the third section, Ferguson affirms that belief in God is universal, so this belief is either part of human nature or suggested by some universal feature of life. After asserting that we perceive, plainly, final causes in nature, Ferguson explains how the goodness of God is compatible with physical or moral evil.

After the publication of the *Essay* and *Institutes*, Ferguson's next great work is a traditional narrative history, not a conjectural one. His *History of the Progress and Termination of the Roman Republic*, delineating how a republican government degenerates into despotism, joins other great eighteenth-century histories, including David Hume's *The History of England* (1754–1762), William Robertson's *History of Scotland* (1759) and his *History of Charles V* (1769), and Edward Gibbon's classic, *The Decline and Fall of the Roman Empire* (1776–88). A brief excerpt of Ferguson's *History* is included in this collection to remind the reader of the breadth of his interests and to illustrate how Ferguson understood the distinct philosophies of Epicureanism and Stoicism to have affected the Romans.

Ferguson, of course, favors the Stoic doctrine, and he admits as much in the Introduction to *Principles of Moral and Political Science*. His aim, in these two volumes, is "not novelty, but benefit to the student." Any normative benefit requires that one recognize the ultimate facts of human nature and society, gleaned from history and experience. These are taken up in the first volume, the second addressing normative obligations. In his account of the operations of mind, Ferguson discusses four sources of knowledge. Conscious reflection and sensory perception are primary sources, but testimony and inference are also crucial (though each is dependent on a prior act of consciousness or perception). Ferguson's account of perception recalls, again, Reid's realism: In the case of a "clear and determinate" act of consciousness or perception, it is not necessary to search for additional reasons or evidence. Ferguson points out, for example, that one need not seek, as René Descartes had suggested, for a reason to establish one's own existence.

Of course, for Ferguson, the goodness of human existence lies not so much in the contemplative as in the active life. However, action need not assume only a rational or purposive form, but may include individual and social habits. These render us at ease in a variety of circumstances, and help to ensure a regularity and stability that bonds individuals within a whole. Along with his discussion of habit, Ferguson revisits and extends his discussion of ambition — "the desire of something better than is possessed at present." Unlike Hume or Smith, who also take up the topic, Ferguson focuses on a mode of proper ambition whose motivating force draws less from the acclaim of spectators than from a sense of excellence discernable within any field of endeavor. Even when ambition is not aimed toward its true end, it remains a powerful and generally beneficent propensity.

Our true moral qualities are not, however, reducible to habit or custom. It is by rational intelligence that we discern distinctions between moral excellence and defect, as they exist in qualities of character (wisdom, justice, self-control, courage, and benevolence). Since our judgments neither reflect any agreement or convention, or reduce to some sentiment or aggregation of sentiments, Ferguson is an objectivist or realist about morals. Yet he maintains that the act of discernment also generates, in some way, a moral sentiment (which would appear to affect motivation and to find expression in praise or blame). His account is not as full as one might wish, but he obviously rejects, both here and elsewhere, some of the leading eighteenth-century accounts of moral judgment, including Samuel Clarke's rationalism, utilitarianism (which Ferguson elsewhere attributes to Hume), Smith's conception of sympathy and the impartial spectator, and the doctrine of moral sense (which, he suggests, is but a figurative expression).

In the last selection included from the *Principles,* Ferguson contends that compulsion should be utilized only to protect a right. He does not explicitly preclude the use of compulsion to obtain other goods but, he maintains, it is an inadequate means for achieving religious or moral ends: "Benefits extorted by *force* are robberies, not acts of beneficence." The rights to be protected may be understood as personal or real, natural or artificial. All natural rights are personal, but real rights, including those of property, are artificial. Property may be established either by occupancy or by labor. In the case of property secured by labor, if one expends one's labor on some unoccupied or otherwise unappropriated resource, then so long as one's effort is "productive of some permanent effect", one secures a right to that effect. This suggests that when one's labor generates a property right, one's right does not extend to the *substance* underlying one's productive *effects!* As a solution, Ferguson proposes that if the substance cannot be occupied without encroachment on the effects, then one may exclude others from the substance.

After the publication of his *Principles,* Ferguson continued to write, and between 1799 and 1810, he penned numerous essays (including two dialogues), many of which were left in a fragmentary state. The last entry in this collection is a more polished dialogue that revisits the discussion, in the *Principles,* on moral judgment. It is largely a matter of speculation as to whether this dialogue is based on an actual conversation or is a fictional or imaginative reconstruction. There are three characters in conversation: General Robert Clerk, David Hume, and Adam Smith. As a matter of fact, General Clerk served with Ferguson and Hume on an ill-starred military expedition in 1746. It would appear that Ferguson intends Clerk to give voice to his (Ferguson's) views, though the General dismisses brusquely the work of both Hume and Smith. Clerk portrays Hume's moral theory as utilitarian, though it would seem to be something more than that. Clerk also suggests that Hume holds that moral approval attaches to the external consequences of one's intentions—a suggestion that fails to capture Hume's view that we judge an intention when it tends to give rise to certain effects. When Adam Smith enters he is quickly apprised of Clerk's view of his moral theory—"a heap of absolute nonsense." Clerk follows this rude dismissal with several interesting reasons as to why Smith's use of sympathy—the agreement of passions or sentiments between spectator and agent—could scarcely generate a moral standard or a moral sentiment.

## V

Ferguson achieved wide fame in his time. Of all of Ferguson's works, it is the *Essay* that has wielded the greatest influence, for it was read well into the nineteenth century, especially among German readers, including G.W.F. Hegel and Karl Marx. For many contemporary philosophers, Ferguson's legacy has faded. Nonetheless, his readers still include philosophers, and a wide array of sociologists, political theorists, and historians. His insights, observations, concerns, and arguments remain valuable for all. His recognition of the contingencies of circumstance and history, his observation of the social (and anti-social) aspects of human beings, his unrelenting adherence to the idea of improvement, his advocacy of a life lived vigorously and with an eye to the good, and his attention to the interplay between culture and commerce, alert us to the tension between the demands of progress and the facts of imperfectability. That the establishments of society often emerge in an unintended fashion serves as a useful reminder that systematizing reason has its limits, that not everything is possible, and that good societies require good persons more than wise legislators—citizens who recognize excellence, understand the limits of history, and possess the will to act.

# An Essay on the History of Civil Society

## 1767[1]

---

**PART I**
**Of the General Characteristics of Human Nature**

*Section I: Of the question relating to the State of Nature*

Natural productions are generally formed by degrees. Vegetables grow
from a tender shoot, and animals from an infant state. The latter being
destined to act, extend their operations as their powers increase: they
exhibit a progress in what they perform, as well as in the faculties they
acquire. This progress in the case of man is continued to a greater extent
than in that of any other animal. Not only the individual advances from
infancy to manhood, but the species itself from rudeness to civilization.
Hence the supposed departure of mankind from the state of their nature;
hence our conjectures and different opinions of what man must have
been in the first age of his being. The poet, the historian, and the moralist,
frequently allude to this ancient time; and under the emblems of gold, or
of iron, represent a condition, and a manner of life, from which mankind
have either degenerated, or on which they have greatly improved. On
either supposition, the first state of our nature must have borne no
resemblance to what men have exhibited in any subsequent period; historical monuments, even of the earliest date, are to be considered as nov-
elties; and the most common establishments of human society are to be
classed among the encroachments which fraud, oppression, or a busy

---

[1]   *An Essay on the History of Civil Society*, Duncan Forbes, ed. (Edinburgh: Edinburgh
      University Press, 1966). Forbes' edition is based on the first (1767) edition.

invention, have made upon the reign of nature, by which the chief of our grievances or blessings were equally withheld.

Among the writers who have attempted to distinguish, in the human character, its original qualities, and to point out the limits between nature and art, some have represented mankind in their first condition, as possessed of mere animal sensibility, without any exercise of the faculties that render them superior to the brutes, without any political union, without any means of explaining their sentiments, and even without possessing any of the apprehensions and passions which the voice and the gesture are so well fitted to express. Others have made the state of nature to consist in perpetual wars, kindled by competition for dominion and interest, where every individual had a separate quarrel with his kind, and where the presence of a fellow-creature was the signal of battle.

The desire of laying the foundation of a favorite system, or a fond expectation, perhaps, that we may be able to penetrate the secrets of nature, to the very source of existence, have, on this subject, led to many fruitless inquiries, and given rise to many wild suppositions. Among the various qualities which mankind possess, we select one or a few particulars on which to establish a theory, and in framing our account of what man was in some imaginary state of nature, we overlook what he has always appeared within the reach of our own observation, and in the records of history.

In every other instance, however, the natural historian thinks himself obliged to collect facts, not to offer conjectures. When he treats of any particular species of animals, he supposes, that their present dispositions and instincts are the same they originally had, and that their present manner of life is a continuance of their first destination. He admits, that his knowledge of the material system of the world consists in a collection of facts, or at most, in general tenets derived from particular observations and experiments. It is only in what relates to himself, and in matters the most important, and the most easily known, that he substitutes hypothesis instead of reality, and confounds the provinces of imagination and reason, of poetry and science.

But without entering any farther on questions either in moral or physical subjects, relating to the manner or to the origin of our knowledge; without any disparagement to that subtlety which would analyze every sentiment, and trace every mode of being to its source; it may be safely affirmed, that the character of man, as he now exists, that the laws of this animal and intellectual system, on which his happiness now depends, deserve our principal study; and that general principles relating to this, or any other subject, are useful only so far as they are founded on just observation, and lead to the knowledge of important consequences, or so far as they enable us to act with success when we would apply either the intellectual or the physical powers of nature, to the great purposes of human life.

If both the earliest and the latest accounts collected from every quarter of the earth, represent mankind as assembled in troops and companies; and the individual always joined by affection to one party, while he is possibly opposed to another; employed in the exercise of recollection and foresight; inclined to communicate his own sentiments, and to be made acquainted with those of others; these facts must be admitted as the foundation of all our reasoning relative to man. His mixed disposition to friendship or enmity, his reason, his use of language and articulate sounds, like the shape and the erect position of his body, are to be considered as so many attributes of his nature: they are to be retained in his description, as the wing and the paw are in that of the eagle and the lion, and as different degrees of fierceness, vigilance, timidity, or speed, are made to occupy a place in the natural history of different animals.

If the question be put [as to] what the mind of man could perform, when left to itself, and without the aid of any foreign direction, we are to look for our answer in the history of mankind. Particular experiments which have been found so useful in establishing the principles of other sciences, could probably, on this subject, teach us nothing important, or new. We are to take the history of every active being from his conduct in the situation to which he is formed, not from his appearance in any forced or uncommon condition; a wild man therefore, caught in the woods, where he had always lived apart from his species, is a singular instance, not a specimen of any general character. As the anatomy of an eye which had never received the impressions of light, or that of an ear which had never felt the impulse of sounds, would probably exhibit defects in the very structure of the organs themselves, arising from their not being applied to their proper functions; so any particular case of this sort would only show in what degree the powers of apprehension and sentiment could exist where they had not been employed, and what would be the defects and imbecilities of a heart in which the emotions that pertain to society had never been felt.

Mankind are to be taken in groups, as they have always subsisted. The history of the individual is but a detail of the sentiments and thoughts he has entertained in the view of his species, and every experiment relative to this subject should be made with entire societies, not with single men. We have every reason, however, to believe, that in the case of such an experiment made, we shall suppose, with a colony of children transplanted from the nursery, and left to form a society apart, untaught, and undisciplined, we should only have the same things repeated, which, in so many different parts of the earth, have been transacted already. The members of our little society would feed and sleep, would herd together and play, would have a language of their own, would quarrel and divide, would be to one another the most important objects of the scene, and, in the ardor of their friendships and competitions, would overlook their personal danger, and suspend the care of their self-preservation. Has not the human race been planted like the colony in question? Who has directed their course? Whose instruction have they heard? Or whose example have they followed?

Nature, therefore, we shall presume, having given to every animal its mode of existence, its dispositions and manner of life, has dealt equally with those of the human race; and the natural historian who would collect the properties of this species, may fill up every article now, as well as he could have done in any former age. Yet one property by which man is distinguished, has been sometimes overlooked in the account of his nature, or has only served to mislead our attention. In other classes of animals, the individual advances from infancy to age or maturity; and he attains, in the compass of a single life, to all the perfection his nature can reach. But, in the human kind, the species has a progress as well as the individual; they build in every subsequent age on foundations formerly laid; and, in a succession of years, tend to a perfection in the application of their faculties, to which the aid of long experience is required, and to which many generations must have combined their endeavors. We observe the progress they have made; we distinctly enumerate many of its steps; we can trace them back to a distant antiquity; of which no record remains, nor any monument is preserved, to inform us what were the openings of this wonderful scene. The consequence is, that instead of attending to the character of our species, where the particulars are vouched by the surest authority, we endeavor to trace it through ages and scenes unknown; and, instead of supposing that the beginning of our story was nearly of a piece with the sequel, we think ourselves warranted to reject every circumstance of our present condition and frame, as adventitious, and foreign to our nature. The progress of mankind from a supposed state of animal sensibility, to the attainment of reason, to the use of language, and to the habit of society, has been accordingly painted with a force of imagination, and its steps have been marked with a boldness of invention, that would tempt us to admit, among the materials of history, the suggestions of fancy, and to receive, perhaps, as the model of our nature in its original state, some of the animals whose shape has the greatest resemblance to ours.[2]

It would be ridiculous to affirm, as a discovery, that the species of the horse was probably never the same with that of the lion; yet, in opposition to what has dropped from the pens of eminent writers, we are obliged to observe, that men have always appeared among animals a distinct and a superior race; that neither the possession of similar organs, nor the approximation of shape, nor the use of the hand, nor the continued intercourse with this sovereign artist, has enabled any other species to blend their nature or their inventions with his; that in his rudest state, he is found to be above them; and in his greatest degeneracy, never descends to their level. He is, in short, a man in every condition; and we can learn nothing of his nature from the analogy of other ani-

---

[2]    Rousseau, *On the Origin of Inequality among Men.*

mals. If we would know him, we must attend to himself, to the course of his life, and the tenor of his conduct. With him society appears to be as old as the individual, and the use of the tongue as universal as that of the hand or the foot. If there was a time in which he had his acquaintance with his own species to make, and his faculties to acquire, it is a time of which we have no record, and in relation to which our opinions can serve no purpose, and are supported by no evidence.

We are often tempted into these boundless regions of ignorance or conjecture, by a fancy which delights in creating rather than in merely retaining the forms which are presented before it; we are the dupes of a subtlety, which promises to supply every defect of our knowledge, and, by filling up a few blanks in the story of nature, pretends to conduct our apprehension nearer to the source of existence. On the credit of a few observations we are apt to presume, that the secret may soon be laid open, and that what is termed *wisdom* in nature, may be referred to operation of physical powers. We forget that physical powers, employed in succession, and combined to a salutary purpose, constitute those very proofs of design from which we infer the existence of God; and that this truth being once admitted, we are no longer to search for the source of existence; we can only collect the laws which the author of nature has established; and in our latest as well as our earliest discoveries, only come to perceive a mode of creation or providence before unknown.

We speak of art as distinguished from nature; but art itself is natural to man. He is in some measure the artificer of his own frame, as well as his fortune, and is destined, from the first age of his being, to invent and contrive. He applies the same talents to a variety of purposes, and acts nearly the same part in very different scenes. He would be always improving on his subject, and he carries this intention wherever he moves, through the streets of the populous city, or the wilds of the forest. While he appears equally fitted to every condition, he is upon this account unable to settle in any. At once obstinate and fickle, he complains of innovations, and is never sated with novelty. He is perpetually busied in reformations, and is continually wedded to his errors. If he dwell in a cave, he would improve it into a cottage; if he has already built, he would still build to a greater extent. But he does not propose to make rapid and hasty transitions; his steps are progressive and slow; and his force, like the power of a spring, silently presses on every resistance; an effect is sometimes produced before the cause is perceived; and with all his talent for projects, his work is often accomplished before the plan is devised. It appears, perhaps, equally difficult to retard or to quicken his pace; if the projector complain he is tardy, the moralist thinks him unstable; and whether his motions be rapid or slow, the scenes of human affairs perpetually change in his management: his emblem is a passing stream, not a stagnating pool. We may desire to direct his love of improvement to its proper object, we may wish for stability of conduct; but we mistake human nature, if we wish for a termination of labor, or a scene of repose.

The occupations of men, in every condition, bespeak their freedom of choice, their various opinions, and the multiplicity of wants by which they are urged: but they enjoy, or endure, with a sensibility, or a phlegm, which are nearly the same in every situation. They possess the shores of the Caspian, or the Atlantic, by a different tenure, but with equal ease. On the one they are fixed to the soil, and seem to be formed for settlement, and the accommodation of cities: The names they bestow on a nation, and on its territory, are the same. On the other they are mere animals of passage, prepared to roam on the face of the earth, and with their herds, in search of new pasture and favorable seasons, to follow the sun in his annual course.

Man finds his lodgment alike in the cave, the cottage, and the palace; and his subsistence equally in the woods, in the dairy, or the farm. He assumes the distinction of titles, equipage, and dress; he devises regular systems of government, and a complicated body of laws: or, naked in the woods, has no badge of superiority but the strength of his limbs and the sagacity of his mind; no rule of conduct but choice; no tie with his fellow-creatures but affection, the love of company, and the desire of safety. Capable of a great variety of arts, yet dependent on none in particular for the preservation of his being; to whatever length he has carried his artifice, there he seems to enjoy the conveniences that suit his nature, and to have found the condition to which he is destined. The tree which an American, on the banks of the Orinoco, has chosen to climb for the retreat, and the lodging of his family, is to him a convenient dwelling. The sofa, the vaulted dome, and the colonnade, do not more effectually content their native inhabitant.

If we are asked therefore, where the state of nature is to be found, we may answer: It is here; and it matters not whether we are understood to speak in the island of Great Britain, at the Cape of Good Hope, or the Straits of Magellan. While this active being is in the train of employing his talents, and of operating on the subjects around him, all situations are equally natural. If we are told, that vice, at least, is contrary to nature, we may answer: It is worse; it is folly and wretchedness. But if nature is only opposed to art, in what situation of the human race are the footsteps of art unknown? In the condition of the savage, as well as in that of the citizen, are many proofs of human invention; and in either is not any permanent station, but a mere stage through which this traveling being is destined to pass. If the palace be unnatural, the cottage is so no less; and the highest refinements of political and moral apprehension, are not more artificial in their kind, than the first operations of sentiment and reason.

If we admit that man is susceptible of improvement, and has in himself a principle of progression, and a desire of perfection, it appears improper to say, that he has quitted the state of his nature, when he has begun to proceed; or that he finds a station for which he was not intended, while, like other animals, he only follows the disposition, and employs the powers that nature has given.

The latest efforts of human invention are but a continuation of certain devices which were practiced in the earliest ages of the world, and in the rudest state of mankind. What the savage projects, or observes, in the forest, are the steps which led nations, more advanced, from the architecture of the cottage to that of the palace, and conducted the human mind from the perceptions of sense, to the general conclusions of science.

Acknowledged defects are to man in every condition a matter of dislike. Ignorance and imbecility are objects of contempt; penetration and conduct give eminence, and procure esteem. Whither should his feelings and apprehensions on these subjects lead him? To a progress, no doubt, in which the savage, as well as the philosopher, is engaged; in which they have made different advances, but in which their ends are the same. The admiration Cicero entertained for literature, eloquence, and civil accomplishments, was not more real than that of a Scythian for such a measure of similar endowments as his own apprehension could reach. "Were I to boast", says a Tartar prince, "it would be of that wisdom I have received from God. For as, on the one hand, I yield to none in the conduct of war, in the disposition of armies, whether of horse or of foot, and in directing the movements of great or small bodies; so, on the other, I have my talent in writing, inferior perhaps only to those who inhabit the great cities of Persia or India. Of other nations, unknown to me, I do not speak."

Man may mistake the objects of his pursuit; he may misapply his industry, and misplace his improvements. If under a sense of such possible errors, he would find a standard by which to judge of his own proceedings, and arrive at the best state of his nature, he cannot find it perhaps in the practice of any individual, or of any nation whatever; not even in the sense of the majority, or the prevailing opinion of his kind. He must look for it in the best conceptions of his understanding, in the best movements of his heart; he must thence discover what is the perfection and the happiness of which he is capable. He will find, on the scrutiny, that the proper state of his nature, taken in this sense, is not a condition from which mankind are forever removed, but one to which they may now attain; not prior to the exercise of their faculties, but procured by their just application.

Of all the terms that we employ in treating of human affairs those of *natural* and *unnatural* are the least determinate in their meaning. Opposed to affectation, frowardness, or any other defect of the temper of character, the natural is an epithet of praise; but employed to specify a conduct which proceeds from the nature of man, can serve to distinguish nothing: for all the actions of men are equally the result of their nature. At most, this language can only refer to the general and prevailing sense or practice of mankind; and the purpose of every important inquiry on this subject may be served by the use of a language equally familiar and more precise. What is just, or unjust? What is happy, or wretched, in the manners of men? What, in their various situations, is favorable or adverse to their amiable qualities? [These] are questions to which we may expect a satisfactory answer; and whatever may have been the original state of our species, it is of more importance to know the condition to which we ourselves should aspire, than that which our ancestors may be supposed to have left.

## Section II: Of the principles of Self-preservation

If in human nature there are qualities by which it is distinguished from every other part of the animal creation, men are themselves in different climates and in different ages greatly diversified. So far as we are able to account for this diversity on principles either moral or physical, we perform a task of great curiosity or signal utility. It appears necessary, however, that we attend to the universal qualities of our nature, before we regard its varieties, or attempt to explain differences consisting in the unequal possession or application of dispositions and powers that are in some measure common to all mankind.

Man, like the other animals, has certain instinctive propensities, which, prior to the perception of pleasure or pain, and prior to the experience of what is pernicious or useful, lead him to perform many functions of nature relative to himself and to his fellow-creatures. He has one set of dispositions which refer to his animal preservation, and to the continuance of his race; another which lead to society, and by enlisting him on the side of one tribe or community, frequently engage him in war and contention with the rest of mankind. His powers of discernment, or his intellectual faculties, which, under the appellation of *reason,* are distinguished from the analogous endowments of other animals, refer to the objects around him, either as they are subjects of mere knowledge, or as they are subjects of approbation or censure. He is formed not only to know, but likewise to admire and to contemn; and these proceedings of his mind have a principal reference to his own character, and to that of his fellow creatures, as being the subjects on which he is chiefly concerned to distinguish what is right from what is wrong. He enjoys his felicity likewise on certain fixed and determinate conditions; and either as an individual apart, or as a member of civil society, must take a particular course in order to reap the advantages of his nature. He is, withal, in a very high degree susceptible of habits; and can, by forbearance or exercise, so far weaken, confirm, or even diversify his talents, and his dispositions, as to appear, in a great measure, the arbiter of his own rank in nature, and the author of all the varieties which are exhibited in the actual history of his species. The universal characteristics, in the mean time, to which we have now referred, must, when we would treat of any part of this history, constitute the first subject of our attention; and they require not only to be enumerated, but to be distinctly considered.

The dispositions which refer to the preservation of the individual, while they continue to operate in the manner of instinctive desires, are nearly the same in man that they are in the other animals, but in him they are sooner or later combined with reflection and foresight; they give rise to his apprehensions on the subject of property, and make him acquainted with that object of care which he calls his interest. Without the instincts which teach the beaver and the squirrel, the ant and the bee, to make up their little hoards for winter, at first improvident, and, where no immediate object of passion is near, addicted to sloth, he becomes, in process of time, the great store master among animals. He finds in a provision of wealth, which he is probably never to employ, an object of his greatest solicitude, and the principal idol of his mind. He apprehends a relation between his person and his property, which renders what he calls his own in a manner a part of himself, a constituent of his rank, his condition, and his character, in which, independent of any real enjoyment, he may be fortunate or unhappy; and, independent of any personal merit, he may be an object of consideration or neglect; and in which he may be wounded and injured, while his person is safe, and every want of his nature completely supplied.

In these apprehensions, while other passions only operate occasionally, the interested find the object of their ordinary cares; their motive to the practice of mechanic and commercial arts; their temptation to trespass on the laws of justice; and, when extremely corrupted, the price of their prostitutions, and the standard of their opinions on the subject of good and of evil. Under this influence, they would enter, if not restrained by the laws of civil society, on a scene of violence or meanness, which would exhibit our species, by turns, under an aspect more terrible and odious, or more vile and contemptible, than that of any animal which inherits the earth.

Although the consideration of interest is founded on the experience of animal wants and desires, its object is not to gratify any particular appetite, but to secure the means of gratifying all; and it imposes frequently a restraint on the very desires from which it arose, more powerful and more severe than those of religion or duty. It arises from the principles of self-preservation in the human frame; but is a corruption, or at least a partial result, of those principles, and is upon many accounts very improperly termed *self-love.*

Love is an affection which carries the attention of the mind beyond itself, and has a quality, which we call *tenderness,* that never can accompany the considerations of interest. This affection being a complacency and a continued satisfaction in its object, independent of any external event, it has, in the midst of disappointment and sorrow, pleasures and triumphs unknown to those who act without any regard to their fellow-creatures; and in every change of condition, it continues entirely distinct from the sentiments which we feel on the subject of personal success or adversity. But as the care a man entertains for his own interest, and the attention his affection makes him pay to that of another, may have similar effects, the one on his own fortune, the other on that of his friend, we confound the principles from which he acts; we suppose that they are the same in kind, only referred to different objects; and we not only misapply the name of love, in conjunction with self, but, in a manner tending to degrade our nature, we limit the aim of this supposed selfish affection to the securing or accumulating the constituents of interest, or the means of mere animal life.

It is somewhat remarkable, that notwithstanding men value themselves so much on qualities of the mind, on parts, learning and wit, on courage, generosity, and honor, those men are still supposed to be in the highest degree selfish or attentive to themselves, who are most careful of animal life, and who are least mindful of rendering that life an object worthy of care. It will be difficult, however, to tell why a good understanding, a resolute and generous mind, should not, by every man in his senses, be reckoned as much parts of himself, as either his stomach or his palate, and much more than his estate or his dress. The epicure, who consults his physician, how he may restore his relish for food, and by creating an appetite, may increase the means of enjoyment, might at least with an equal regard to himself, consult how he might strengthen his affection to a parent or a child, to his country or to mankind; and it is probable that an appetite of this sort would prove a source of enjoyment not less than the former.

By our supposed selfish maxims, notwithstanding, we generally exclude from among the objects of our personal cares, many of the happier and more respectable qualities of human nature. We consider affection and courage as mere follies, that lead us to neglect or expose ourselves; we make wisdom consist in a regard to our interest; and without explaining what interest means, we would have it understood as the only reasonable motive of action with mankind. There is even a system of philosophy founded upon tenets of this sort, and such is our opinion of what men are likely to do upon selfish principles, that we think it must have a tendency very dangerous to virtue. But the errors of this system do not consist so much in general principles, as in their particular applications; not so much in teaching men to regard themselves, as in leading them to forget that their happiest affections, their candor, and their independence of mind, are in reality parts of themselves. And the adversaries of this supposed selfish philosophy, where it makes self-love the ruling passion with mankind, have had reason to find fault, not so much with its general representations of human nature, as with the obtrusion of a mere innovation in language for a discovery in science.

When the vulgar speak of their different motives, they are satisfied with ordinary names, which refer to known and obvious distinctions. Of this kind are the terms *benevolence* and *selfishness*, by which they express their desire of the welfare of others, or the care of their own. The speculative are not always satisfied with this proceeding; they would analyze, as well as enumerate the principles of nature; and the chance is, that, merely to gain the appearance of something new, without any prospect of real advantage, they will disturb the order of vulgar apprehension. In the case before us, they have actually found that benevolence is no more than a species of self-love; and would oblige us, if possible, to look out for a new set of words, by which we may distinguish the selfishness of the parent when he takes care of his child, from his selfishness when he only takes care of himself. For according to this philosophy, as in both cases he only means to gratify a desire of his own, he is in both cases equally selfish. The term *benevolent*, in the mean time, is not employed to characterise persons who have no desires of their own, but persons whose own desires prompt them to procure the welfare of others. The fact is, that we should need only a fresh supply of language, instead of that which by this seeming discovery we should have lost, in order to make the reasonings of men proceed as they formerly did. But it is certainly impossible to live and to act with men, without employing different names to distinguish the humane from the cruel, and the benevolent from the selfish.

These terms have their equivalents in every tongue; they were invented by men of no refinement, who only meant to express what they distinctly perceived or strongly felt. And if a man of speculation should prove that we are selfish in a sense of his own, it does not follow that we are so in the sense of the vulgar; or, as ordinary men would understand his conclusion, that we are condemned in every instance to act on motives of interest, covetousness, pusillanimity, and cowardice; for such is conceived to be the ordinary import of selfishness in the character of man.

An affection or passion of any kind is sometimes said to give us an interest in its object; and humanity itself gives an interest in the welfare of mankind. This term *interest*, which commonly implies little more than our regard to property, is sometimes put for utility in general, and this for happiness; insomuch that, under these ambiguities, it is not surprising we are still unable to determine whether interest is the only motive of human action, and the standard by which to distinguish our good from our ill.

So much is said in this place, not from any desire to have a share in any controversy of this sort, but merely to confine the meaning of the term *interest* to its most common acceptation, and to intimate our intention of employing it in expressing those objects of care which refer to our external condition, and the preservation of our animal nature. When taken in this sense, it will not surely be thought to comprehend at once all the motives of human conduct. If men be not allowed to have disinterested benevolence, they will not be denied to have disinterested passions of another kind. Hatred, indignation, and rage, frequently urge them to act in opposition to their known interest, and even to hazard their lives, without any hopes of compensation in any future returns of preferment or profit.

### Section III: Of the principles of Union among Mankind

Mankind have always wandered or settled, agreed or quarrelled, in troops and companies. The cause of their assembling, whatever it be, is the principle of their alliance or union.

In collecting the materials of history, we are seldom willing to put up with our subject merely as we find it. We are loath to be embarrassed with a multiplicity of particulars, and apparent inconsistencies. In theory we profess the investigation of general principles; and in order to bring the matter of our inquiries within the reach of our comprehension, are disposed to adopt any system. Thus, in treating of human affairs, we would draw every consequence from a principle of union, or a principle of dissension. The state of nature is a state of war or of amity, and men are made to unite from a principle of affection, or from a principle of fear, as is most suitable to the system of different writers. The history of our species indeed abundantly shows, that they are to one another mutual objects both of fear and of love; and they who prove them to have been originally either in a state of alliance, or of war, have arguments in store to maintain their assertions. Our attachment to one division, or to one sect, seems often to derive much of its force from an animosity conceived to an opposite one; and this animosity in its turn, as often arises from a zeal in behalf of the side we espouse, and from a desire to vindicate the rights of our party.

"Man is born in society", says Montesquieu, "and there he remains." The charms that detain him are known to be manifold. We may reckon the parental affection, which, instead of deserting the adult, as among the brutes, embraces more [closely], as it becomes mixed with esteem, and the memory of its early effects, together with a propensity common to man and other animals, to mix with the herd, and, without reflection, to follow the crowd of his species. What this propensity was in the first moment of its operation, we know not; but with men accustomed to company, its enjoyments and. disappointments are reckoned among the principal pleasures or pains of human life. Sadness and melancholy are connected with solitude; gladness and pleasure with the concourse of men. The track of a Laplander on the snowy shore gives joy to the lonely mariner, and the mute signs of cordiality and kindness which are made to him, awaken the memory of pleasures which he felt in society. In fine, says the writer of a voyage to the north, after describing a mute scene of this sort, "We were extremely pleased to converse with men, since in thirteen months we had seen no human creature." But we need no remote observation to confirm this position: The wailings of the infant, and the languors of the adult, when alone; the lively joys of the one, and the cheerfulness of the other, upon the return of company, are a sufficient proof of its solid foundations in the frame of our nature.

In accounting for actions we often forget that we ourselves have acted; and instead of the sentiments which stimulate the mind in the presence of its object, we assign as the motives of conduct with men, those considerations which occur in the hours of retirement and cold reflection. In this mood frequently we can find nothing important, besides the deliberate prospects of interest; and a great work, like that of forming society, must in our apprehension arise from deep reflections, and be carried on with a view to the advantages which mankind derive from commerce and mutual support. But neither a propensity to mix with the herd, nor the sense of advantages enjoyed in that condition, comprehend all the principles by which men are united together. Those bands are even of a feeble texture, when compared to the resolute ardor with which a man adheres to his friend, or to his tribe, after they have for some time run the career of fortune together. Mutual discoveries of generosity, joint trials of fortitude, redouble the ardors of friendship, and kindle a flame in the human breast, which the considerations of personal interest or safety cannot suppress. The most lively transports of joy are seen, and the loudest shrieks of despair are heard, when the objects of a tender affection are beheld in a state of triumph or of suffering. An Indian recovered his friend unexpectedly on the island of Juan Fernandes; he prostrated himself on the ground, at his feet: "We stood gazing in silence", says [William] Dampier, "at this tender scene." If we would know what is the religion of a wild American, what it is in his heart that most resembles devotion: it is not his fear of the sorcerer, nor his hope of protection from the spirits of the air or the wood; it is the ardent affection with which he selects and embraces his friend; with which he clings to his side in every season of peril; and with which he invokes his spirit from a distance, when dangers surprise him alone. Whatever proofs we may have of the social disposition of man in familiar and contiguous scenes, it is possibly of importance, to draw our observations from the examples of men who live in the simplest condition, and who have not learned to affect what they do not actually feel.

Mere acquaintance and habitude nourish affection, and the experience of society brings every passion of the human mind upon its side. Its triumphs and prosperities, its calamities and distresses, bring a variety and a force of emotion, which can only have place in the company of our fellow-creatures. It is here that a man is made to forget his weakness, his cares of safety, and his subsistence; and to act from those passions which make him discover his force. It is here he finds that his arrows fly swifter than the eagle, and his weapons wound deeper than the paw of the lion, or the tooth of the boar. It is not alone his sense of a support which is near, nor the love of distinction in the opinion of his tribe, that inspire his courage, or swell his heart with a confidence that exceeds what his natural force should bestow. Vehement passions of animosity or attachment are the first exertions of vigor in his breast; under their influence, every consideration, but that of his object, is forgotten; dangers and difficulties only excite him the more.

That condition is surely favorable to the nature of any being, in which his force is increased; and if courage be the gift of society to man, we have reason to consider his union with his species as the noblest part of his fortune. From this source are derived, not only the force, but the very existence of his happiest emotions; not only the better part, but almost the whole of his rational character. Send him to the desert alone, he is a plant torn from its roots: the form indeed may remain, but every faculty droops and withers; the human personage and the human character cease to exist.

Men are so far from valuing society on account of its mere external conveniences, that they are commonly most attached where those conveniences are least frequent; and are there most faithful, where the tribute of their allegiance is paid in blood. Affection operates with the greatest force, where it meets with the greatest difficulties. In the breast of the parent, it is most solicitous amidst the dangers and distresses of the child; in the breast of a man, its flame redoubles where the wrongs or sufferings of his friend, or his country, require his aid. It is, in short from this principle alone that we can account for the obstinate attachment of a savage to his unsettled and defenseless tribe when temptations on the side of ease and of safety might induce him to fly from famine and danger, to a station more affluent and more secure. Hence the sanguine affection which every Greek bore to his country, and hence the devoted patriotism of an early Roman. Let those examples be compared with the spirit which reigns in a commercial state, where men may be supposed to have experienced, in its full extent, the interest which individuals have in the preservation of their country. It is here indeed if ever, that man is sometimes found a detached and a solitary being: he has found an object which sets him in competition with his fellow-creatures, and he deals with them as he does with his cattle and his soil, for the sake of the profits they bring. The mighty engine which we suppose to have formed society, only tends to set its members at variance, or to continue their intercourse after the bands of affection are broken.

## Section IV: Of the principles of War and Dissension

"There are some circumstances in the lot of mankind", says Socrates, "that show them to be destined to friendship and amity: Those are, their mutual need of one another; their mutual compassion; their sense of mutual benefits; and the pleasures arising in company. There are other circumstances which prompt them to war and dissension; the admiration and the desire which they entertain for the same subjects; their opposite pretensions; and the provocations which they mutually offer in the course of their competitions."

When we endeavor to apply the maxims of natural justice to the solution of difficult questions, we find that some cases may be supposed, and actually happen, where oppositions take place, and are lawful, prior to any provocation, or act of injustice; that where the safety and preservation of numbers are mutually inconsistent, one party may employ his right of defense, before the other has begun an attack. And when we join with such examples, the instances of mistake, and misunderstanding, to which mankind are exposed, we may be satisfied that war does not always proceed from an intention to injure; and that even the best qualities of men, their candor, as well as their resolution, may operate in the midst of their quarrels.

There is still more to be observed on this subject. Mankind not only find in their condition the sources of variance and dissension; they appear to have in their minds the seeds of animosity, and to embrace the occasions of mutual opposition, with alacrity and pleasure. In the most pacific situation there are few who have not their enemies, as well as their friends; and who are not pleased with opposing the proceedings of one, as much as with favoring the designs of another. Small and simple tribes, who in their domestic society have the firmest union, are in their state of opposition as separate nations, frequently animated with the most implacable hatred. Among the citizens of Rome, in the early ages of that republic, the name of a foreigner, and that of an enemy, were the same. Among the Greeks, the name of Barbarian, under which that people comprehended every nation that was of a race, and spoke a language, different from their own, became a term of indiscriminate contempt and aversion. Even where no particular claim to superiority is formed, the repugnance to union, the frequent wars, or rather the perpetual hostilities, which take place among rude nations and separate clans, discover how much our species is disposed to opposition, as well as to concert.

Late discoveries have brought us to the knowledge of almost every situation in which mankind are placed. We have found them spread over large and extensive continents, where communications are open, and where national confederacy might be easily formed. We have found them in narrower districts, circumscribed by mountains, great rivers, and arms of the sea. They have been found in small and remote islands, where the inhabitants might be easily assembled, and derive an advantage from their union. But in all those situations, alike, they were broke into cantons, and affected a distinction of name and community. The titles of *fellow-citizen* and *countryman*, unopposed to those of *alien* and *foreigner*, to which they refer, would fall into disuse, and lose their meaning. We love individuals on account of personal qualities; but we love our country, as it is a party in the divisions of mankind; and our zeal for its interest, is a predilection in behalf of the side we maintain.

In the promiscuous concourse of men, it is sufficient that we have an opportunity of selecting our company. We turn away from those who do not engage us, and we fix our resort where the society is more to our mind. We are fond of distinctions; we place ourselves in opposition, and quarrel under the denominations of faction and party, without any material subject of controversy. A version, like affection, is fostered by a continued direction to its particular object. Separation and estrangement, as well as opposition, widen a breach which did not owe its beginnings to any offense. And it would seem, that until we have reduced mankind to the state of a family, or found some external consideration to maintain their connection in greater numbers, they will be for ever separated into bands, and form a plurality of nations.

The sense of a common danger, and the assaults of an enemy, have been frequently useful to nations, by uniting their members more firmly together, and by preventing the secessions and actual separations in which their civil discord might otherwise terminate. And this motive to union which is offered from abroad, may be necessary, not only in the case of large and extensive nations, where coalitions are weakened by distance, and the distinction of provincial names, but even in the narrow society of the smallest states. Rome itself was founded by a small party, which took its flight from Alba; her citizens were often in danger of separating; and if the villages and cantons of the Volsci had been further removed from the scene of their dissensions, the Mons Sacer might have received a new colony before the mother country was ripe for such a discharge. She continued long to feel the quarrels of her nobles and her people; and the gates of Janus were frequently opened, to remind her inhabitants of the duties they owed to their country.

…

These observations seem to arraign our species, and to give an unfavorable picture of mankind; and yet the particulars we have mentioned are consistent with the most amiable qualities of our nature, and often furnish a scene for the exercise of our greatest abilities. They are sentiments of generosity and self-denial that animate the warrior in defense of his country; and they are dispositions most favorable to mankind, that become the principles of apparent hostility to men. Every animal is made to delight in the exercise of his natural talents and forces: The lion and the tiger sport with the paw; the horse delights to commit his mane to the wind, and forgets his pasture to try his speed in the field; the bull even before his brow is armed, and the lamb while yet an emblem of innocence, have a disposition to strike with the forehead, and anticipate, in play, the conflicts they are doomed to sustain. Man too is disposed to opposition, and to employ the forces of his nature against an equal antagonist; he loves to bring his reason, his eloquence, his courage, even his bodily strength, to the proof. His sports are frequently an image of war; sweat and blood are freely expended in play; and fractures or death are often made to terminate the pastimes of idleness and festivity. He was not made to live forever, and even his love of amusement has opened a path that leads to the grave.

Without the rivalry of nations, and the practice of war, civil society itself could scarcely have found an object, or a form. Mankind might have traded without any formal convention, but they cannot be safe without a national concert. The necessity of a public defense, has given rise to many departments of state, and the intellectual talents of men have found their busiest scene in wielding their national forces. To overawe, or intimidate, or, when we cannot persuade with reason, to resist with fortitude, are the occupations which give its most animating exercise, and its greatest triumphs, to a vigorous mind; and he who has never struggled with his fellow-creatures, is a stranger to half the sentiments of mankind.

The quarrels of individuals, indeed, are frequently the operations of unhappy and detestable passions: malice, hatred, and rage. If such passions alone possess the breast, the scene of dissension becomes an object of horror; but a common opposition maintained by numbers, is always allayed by passions of another sort. Sentiments of affection and friendship mix with animosity; the active and strenuous become the guardians of their society; and violence itself is, in their case, an exertion of generosity as well as of courage. We applaud, as proceeding from a national or party spirit, what we could not endure as the effect of a private dislike; and amidst the competitions of rival states, think we have found, for the patriot and the warrior, in the practice of violence and stratagem, the most illustrious career of human virtue. Even personal opposition here does not divide our judgment on the merits of men. The rival names of Agesilaus and Epaminondas, of Scipio and Hannibal, are repeated with equal praise; and war itself, which in one view appears so fatal, in another is the exercise of a liberal spirit; and in the very effects which we regret, is but one distemper more by which the author of nature has appointed our exit from human life.

These reflections may open our view into the state of mankind; but they tend to reconcile us to the conduct of Providence, rather than to make us change our own, where, from a regard to the welfare of our fellow-creatures, we endeavor to pacify their animosities, and unite them by the ties of affection. In the pursuit of this amiable intention, we may hope, in some instances, to disarm the angry passions of jealousy and envy; we may hope to instill into the breasts of private men sentiments of candor toward their fellow creatures, and a disposition to humanity and justice. But it is vain to expect that we can give to the multitude of a people a sense of union among themselves, without admitting hostility to those who oppose them. Could we at once, in the case of any nation, extinguish the emulation which is excited from abroad, we should probably break or weaken the bands of society at home, and close the busiest scenes of national occupations and virtues.

## Section VII: Of Happiness

Having had under our consideration the active powers and the moral qualities which distinguish the nature of man, is it still necessary that we should treat of his happiness apart? This significant term, the most frequent, and the most familiar, in our conversation, is, perhaps, on reflection, the least understood. It serves to express our satisfaction, when any desire is gratified; it is pronounced with a sigh, when our object is distant; it means what we wish to obtain, and what we seldom stay to examine. We estimate the value of every subject by its utility, and its influence on happiness; but we think that utility itself, and happiness, require no explanation.

Those men are commonly esteemed the happiest, whose desires are most frequently gratified. But if, in reality, the possession of what we desire, and a continued fruition, were requisite to happiness, mankind for the most part would have reason to complain of their lot. What they call their enjoyments, are generally momentary; and the object of sanguine expectation, when obtained, no longer continues to occupy the mind: A new passion succeeds, and the imagination, as before, is intent on a distant felicity.

...

The very terms pleasure and pain, perhaps, are equivocal; but if they are confined, as they appear to be in many of our reasonings, to the mere sensations which have a reference to external objects, either in the memory of the past, the feeling of the present, or the apprehension of the future, it is a great error to suppose that they comprehend all the constituents of happiness or misery; or that the good humor of an ordinary life is maintained by the prevalence of those pleasures which have their separate names, and are, on reflection, distinctly remembered.

The mind, during the greater part of its existence, is employed in active exertions, not in merely attending to its own feelings of pleasure or pain; and the list of its faculties, understanding, memory, foresight, sentiment, will, and intention, only contains the names of its different operations.

In the absence of every sensation to which we commonly give the names either of *enjoyment* or *suffering,* our very existence may have its opposite qualities of *happiness* or *misery;* and if what we call *pleasure* or *pain* occupies but a small part of human life, compared to what passes in contrivance and execution, in pursuits and expectations, in conduct, reflection, and social engagements; it must appear that our active pursuits, at least on account of their duration, deserve the greater part of our attention. When their occasions have failed, the demand is not for pleasure, but for something to do; and the very complaints of a sufferer are not so sure a mark of distress, as the stare of the languid.

...

In devising, or in executing a plan, in being carried on the tide of emotion and sentiment, the mind seems to unfold its being, and to enjoy itself. Even where the end and the object are known to be of little avail, the talents and the fancy are often intensely applied, and business or play may amuse them alike. We only desire repose to recruit our limited and our wasting force: when business fatigues, amusement is often but a change of occupation. We are not always unhappy, even when we complain. There is a kind of affliction which makes an agreeable state of the mind; and lamentation itself is sometimes an expression of pleasure. The painter and the poet have laid hold of this handle, and find, among the means of entertainment, a favorable reception for works that are composed to awaken our sorrows.

To a being of this description, therefore, it is a blessing to meet with incentives to action, whether in the desire of pleasure, or the aversion to pain. His activity is of more importance than the very pleasure he seeks, and languor a greater evil than the suffering he shuns.

The gratifications of animal appetite are of short duration; and sensuality is but a distemper of the mind, which ought to be cured by remembrance, if it were not perpetually inflamed by hope. The chase is not more surely terminated by the death of the game, than the joys of the voluptuary by the means of completing his debauch. As a bond of society, as a matter of distant pursuit, the objects of sense make an important part in the system of human life. They lead us to fulfill the purpose of nature, in preserving the individual, and in perpetuating the species; but to rely on their use as a principal constituent of human felicity, were an error in speculation, and would be still more an error in practice. Even the master of the seraglio, for whom all the treasures of empire are extorted from the hoards of its frightened inhabitants, for whom alone the choicest emerald and the diamond are drawn from the mine, for whom every breeze is enriched with perfumes, for whom beauty is assembled from every quarter, and, animated by passions that ripen under the vertical sun, is confined to the grate for his use, is still, perhaps, more wretched than the very herd of the people, whose labors and properties are devoted to relieve him of trouble, and to procure him enjoyment.

Sensuality is easily overcome by any of the habits of pursuit which usually engage an active mind. When curiosity is awake, or when passion is excited, even in the midst of the feast when conversation grows warm, grows jovial, or serious, the pleasures of the table we know are forgotten. The boy contemns them for play, and the man of age declines them for business.

When we reckon the circumstances that correspond to the nature of any animal, or to that of man in particular, such as safety, shelter, food, and the other means of enjoyment or preservation, we sometimes think that we have found a sensible and a solid foundation on which to rest his felicity. But those who are least disposed to moralize, observe that happiness is not connected with fortune, although fortune includes at once all the means of subsistence, and the means of sensual indulgence. The circumstances that require abstinence, courage, and conduct, expose us to hazard, and are in description of the painful kind; yet the able, the brave, and the ardent, seem most to enjoy themselves when placed in the midst of difficulties, and obliged to employ the powers they possess.

Spinola being told, that Sir Francis Vere died of having nothing to do, said, "That was enough to kill a general." How many are there to whom war itself is a pastime, who choose the life of a soldier, exposed to dangers and continued fatigues; of a mariner, in conflict with every hardship, and bereft of every convenience; of a politician, whose sport is the conduct of parties and factions; and who, rather than be idle, will do the business of men and of nations for whom he has not the smallest regard. Such men do not choose pain as preferable to pleasure, but they are incited by a restless disposition to make continued exertions of capacity and resolution; they triumph in the midst of their struggles; they droop, and they languish, when the occasion of their labor has ceased.

What was enjoyment, in the sense of that youth, who, according to Tacitus, loved danger itself, not the rewards of courage? What is the prospect of pleasure, when the sound of the horn or the trumpet, the cry of the dogs, or the shout of war, awaken the ardor of the sportsman and the soldier? The most animating occasions of human life, are calls to danger and hardship, not invitations to safety and ease. And man himself, in his excellence, is not an animal of pleasure, nor destined merely to enjoy what the elements bring to his use; but, like his associates, the dog and the horse, to follow the exercises of his nature, in preference to what are called its enjoyments; to pine in the lap of ease and of affluence, and to exult in the midst of alarms that seem to threaten his being. In all which, his disposition to action only keeps pace with the variety of powers with which he is furnished; and the most respectable attributes of his nature, magnanimity, fortitude, and wisdom, carry a manifest reference to the difficulties with which he is destined to struggle.

...

## Section VIII: The same subject continued

...

What, then, is that mysterious thing called *happiness*, which may have place in such a variety of stations, and to which circumstances in one age or nation thought necessary, are in another held to be destructive, or of no effect? It is not the succession of mere animal pleasures, which, apart from the occupation or the company in which they serve to engage the mind, can fill up but a few moments in the duration of life. On too frequent a repetition, those pleasures turn to satiety and disgust; they tear the constitution to which they are applied in excess, and, like the lightning of night, only serve to darken the gloom through which they occasionally break. Happiness is not that state of repose, or that imaginary freedom from care, which at a distance is so frequent an object of desire, but with its approach brings a tedium, or a languor, more unsupportable than pain itself. If the preceding observations on this subject be just, it arises more from the pursuit, than from the attainment of any end whatever; and in every new situation to which we arrive, even in the course of a prosperous life, it depends more on the degree in which our minds are properly employed, than it does on the circumstances in which we are destined to act, on the materials which are placed in our hands, or the tools with which we are furnished.

...

Whoever has the force of mind steadily to view human life under this aspect, has only to choose well his occupations, in order to command that state of enjoyment, and freedom of soul, which probably constitute the peculiar felicity to which his active nature is destined.

The dispositions of men, and consequently their occupations, are commonly divided into two principal classes: the selfish, and the social. The first are indulged in solitude; and if they carry a reference to mankind, it is that of emulation, competition, and enmity. The second incline us to live with our fellow-creatures, and to do them good; they tend to unite the members of society together; they terminate in a mutual participation of their cares and enjoyments, and render the presence of men an occasion of joy. Under this class may be enumerated the passions of the sexes, the affections of parents and children, general humanity, or singular attachments; above all, that habit of the soul by which we consider ourselves as but a part of some beloved community, and as but individual members of some society, whose general welfare is to us the supreme object of zeal, and the great rule of our conduct. This affection is a principle of candor, which knows no partial distinctions, and is confined to no bounds: it may extend its effects beyond our personal acquaintance; it may, in the mind, and in thought, at least, make us feel a relation to the universe, and to the whole creation of God. "Shall any one", says Antoninus, "love the city of Cecrops, and you not love the city of God?"

No emotion of the heart is indifferent. It is either an act of vivacity and joy, or a feeling of sadness; a transport of pleasure, or a convulsion of anguish. And the exercises of our different dispositions, as well as their gratifications, are likely to prove matter of the greatest importance to our happiness or misery.

The individual is charged with the care of his animal preservation. He may exist in solitude, and, far removed from society, perform many functions of sense, imagination, and reason. He is even rewarded for the proper discharge of those functions; and all the natural exercises which relate to himself, as well as to his fellow-creatures, not only occupy without distressing him, but in many instances are attended with positive pleasures, and fill up the hours of life with agreeable occupation.

There is a degree, however, in which we suppose that the care of our-selves becomes a source of painful anxiety and cruel passions; in which it degenerates into avarice, vanity, or pride; and in which, by fostering habits of jealousy and envy, of fear and malice, it becomes as destructive of our own enjoyments, as it is hostile to the welfare of mankind. This evil, however, is not to be charged upon any excess in the care of our-selves, but upon a mere mistake in the choice of our objects. We look abroad for a happiness which is to be found only in the qualities of the heart. We think ourselves dependent on accidents; and are therefore kept in suspense and solicitude. We think ourselves dependent on the will of other men; and are therefore servile and timid. We think our felic-ity is placed in subjects for which our fellow-creatures are rivals and competitors; and in pursuit of happiness, we engage in those scenes of emulation, envy, hatred, animosity, and revenge, that lead to the highest pitch of distress. We act, in short, as if to preserve ourselves were to retain our weakness, and perpetuate our sufferings. We charge the ills of a distempered imagination, and a corrupt heart, to the account of our fel-low-creatures, to whom we refer the pangs of our disappointment or malice; and while we foster our misery, are surprised that the care of ourselves is attended with no better effects. But he who remembers that he is by nature a rational being, and a member of society, that to preserve himself, is to preserve his reason, and to preserve the best feelings of his heart, will encounter with none of these inconveniences; and in the care of himself, will find subjects only of satisfaction and triumph.

The division of our appetites into benevolent and selfish, has proba-bly, in some degree, helped to mislead our apprehension on the subject of personal enjoyment and private good; and our zeal to prove that vir-tue is disinterested has not greatly promoted its cause. The gratification of a selfish desire, it is thought, brings advantage or pleasure to our-selves; that of benevolence terminates in the pleasure or advantage of others. Whereas, in reality, the gratification of every desire is a personal enjoyment, and its value being proportioned to the particular quality or force of the sentiment, it may happen that the same person may reap a greater advantage from the good fortune he has procured to another, than from that he has obtained for himself.

While the gratifications of benevolence, therefore, are as much our own as those of any other desire whatever, the mere exercises of this dis-position are, on many accounts, to be considered as the first and the prin-cipal constituent of human happiness. Every act of kindness, or of care, in the parent to his child; every emotion of the heart, in friendship or in love, in public zeal, or general humanity, are so many acts of enjoyment and satisfaction. Pity itself, and compassion, even grief and melancholy, when grafted on some tender affection, partake of the nature of the stock; and if they are not positive pleasures, are at least pains of a pecu-liar nature, which we do not even wish to exchange but for a very real enjoyment, obtained in relieving our object. Even extremes, in this class of our dispositions, as they are the reverse of hatred, envy, and malice, so they are never attended with those excruciating anxieties, jealousies, and fears, which tear the interested mind; or if, in reality, any ill passion arise from a pretended attachment to our fellow-creatures, that attachment may be safely condemned, as not genuine. If we be distrustful or jealous, our pretended affection is probably no more than a desire of attention and personal consideration, a motive which frequently inclines us to be connected with our fellow-creatures; but to which we are as frequently willing to sacrifice their happiness. We consider them as the tools of our vanity, pleasure, or interest; not as the parties on whom we may bestow the effects of our good will, and our love.

A mind devoted to this class of its affections, being occupied with an object that may engage it habitually, is not reduced to court the amusements or pleasures with which persons of an ill temper are obliged to repair their disgusts; and temperance becomes an easy task when gratifications of sense are supplanted by those of the heart. Courage too is most easily assumed, or is rather inseparable from that ardor of the mind, in society, friendship, or in public action, which makes us forget subjects of personal anxiety or fear, and attend chiefly to the object of our zeal or affection, not to the trifling inconveniences, dangers, or hardships, which we ourselves may encounter in striving to maintain it.

It should seem, therefore, to be the happiness of man, to make his social dispositions the ruling spring of his occupations; to state himself as the member of a community, for whose general good his heart may glow with an ardent zeal, to the suppression of those personal cares which are the foundation of painful anxieties, fear, jealousy, and envy; or, as Mr. Pope expresses the same sentiment,

> Man, like the generous vine, supported lives;
> The strength he gains, is from the embrace he gives.

If this be the good of the individual, it is likewise that of mankind; and virtue no longer imposes a task by which we are obliged to bestow upon others that good from which we ourselves refrain; but supposes, in the highest degree, as possessed by ourselves, that state of felicity which we are required to promote in the world.

We commonly apprehend, that it is our duty to do kindnesses, and our happiness to receive them. But if, in reality, courage, and a heart devoted to the good of mankind, are the constituents of human felicity, the kindness which is done infers a happiness in the person from whom it proceeds, not in him on whom it is bestowed; and the greatest good which men possessed of fortitude and generosity can procure to their fellow-creatures, is a participation of this happy character. "You will confer the greatest benefit on your city", says Epictetus, "not by raising the roofs, but by exalting the souls of your fellow-citizens; for it is better that great souls should live in small habitations, than that abject slaves should burrow in great houses."

To the benevolent, the satisfaction of others is a ground of enjoyment; and existence itself, in a world that is governed by the wisdom of God, is a blessing. The mind, freed from cares that lead to pusillanimity and meanness, becomes calm, active, fearless, and bold; capable of every enterprise, and vigorous in the exercise of every talent, by which the nature of man is adorned. On this foundation was raised the admirable character, which, during a certain period of their story, distinguished the celebrated nations of antiquity, and rendered familiar and ordinary in their manners, examples of magnanimity, which, under governments less favorable to the public affections, rarely occur; or which, without being much practiced, or even understood, are made subjects of admiration and swelling panegyric. "Thus", says Xenophon, "died Thrasybulus; who indeed appears to have been a good man." What valuable praise, and how significant to those who know the story of this admirable person! The members of those illustrious states, from the habit of considering themselves as part of a community, or at least as deeply involved with some order of men in the state, were regardless of personal considerations: they had a perpetual view to objects which excite a great ardor in the soul; which led them to act perpetually in the view of their fellow-citizens, and to practice those arts of deliberation, elocution, policy, and war, on which the fortunes of nations, or of men, in their collective body, depend. To the force of mind collected in this career, and to the improvements of wit which were made in pursuing it, these nations owed, not only their magnanimity, and the superiority of their political and military conduct, but even the arts of poetry and literature, which among them were only the inferior appendages of a genius otherwise excited, cultivated, and refined.

To the ancient Greek, or the Roman, the individual was nothing, and the public everything. To the modern, in too many nations of Europe, the individual is everything, and the public nothing...

## PART II
## Of the History of Rude Nations

*Section II: Of Rude Nations prior to the Establishment of Property*

From one to the other extremity of America; from Kamchatka westward to the river Oby, and from the Northern sea, over that length of country, to the confines of China, of India, and Persia; from the Caspian to the Red sea, with little exception, and from thence over the inland continent and the western shores of Africa; we everywhere meet with nations on whom we bestow the appellations of barbarous or savage. That extensive tract of the earth, containing so great a variety of situation, climate, and soil, should, in the manners of its inhabitants, exhibit all the diversities which arise from the unequal influence of the sun, joined to a different nourishment and manner of life. Every question, however, on this subject is premature, until we have first endeavored to form some general conception of our species in its rude state, and have learned to distinguish mere ignorance from dullness, and the want of arts from the want of capacity.

Of the nations who dwell in those, or any other of the less cultivated parts of the earth, some entrust their subsistence chiefly to hunting, fishing, or the natural produce of the soil. They have little attention to property, and scarcely any beginnings of subordination or government. Others having possessed themselves of herds, and depending for their provision on pasture, know what it is to be poor and rich. They know the relations of patron and client, of servant and master, and suffer themselves to be classed according to their measures of wealth. This distinction must create a material difference of character, and may furnish two separate heads, under which to consider the history of mankind in their rudest state; that of the savage, who is not yet acquainted with property; and that of the barbarian, to whom it is, although not ascertained by laws, a principal object of care and desire.

It must appear very evident, that property is a matter of progress. It requires, among other particulars which are the effects of time, some method of defining possession. The very desire of it proceeds from experience; and the industry by which it is gained, or improved, requires such a habit of acting with a view to distant objects, as may overcome the present disposition either to sloth or to enjoyment. This habit is slowly acquired, and is in reality a principal distinction of nations in the advanced state of mechanic and commercial arts.

In a tribe which subsists by hunting and fishing, the arms, the utensils, and the fur, which the individual carries, are to him the only subjects of property. The food of tomorrow is yet wild in the forest, or hid in the lake; cannot be appropriated before it is caught; and even then, being the purchase of numbers, who fish or hunt in a body, it accrues to the community, and is applied to immediate use, or becomes an accession to the stores of the public.

Where savage nations, as in most parts of America, mix with the practice of hunting some species of rude agriculture, they still follow, with respect to the soil and the fruits of the earth, the analogy of their principal object. As the men hunt, so the women labor together; and, after they have shared the toils of the seed-time, they enjoy the fruits of the harvest in common. The field in which they have planted, like the district over which they are accustomed to hunt, is claimed as a property by the nation, but is not parceled in lots to its members. They go forth in parties to prepare the ground, to plant, and to reap. The harvest is gathered into the public granary, and from thence, at stated times, is divided into shares for the maintenance of separate families. Even the returns of the market, when they trade with foreigners, are brought home to the stock of the nation.

As the fur and the bow pertain to the individual, the cabin and its utensils are appropriated to the family; and as the domestic cares are committed to the women, so the property of the household seems likewise to be vested in them. The children are considered as pertaining to the mother, with little regard to descent on the father's side. The males, before they are married, remain in the cabin in which they are born; but after they have formed a new connection with the other sex, they change their habitation, and become an accession to the family in which they have found their wives. The hunter and the warrior are numbered by the matron as a part of her treasure; they are reserved for perils and trying occasions; and in the recess of public councils, in the intervals of hunting or war, are maintained by the cares of the women, and loiter about in mere amusement or sloth.

While one sex continue to value themselves chiefly on their courage, their talent for policy, and their warlike achievements, this species of property which is bestowed on the other, is in reality a mark of subjection; not, as some writers allege, of their having acquired an ascendant. It is the care and trouble of a subject with which the warrior does not choose to be embarrassed. It is a servitude, and a continual toil, where no honors are won; and they whose province it is, are in fact the slaves and the helots of their country. If in this destination of the sexes, while the men continue to indulge themselves in the contempt of sordid and mercenary arts, the cruel establishment of slavery is for some ages deferred; if in this tender, though unequal alliance, the affections of the heart prevent the severities practiced on slaves; we have in the custom itself, as perhaps in many other instances, reason to prefer the first suggestions of nature, to many of her after refinements.

If mankind, in any instance, continue the article of property on the footing we have now represented, we may easily credit what is farther reported by travelers, that they admit of no distinctions of rank or condition; and that they have in fact no degree of subordination different from the distribution of function, which follows the differences of age, talents, and dispositions. Personal qualities give an ascendant in the midst of occasions which require their exertion; but in times of relaxation, leave no vestige of power or prerogative. A warrior who has led the youth of his nation to the slaughter of their enemies, or who has been foremost in the chase, returns upon a level with the rest of his tribe; and when the only business is to sleep, or to feed, can enjoy no pre-eminence; for he sleeps and he feeds no better than they.

Where no profit attends dominion, one party is as much averse to the trouble of perpetual command, as the other is to the mortification of perpetual submission. "I love victory, I love great actions", says Montesquieu in the character of Sylla, "but have no relish for the languid detail of pacific government, or the pageantry of high station." He has touched perhaps what is a prevailing sentiment in the simplest state of society, when the weakness of motives suggested by interest, and the ignorance of any elevation not founded on merit, supplies the place of disdain.

The character of the mind, however, in this state, is not founded on ignorance alone. Men are conscious of their equality, and are tenacious of its rights. Even when they follow a leader to the field, they cannot brook the pretensions to a formal command: they listen to no orders; and they come under no military engagements, but those of mutual fidelity, and equal ardor in the enterprise.

...

In these happy, though informal, proceedings, where age alone gives a place in the council; where youth, ardor, and valor in the field, give a title to the station of leader; where the whole community is assembled on any alarming occasion, we may venture to say, that we have found the origin of the senate, the executive power, and the assembly of the people; institutions for which ancient legislators have been so much renowned. The senate among the Greeks, as well as the Latins, appears, from the etymology of its name, to have been originally composed of elderly men. The military leader at Rome, in a manner not unlike to that of the American warrior, proclaimed his levies, and the citizen prepared for the field, in consequence of a voluntary engagement. The suggestions of nature, which directed the policy of nations in the wilds of America, were followed before on the banks of the Eurotas and the Tiber; and Lycurgus and Romulus found the model of their institutions where the members of every rude nation find the earliest mode of uniting their talents, and combining their forces.

Among the North-American nations, every individual is independent; but he is engaged by his affections and his habits in the cares of a family. Families, like so many separate tribes, are subject to no inspection or government from abroad; whatever passes at home, even bloodshed and murder, are only supposed to concern themselves. They are, in the mean time, the parts of a canton; the women assemble to plant their maize; the old men go to council; the huntsman and the warrior joins the youth of his village in the field. Many such cantons assemble to constitute a national council, or to execute a national enterprise. When the Europeans made their first settlements in America, six such nations had formed a league, had their amphictyonies or states-general, and, by the firmness of their union, and the ability of their councils, had obtained an ascendant from the mouth of the St. Laurence to that of the Mississippi. They appeared to understand the objects of the confederacy, as well as those of the separate nation; they studied a balance of power; the statesman of one country watched the designs and proceedings of another; and occasionally threw the weight of his tribe into a different scale. They had their alliances and their treaties, which, like the nations of Europe, they maintained, or they broke, upon reasons of state; and remained at peace from a sense of necessity or expediency, and went to war upon any emergence of provocation or jealousy.

Thus, without any settled form of government, or any bond of union, but what resembled more the suggestion of instinct, than the invention of reason, they conducted themselves with the concert, and the force, of nations. Foreigners, without being able to discover who is the magistrate, or in what manner the senate is composed, always find a council with whom they may treat, or a band of warriors with whom they may fight. Without police or compulsory laws, their domestic society is conducted with order, and the absence of vicious dispositions, is a better security than any public establishment for the suppression of crimes.

Disorders, however, sometimes occur, especially in times of debauch, when the immoderate use of intoxicating liquors, to which they are extremely addicted, suspends the ordinary caution of their demeanor, and inflaming their violent passions, engages them in quarrels and bloodshed. When a person is slain, his murderer is seldom called to an immediate account, but he has a quarrel to sustain with the family and the friends—or, if a stranger, with the countrymen of the deceased, sometimes even with his own nation at home, if the injury committed be of a kind to alarm the society. The nation, the canton, or the family, endeavor, by presents, to atone for the offence of any of their members; and, by pacifying the parties aggrieved, endeavor to prevent what alarms the community more than the first disorder, the subsequent effects of revenge and animosity. The shedding of blood, however, if the guilty person remain where he has committed the crime, seldom escapes unpunished: the friend of the deceased knows how to disguise, though not to suppress, his resentment; and even after many years have elapsed, is sure to repay the injury that was done to his kindred or his house.

These considerations render them cautious and circumspect, put them on their guard against their passions, and give to their ordinary deportment an air of phlegm and composure superior to what is possessed among polished nations. They are, in the mean time, affectionate in their carriage, and in their conversations pay a mutual attention and regard, says Charlevoix, more tender and more engaging, than what we profess in the ceremonial of polished societies.

This writer has observed, that the nations among whom he traveled in North America, never mentioned acts of generosity or kindness under the notion of duty. They acted from affection, as they acted from appetite, without regard to its consequences. When they had done a kindness, they had gratified a desire; the business was finished, and passed from the memory. When they received a favor, it might, or it might not, prove the occasion of friendship: if it did not, the parties appeared to have no apprehensions of gratitude, as a duty by which the one was bound to make a return, or the other entitled to reproach the person who had failed in his part. The spirit with which they give or receive presents, is the same which Tacitus observed among the ancient Germans: They delight in them, but do not consider them as matter of obligation. Such gifts are of little consequence, except when employed as the seal of a bargain or treaty.

It was their favorite maxim, that no man is naturally indebted to another; that he is not, therefore, obliged to bear with any imposition, or unequal treatment. Thus, in a principle apparently sullen and inhospitable, they have discovered the foundation of justice, and observe its rules, with a steadiness and candor which no cultivation has been found to improve. The freedom which they give in what relates to the supposed duties of kindness and friendship, serves only to engage the heart more entirely, where it is once possessed with affection. We love to choose our object without any restraint, and we consider kindness itself as a task, when the duties of friendship are exacted by rule. We therefore, by our demand for attentions, rather corrupt than improve the system of morality; and by our exactions of gratitude, and our frequent proposals to enforce its observance, we only show that we have mistaken its nature; we only give symptoms of that growing sensibility to interest, from which we measure the expediency of friendship and generosity itself; and by which we would introduce the spirit of traffic into the commerce of affection. In consequence of this proceeding, we are often obliged to decline a favor with the same spirit that we throw off a servile engagement, or reject a bribe. To the unrefined savage every favor is welcome, and every present received without reserve or reflection.

The love of equality, and the love of justice, were originally the same. And although, by the constitution of different societies, unequal privileges are bestowed on their members; and although justice itself requires a proper regard to be paid to such privileges; yet he who has forgotten that men were originally equal, easily degenerates into a slave; or in the capacity of a master, is not to be trusted with the rights of his fellow-creatures. This happy principle gives to the mind its sense of independence, renders it indifferent to the favors which are in the power of other men, checks it in the commission of injuries, and leaves the heart open to the affections of generosity and kindness. It gives to the untutored American that air of candor, and of regard to the welfare of others, which, in some degree, softens the arrogant pride of his carriage, and in times of confidence and peace, without the assistance of government or law, renders the approach and commerce of strangers secure.

Among this people, the foundations of honor are eminent abilities and great fortitude; not the distinctions of equipage and fortune. The talents in esteem are such as their situation leads them to employ, the exact knowledge of a country, and stratagem in war. On these qualifications, a captain among the Caribbean underwent an examination. When a new leader was to be chosen, a scout was sent forth to traverse the forests which led to the enemy's country, and, upon his return, the candidate was desired to find the track in which he had traveled. A brook, or a fountain, was named to him on the frontier, and he was desired to find the nearest path to a particular station, and to plant a stake in the place.

They can, accordingly, trace a wild beast, or the human foot, over many leagues of a pathless forest, and find their way across a woody and uninhabited continent, by means of refined observations, which escape the traveler who has been accustomed to different aids. They steer in slender canoes, across stormy seas, with a dexterity equal to that of the most experienced pilot. They carry a penetrating eye for the thoughts and intentions of those with whom they have to deal; and when they mean to deceive, they cover themselves with arts which the most subtle can seldom elude. They harangue in their public councils with a nervous and figurative elocution; and conduct themselves in the management of their treaties with a perfect discernment of their national interests.

Thus being able masters in the detail of their own affairs, and well qualified to acquit themselves on particular occasions, they study no science, and go in pursuit of no general principles. They even seem incapable of attending to any distant consequences, beyond those they have experienced in hunting or war. They entrust the provision of every season to itself; consume the fruits of the earth in summer; and, in winter, are driven in quest of their prey, through woods, and over deserts covered with snow. They do not form in one hour those maxims which may prevent the errors of the next; and they fail in those apprehensions, which, in the intervals of passion, produce ingenuous shame, compassion, remorse, or a command of appetite. They are seldom made to repent of any violence; nor is a person, indeed, thought accountable in his sober mood, for what he did in the heat of a passion, or in a time of debauch.

...

## Section III
### Of Rude Nations under the Impressions of Property and Interest

It was a proverbial imprecation in use among the hunting nations on the confines of Siberia, that their enemy might be obliged to live like a Tartar, and be seized with the folly of breeding and attending his cattle. Nature, it seems, in their apprehension, by storing the woods and the desert with game, rendered the task of the herdsman unnecessary, and left to man only the trouble of selecting and of seizing his prey.

The indolence of mankind, or rather their aversion to any application in which they are not engaged by immediate instinct and passion, retards their progress in extending the notion of property. It has been found, however, even while the means of subsistence are left in common, and the stock of the public is yet undivided, that this notion is already applied to different subjects; as the fur and the bow pertain to the individual, the cottage, with its furniture, are appropriated to the family.

When the parent begins to desire a better provision for his children than is found under the promiscuous management of many co-partners, when he has applied his labor and his skill apart, he aims at an exclusive possession, and seeks the property of the soil, as well as the use of its fruits.

When the individual no longer finds among his associates the same inclination to commit every subject to public use, he is seized with concern for his personal fortune; and is alarmed by the cares which every person entertains for himself. He is urged as much by emulation and jealousy, as by the sense of necessity. He suffers considerations of interest to rest on his mind, and when every present appetite is sufficiently gratified, he can act with a view to futurity, or rather finds an object of vanity in having amassed what is become a subject of competition, and a matter of universal esteem. Upon this motive, where violence is restrained, he can apply his hand to lucrative arts, confine himself to a tedious task, and wait with patience for the distant returns of his labor.

Thus mankind acquire industry by many and by slow degrees. They are taught to regard their interest; they are taught to abstain from unlawful profits; they are secured in the possession of what they fairly obtain; and by these methods the habits of the laborer, the mechanic, and the trader, are gradually formed. A hoard, collected from the simple productions of nature, or a herd of cattle, are, in every rude nation, the first species of wealth. The circumstances of the soil, and the climate, determine whether the inhabitant shall apply himself chiefly to agriculture or pasture; whether he shall fix his residence, or be moving continually about with all his possessions.

In the west of Europe; in America, from south to north, with a few exceptions; in the torrid zone, and everywhere within the warmer climates, mankind have generally applied themselves to some species of agriculture, and have been disposed to settlement. In the east and the north of Asia, they depended entirely on their herds, and were perpetually shifting their ground in search of new pasture. The arts which pertain to settlement have been practiced, and variously cultivated, by the inhabitants of Europe. Those which are consistent with perpetual migration, have, from the earliest accounts of history, remained nearly the same with the Scythian or Tartar. The tent pitched on a moveable carriage, the horse applied to every purpose of labor, and of war, of the dairy, and of the butcher's stall, from the earliest to the latest accounts, have made up the riches and equipage of this wandering people.

But in whatever way rude nations subsist, there are certain points in which, under the first impressions of property, they nearly agree. Homer either lived with a people in this stage of their progress, or found himself engaged to exhibit their character. Tacitus has made them the subject of a particular treatise; and if this be an aspect under which mankind deserve to be viewed, it must be confessed, that we have singular advantages in collecting their features. The portrait has already been drawn by the ablest hands, and gives, at one view, in the writings of these celebrated authors, whatever has been scattered in the relations of historians, or whatever we have opportunities to observe in the actual manners of men, who still remain in a similar state.

In passing from the condition we have described, to this we have at present in view, mankind still retain many parts of their earliest character. They are still averse to labor, addicted to war, admirers of fortitude, and, in the language of Tacitus, more lavish of their blood than of their sweat. They are fond of fantastic ornaments in their dress, and endeavor to fill up the listless intervals of a life addicted to violence, with hazardous sports, and with games of chance. Every servile occupation they commit to women or slaves. But we may apprehend, that the individual having now found a separate interest, the bands of society must become less firm, and domestic disorders more frequent. The members of any community, being distinguished among themselves by unequal shares in the distribution of property, the ground of a permanent and palpable subordination is laid.

These particulars accordingly take place among mankind, in passing from the savage to what may be called the barbarous state. Members of the same community enter into quarrels of competition or revenge. They unite in following leaders, who are distinguished by their fortunes, and by the luster of their birth. They join the desire of spoil with the love of glory; and from an opinion, that what is acquired by force, justly pertains to the victor, they become hunters of men, and bring every contest to the decision of the sword.

...

From the descriptions contained in the last section [II], we may incline to believe, that mankind, in their simplest state, are on the eve of erecting republics. Their love of equality, their habit of assembling in public councils, and their zeal for the tribe to which they belong, are qualifications that fit them to act under that species of government; and they seem to have but a few steps to make, in order to reach its establishment. They have only to define the numbers of which their councils shall consist, and to settle the forms of their meeting; they have only to bestow a permanent authority for repressing disorders, and to enact a few rules in favor of that justice they have already acknowledged, and from inclination so strictly observe.

But these steps are far from being so easily made, as they appear on a slight or a transient view. The resolution of choosing, from among their equals, the magistrate to whom they give from thenceforward a right to control their own actions, is far from the thoughts of simple men; and no eloquence, perhaps, could make them adopt this measure, or give them any sense of its use.

Even after nations have chosen a military leader, they do not entrust him with any species of civil authority. The captain, among the Caribbean, did not pretend to decide in domestic disputes; the terms *jurisdiction* and *government* were unknown in their tongue.

Before this important change is admitted, men must be accustomed to the distinction of ranks; and before they are sensible that subordination is matter of choice, must arrive at unequal conditions by chance. In desiring property, they only mean to secure their subsistence, but the brave who lead in war, have likewise the largest share in its spoils. The eminent are fond of devising hereditary honors; and the multitude, who admire the parent, are ready to extend their esteem to his offspring. Possessions descend, and the luster of family grows brighter with age. Hercules, who perhaps was an eminent warrior, became a god with posterity, and his race was set apart for royalty and sovereign power. When the distinctions of fortune and those of birth are conjoined, the chieftain enjoys a pre-eminence, as well at the feast as in the field. His followers take their place in subordinate stations; and instead of considering themselves as parts of a community, they rank as the followers of a chieftain, and take their designation from the name of their leader. They find a new object of public affection, in defending his person, and in supporting his station; they lend of their substance to form his estate; they are guided by his smiles and his frowns; and court, as the highest distinction, a share in the feast which their own contributions have furnished.

As the former state of mankind seemed to point at democracy, this seems to exhibit the rudiments of monarchical government. But it is yet far short of that establishment which is known in after ages by the name of *monarchy*. The distinction between the leader and the follower, the prince and the subject, is still but imperfectly marked: their pursuits and occupations are not different; their minds are not unequally cultivated; they feed from the same dish; they sleep together on the ground; the children of the king, as well as those of the subject, are employed in tending the flock; and the keeper of the swine was a prime counselor at the court of Ulysses.

The chieftain, sufficiently distinguished from his tribe, to excite their admiration, and to flatter their vanity by a supposed affinity to his noble descent, is the object of their veneration, not of their envy; he is considered as the common bond of connection, not as their common master; is foremost in danger, and has a principal share in their troubles. His glory is placed in the number of his attendants, in his superior magnanimity and valor; that of his followers, in being ready to shed their blood in his service.

The frequent practice of war tends to strengthen the bands of society, and the practice of depredation itself engages men in trials of mutual attachment and courage. What threatened to ruin and overset every good disposition in the human breast, what seemed to banish justice from the societies of men, tends to unite the species in clans and fraternities; formidable, indeed, and hostile to one another, but in the domestic society of each, faithful disinterested, and generous. Frequent dangers, and the experience of fidelity and valor, awaken the love of those virtues, render them a subject of admiration, and endear their possessors.

Actuated by great passions, the love of glory, and the desire of victory; roused by the menaces of an enemy, or stung with revenge; in suspense between the prospects of ruin or conquest, the barbarian spends every moment of relaxation in the indulgence of sloth. He cannot descend to the pursuits of industry or mechanical labor: the beast of prey is a sluggard; the hunter and the warrior sleeps, while women or slaves are made to toil for his bread. But show him a quarry at a distance, he is bold, impetuous, artful, and rapacious. No bar can withstand his violence, and no fatigue can allay his activity.

Even under this description mankind are generous and hospitable to strangers, as well as kind, affectionate, and gentle, in their domestic society. Friendship and enmity are to them terms of the greatest importance: they mingle not their functions together; they have singled out their enemy, and they have chosen their friend. Even in depredation, the principal object is glory; and spoil is considered as a badge of victory. Nations and tribes are their prey; the solitary traveler, by whom they can acquire only the reputation of generosity, is suffered to pass unhurt, or is treated with splendid munificence.

Though distinguished into small cantons under their several chieftains, and for the most part separated by jealousy and animosity; yet when pressed by wars and formidable enemies, they sometimes unite in greater bodies. Like the Greeks in their expedition to Troy, they follow some remarkable leader, and compose a kingdom of many separate tribes. But such coalitions are merely occasional; and even during their continuance, more resemble republic than monarchy. The inferior chieftains reserve their importance, and intrude, with an air of equality, into the councils of their leader, as the people of their several clans commonly intrude upon them. Upon what motive indeed could we suppose, that men who live together in the greatest familiarity, and amongst whom the distinctions of rank are so obscurely marked, would resign their personal sentiments and inclinations, or pay an implicit submission to a leader who can neither overawe nor corrupt?
...

There is not disparity of rank among men in rude ages, sufficient to give their communities the form of legal monarchy; and in a territory of considerable extent, when united under one head, the warlike and turbulent spirit of its inhabitants seems to require the bridle of despotism and military force. Where any degree of freedom remains, the powers of the prince are, as they were in most of the rude monarchies of Europe, extremely precarious, and depend chiefly on his personal character; where, on the contrary, the powers of the prince are above the control of his people, they are likewise above the restrictions of law. Rapacity and terror become the predominant motives of conduct, and form the character of the only parties into which mankind are divided, that of the oppressor, and that of the oppressed.

This calamity threatened Europe for ages, under the conquest and settlement of its new inhabitants. It has actually taken place in Asia, where similar conquests have been made; and even without the ordinary opiates of effeminacy, or a servile weakness, founded on luxury, it has surprised the Tartar on his wain, in the rear of his herds. Among this people, in the heart of a great continent, bold and enterprising warriors arose. They subdued, by surprise, or superior abilities, the contiguous hordes; they gained, in their progress, accessions of numbers and of strength; and, like a torrent increasing as it descends, became too strong for any bar that could be opposed to their passage. The conquering tribe, during a succession of ages, furnished the prince with his guards; and while they themselves were allowed to share in its spoils, were the voluntary tools of oppression. In this manner has despotism and corruption made their way into regions so much renowned for the wild freedom of nature: a power which was the terror of every effeminate province is disarmed, and the nursery of nations is itself gone to decay.

Where rude nations escape this calamity, they require the exercise of foreign wars to maintain domestic peace. When no enemy appears from abroad, they have leisure for private feuds, and employ that courage in their dissensions at home, which, in time of war, is employed in defense of their country.

...

We are generally at a loss to conceive how mankind can subsist under customs and manners extremely different from our own; and we are apt to exaggerate the misery of barbarous times, by an imagination of what we ourselves should suffer in a situation to which we are not accustomed. But every age hath its consolations, as well as its sufferings. In the interval of occasional outrages, the friendly intercourses of men, even in their rudest condition, is affectionate and happy. In rude ages, the persons and properties of individuals are secure; because each has a friend, as well as an enemy; and if the one is disposed to molest, the other is ready to protect; and the very admiration of valor, which in some instances tends to sanctify violence, inspires likewise certain maxims of generosity and honor, that tend to prevent the commission of wrongs.

Men bear with the defects of their policy, as they do with hardships and inconveniences in their manner of living. The alarms and the fatigues of war become a necessary recreation to those who are accustomed to them, and who have the tone of their passions raised above less animating or trying occasions. Old men, among the courtiers of Attila, wept when they heard of heroic deeds, which they themselves could no longer perform. And among the Celtic nations, when age rendered the warrior unfit for his former toils, it was the custom, in order to abridge the languors of a listless and inactive life, to sue for death at the hands of his friends.

With all this ferocity of spirit, the rude nations of the West were subdued by the policy and more regular warfare of the Romans. The point of honor, which the barbarians of Europe adopted as individuals, exposed them to a peculiar disadvantage, by rendering them, even in their national wars, averse to assailing their enemy by surprise, or taking the benefit of stratagem; and though separately bold and intrepid, yet, like other rude nations, they were, when assembled in great bodies, addicted to superstition, and subject to panics.

They were, from a consciousness of their personal courage and force, sanguine on the eve of battle; they were, beyond the bounds of moderation, elated on success, and dejected in adversity; and being disposed to consider every event as a judgment of the gods, they were never qualified by an uniform application of prudence, to make the most of their forces, to repair their misfortunes, or to improve their advantages.

Resigned to the government of affection and passion, they were generous and faithful where they had fixed an attachment; implacable, froward, and cruel, where they had conceived a dislike. Addicted to debauchery, and the immoderate use of intoxicating liquors, they deliberated on the affairs of state in the heat of their riot; and in the same dangerous moments, conceived the designs of military enterprise, or terminated their domestic dissensions by the dagger or the sword.

In their wars they preferred death to captivity. The victorious armies of the Romans, in entering a town by assault, or in forcing an encampment, have found the mother in the act of destroying her children, that they might not be taken; and the dagger of the parent, red with the blood of his family, ready to be plunged at last into his own breast.

In all these particulars we perceive that vigor of spirit, which renders disorder itself respectable, and which qualifies men, if fortunate in their situation, to lay the basis of domestic liberty, as well as to maintain against foreign enemies their national independence and freedom.

## PART III
### Of the History of Policy and Arts

#### *Section II: The History of Subordination*

We have hitherto observed mankind, either united together on terms of equality, or disposed to admit of a subordination founded merely on the voluntary respect and attachment which they paid to their leaders; but, in both cases, without any concerted plan of government, or system of laws.

The savage, whose fortune is comprised in his cabin, his fur, and his arms, is satisfied with that provision, and with that degree of security, he himself can procure. He perceives, in treating with his equal, no subject of discussion that should be referred to the decision of a judge; nor does he find in any hand the badges of magistracy, or the ensigns of a perpetual command.

The barbarian, though induced by his admiration of personal qualities, the luster of a heroic race, or a superiority of fortune, to follow the
banners of a leader, and to act a subordinate part in his tribe, knows not,
that what he performs from choice, is to be made a subject of obligation.
He acts from affections unacquainted with forms; and when provoked,
or when engaged in disputes, he recurs to the sword, as the ultimate
means of decision, in all questions of right.

Human affairs, in the mean time, continue their progress. What was in
one generation a propensity to herd with the species, becomes, in the
ages which follow, a principle of national union. What was originally an
alliance for common defense, becomes a concerted plan of political
force; the care of subsistence becomes an anxiety for accumulating
wealth, and the foundation of commercial arts.

Mankind, in following the present sense of their minds, in striving to
remove inconveniences, or to gain apparent and contiguous advantages, arrive at ends which even their imagination could not anticipate,
and pass on, like other animals, in the track of their nature, without perceiving its end. He who first said, "I will appropriate this field: I will
leave it to my heirs", did not perceive, that he was laying the foundation
of civil laws and political establishments. He who first ranged himself
under a leader, did not perceive, that he was setting the example of a permanent subordination, under the pretence of which, the rapacious were
to seize his possessions, and the arrogant to lay claim to his service.

Men, in general, are sufficiently disposed to occupy themselves in
forming projects and schemes, but he who would scheme and project for
others, will find an opponent in every person who is disposed to scheme
for himself. Like the winds, that come we know not whence, and blow
whithersoever they list, the forms of society are derived from an obscure
and distant origin; they arise, long before the date of philosophy, from
the instincts, not from the speculations, of men. The crowd of mankind,
are directed in their establishments and measures, by the circumstances
in which they are placed; and seldom are turned from their way, to follow the plan of any single projector.

Every step and every movement of the multitude, even in what are
termed enlightened ages, are made with equal blindness to the future;
and nations stumble upon establishments, which are indeed the result of
human action, but not the execution of any human design. If Cromwell
said, that a man never mounts higher, than when he knows not whither
he is going; it may with more reason be affirmed of communities, that
they admit of the greatest revolutions where no change is intended, and
that the most refined politicians do not always know whither they are
leading the state by their projects.

If we listen to the testimony of modern history, and to that of the most
authentic parts of the ancient; if we attend to the practice of nations in
every quarter of the world, and in every condition, whether that of the
barbarian or the polished, we shall find very little reason to retract this

assertion. No constitution is formed by concert, no government is copied from a plan. The members of a small state contend for equality; the members of a greater, find themselves classed in a certain manner that lays a foundation for monarchy. They proceed from one form of government to another, by easy transitions, and frequently under old names adopt a new constitution. The seeds of every form are lodged in human nature; they spring up and ripen with the season. The prevalence of a particular species is often derived from an imperceptible ingredient mingled in the soil.

We are therefore to receive, with caution, the traditional histories of ancient legislators, and founders of states. Their names have long been celebrated; their supposed plans have been admired; and what were probably the consequences of an early situation, is, in every instance, considered as an effect of design. An author and a work, like cause and effect, are perpetually coupled together. This is the simplest form under which we can consider the establishment of nations; and we ascribe to a previous design, what came to be known only by experience, what no human wisdom could foresee, and what, without the concurring humor and disposition of his age, no authority could enable an individual to execute.

If men, during ages of extensive reflection, and employed in the search of improvement, are wedded to their institutions; and, laboring under many acknowledged inconveniences, cannot break loose from the trammels of custom; what shall we suppose their humor to have been in the times of Romulus and Lycurgus? They were not surely more disposed to embrace the schemes of innovators, or to shake off the impressions of habit: they were not more pliant and ductile, when their knowledge was less; not more capable of refinement, when their minds were more circumscribed.

We imagine, perhaps, that rude nations must have so strong a sense of the defects under which they labor, and be so conscious that reformations are requisite in their manners, that they must be ready to adopt, with joy, every plan of improvement, and to receive every plausible proposal with implicit compliance. And we are thus inclined to believe, that the harp of Orpheus could effect, in one age, what the eloquence of Plato could not produce in another. We mistake, however, the characteristic of simple ages: mankind then appear to feel the fewest defects, and are then least desirous to enter on reformations.

The reality, in the mean time, of certain establishments at Rome and at Sparta, cannot be disputed. But it is probable, that the government of both these states took its rise from the situation and genius of the people, not from the projects of single men; that the celebrated warrior and statesman, who are considered as the founders of those nations, only acted a superior part among numbers who were disposed to the same institutions; and that they left to posterity a renown, pointing them out as the inventors of many practices which had been already in use, and which helped to form their own manners and genius, as well as those of their countrymen.

It has been formerly observed, that, in many particulars, the customs of simple nations coincide with what is ascribed to the invention of early statesmen; that the model of republican government, the senate, and the assembly of the people; that even the equality of property, or the community of goods, were not reserved to the invention or contrivance of singular men.

If we consider Romulus as the founder of the Roman state, certainly he who killed his brother that he might reign alone, did not desire to come under restraints from the controlling power of the senate, nor to refer the councils of his sovereignty to the decision of a collective body. Love of dominion is, by its nature, averse to constraint; and this chieftain, like every leader in a rude age, probably found a class of men ready to intrude on his councils, and without whom he could not proceed. He met with occasions, on which, as at the sound of a trumpet, the body of the people assembled, and took resolutions, which any individual might in vain dispute, or attempt to control; and Rome, which commenced on the general plan of every artless society, found lasting improvements in the pursuit of temporary expedients, and digested her political frame in adjusting the pretensions of parties which arose in the state.

Mankind, in very early ages of society, learn to covet riches, and to admire distinction. They have avarice and ambition, and are occasionally led by them to depredation and conquest, but in their ordinary conduct, these motives are balanced or restrained by other habits and other pursuits—by sloth, or intemperance; by personal attachments, or personal animosities, which mislead from the attention to interest. These circumstances render man kind, at times, remiss or outrageous: they prove the source of civil peace or disorder, but disqualify those who are actuated by them, from maintaining any fixed usurpation. Slavery and rapine are first threatened from abroad, and war, either offensive or defensive, is the great business of every tribe. The enemy occupy their thoughts; they have no leisure for domestic dissensions. It is the desire of every separate community, however, to secure itself; and in proportion as it gains this object, by strengthening its barrier, by weakening its enemy, or by procuring allies, the individual at home bethinks him of what he may gain or lose for himself. The leader is disposed to enlarge the advantages which belong to his station; the follower becomes jealous of rights which are open to encroachment; and parties who united before, from affection and habit, or from a regard to their common preservation, disagree in supporting their several claims to precedence or profit.

When the animosities of faction are thus awakened at home, and the pretensions of freedom are opposed to those of dominion, the members of every society find a new scene upon which to exert their activity. They had quarreled, perhaps, on points of interest; they had balanced between different leaders; but they had never united as citizens, to withstand the encroachments of sovereignty, or to maintain their common rights as a people. If the prince, in this contest, finds numbers to support, as well as to oppose his pretensions, the sword which was whetted against foreign enemies, may be pointed at the bosom of fellow-subjects, and every interval of peace from abroad, be filled with domestic war. The sacred names of Liberty, Justice, and Civil Order, are made to resound in public assemblies; and, during the absence of other alarms, give a society, within itself, an abundant subject of ferment and animosity.

If what is related of the little principalities which, in ancient times, were formed in Greece, in Italy, and over all Europe, agrees with the character we have given of mankind under the first impressions of property, of interest, and of hereditary distinctions; the seditions and domestic wars which followed in those very states, the expulsion of their kings, or the questions which arose concerning the prerogatives of the sovereign, or privilege of the subject, are agreeable to the representation which we now give of the first step toward political establishment, and the desire of a legal constitution.

What this constitution may be in its earliest form, depends on a variety of circumstances in the condition of nations. It depends on the extent of the principality in its rude state; on the degree of disparity to which mankind had submitted before they began to dispute its abuses. It depends likewise on what we term *accidents*, the personal character of an individual, or the events of a war.

Every community is originally a small one. That propensity by which mankind at first unite, is not the principle from which they afterwards act in extending the limits of empire. Small tribes, where they are not assembled by common objects of conquest or safety, are even averse to a coalition. If, like the real or fabulous confederacy of the Greeks for the destruction of Troy, many nations combine in pursuit of a single object, they easily separate again, and act anew on the maxims of rival states.

There is, perhaps, a certain national extent, within which the passions of men are easily communicated from one, or a few, to the whole; and there are certain numbers of men who can be assembled, and act in a body. If, while the society is not enlarged beyond this dimension, and while its members are easily assembled, political contentions arise, the state seldom fails to proceed on republican maxims, and to establish democracy. In most rude principalities, the leader derived his prerogative from the luster of his race, and from the voluntary attachment of his tribe: the people he commanded, were his friends, his subjects, and his troops. If we suppose, upon any change in their manners, that they cease to revere his dignity, that they pretend to equality among themselves, or are seized with a jealousy of his assuming too much, the foundations of his power are already withdrawn. When the voluntary subject becomes refractory; when considerable parties, or the collective body, choose to act for themselves; the small kingdom, like that of Athens, becomes of course a republic.

The changes of condition, and of manners, which, in the progress of mankind, raise up to nations a leader and a prince, create, at the same time, a nobility, and a variety of ranks, who have, in a subordinate degree, their claim to distinction. Superstition, too, may create an order of men, who, under the title of priesthood, engage in the pursuit of a separate interest; who, by their union and firmness as a body, and by their incessant ambition, deserve to be reckoned in the list of pretenders to power. These different orders of men are the elements of whose mixture the political body is generally formed; each draws to its side some part from the mass of the people. The people themselves are a party upon occasion; and numbers of men, however classed and distinguished, become, by their jarring pretensions and separate views, mutual interruptions and checks; and have, by bringing to the national councils the maxims and apprehensions of a particular order, and by guarding a particular interest, a share in adjusting or preserving the political form of the state.

The pretensions of any particular order, if not checked by some collateral power, would terminate in tyranny; those of a prince, in despotism; those of a nobility or priesthood, in the abuses of aristocracy; of a populace, in the confusions of anarchy. These terminations, as they are never the professed, so are they seldom even the disguised, object of party. But the measures which any party pursues, if suffered to prevail, will lead, by degrees, to every extreme.

In their way to the ascendant they endeavor to gain, and in the midst of interruptions which opposite interests mutually give, liberty may have a permanent or a transient existence; and the constitution may bear a form and a character as various as the casual combination of such multiplied parts can effect.

To bestow on communities some degree of political freedom, it is perhaps sufficient, that their members, either singly, or as they are involved with their several orders, should insist on their rights: that under republics, the citizen should either maintain his own equality with firmness, or restrain the ambition of his fellow-citizen within moderate bounds; that under monarchy, men of every rank should maintain the honors of their private or their public stations; and sacrifice, neither to the impositions of a court, nor to the claims of a populace, those dignities which are destined, in some measure, independent of fortune, to give stability to the throne, and to procure a respect to the subject.

Amidst the contentions of party, the interests of the public, even the maxims of justice and candor, are sometimes forgotten; and yet those fatal consequences which such a measure of corruption seems to portend, do not unavoidably follow. The public interest is often secure, not because individuals are disposed to regard it as the end of their conduct, but because each, in his place, is determined to preserve his own. Liberty is maintained by the continued differences and oppositions of numbers, not by their concurring zeal in behalf of equitable government. In free states, therefore, the wisest laws are never, perhaps, dictated by the interest and spirit of any order of men: they are moved, they are opposed, or amended, by different hands; and come at last to express that medium and composition which contending parties have forced one another to adopt.

When we consider the history of mankind in this view, we cannot be at a loss for the causes which, in small communities, threw the balance on the side of democracy; which, in states more enlarged in respect to territory and numbers of people, gave the ascendant to monarchy; and which, in a variety of conditions and of different ages, enabled mankind to blend and unite the characters of different forms; and, instead of any of the simple constitutions we have mentioned, to exhibit a medley of all.

In emerging from a state of rudeness and simplicity, men must be expected to act from that spirit of equality, or moderate subordination, to which they have been accustomed. When crowded together in cities, or within the compass of a small territory, they act by contagious passions, and every individual feels a degree of importance proportioned to his figure in the crowd, and the smallness of its numbers. The pretenders to power and dominion appear in too familiar a light to impose upon the multitude, and they have no aids at their call, by which they can bridle the refractory humors of a people who resist their pretensions. Theseus, King of Attica, we are told, assembled the inhabitants of its twelve cantons into one city. In this he took an effectual method to unite into one democracy, what were before the separate members of his monarchy, and to hasten the downfall of the regal power.

The monarch of an extensive territory has many advantages in maintaining his station. Without any grievance to his subjects, he can support the magnificence of a royal estate, and dazzle the imagination of his people, by that very wealth which themselves have bestowed. He can employ the inhabitants of one district against those of another; and while the passions that lead to mutiny and rebellion, can at anyone time seize only on a part of his subjects, he feels himself strong in the possession of a general authority. Even the distance at which he resides from many of those who receive his commands, augments the mysterious awe and respect which are paid to his government.

With these different tendencies, accident and corruption, however, joined to a variety of circumstances, may throw particular states from their bias, and produce exceptions to every general rule. This has actually happened in some of the later principalities of Greece, and modern Italy, in Sweden, Poland, and the German empire. But the united states of the Netherlands, and the Swiss cantons, are perhaps the most extensive communities, which maintaining the union of nations, have, for any considerable time, resisted the tendency to monarchical government;

and Sweden is the only instance of a republic established in a great kingdom on the ruins of monarchy.

The sovereign of a petty district, or a single city, when not supported, as in modern Europe, by the contagion of monarchical manners, holds the scepter by a precarious tenure, and is perpetually alarmed by the spirit of mutiny in his people, is guided by jealousy, and supports himself by severity, prevention, and force.

The popular and aristocratic powers in a great nations, as in the case of Germany and Poland, may meet with equal difficulty in maintaining their pretensions; and in order to avoid their danger on the side of kingly usurpation, are obliged to withhold from the supreme magistrate even the necessary trust of an executive power.

The states of Europe, in the manner of their first settlement laid the foundations of monarchy, and were prepared to unite under regular and extensive governments. If the Greeks, whose progress at home terminated in the establishment of so many independent republics, had under Agamemnon effected a conquest and settlement in Asia, it is probable, that they might have furnished an example of the same kind. But the original inhabitants of any country, forming many separate cantons, come by slow degrees to that coalition and union into which conquering tribes are, in effecting their conquests, or in securing their possessions, hurried at once. Caesar encountered some hundreds of independent nations in Gaul, whom even their common danger did not sufficiently unite. The German invaders, who settled in the lands of the Romans, made, in the same district, a number of separate establishments, but far more extensive than what the ancient Gauls, by their conjunctions and treaties, or in the result of their wars, could after many ages have reached.

The seeds of great monarchies, and the roots of extensive dominion, were everywhere planted with the colonies that divided the Roman empire. We have no exact account of the numbers, who, with a seeming concert, continued, during some ages, to invade and to seize this tempting prize. Where they expected resistance, they endeavored to muster up a proportional force; and when they proposed to settle, entire nations removed to share in the spoil. Scattered over an extensive province, where they could not be secure, without maintaining their union, they continued to acknowledge the leader under whom they had fought; and, like an army sent by divisions into separate stations, were prepared to assemble whenever occasion should require their united operations or counsels.

Every separate party had its post assigned, and every subordinate chieftain his possessions, from which he was to provide his own subsistence, and that of his followers. The model of government was taken from that of a military subordination, and a fief was the temporary pay of an officer proportioned to his rank. There was a class of the people destined to military service, another to labor, and to cultivate lands for the benefit of their masters. The officer improved his tenure by degrees, first changing a temporary grant into a tenure for his life; and this also, upon the observance of certain conditions, into a grant including his heirs.

The rank of the nobles became hereditary in every quarter, and formed a powerful and permanent order of men in every state. While they held the people in servitude, they disputed the claims of their sovereign; they withdrew their attendance upon occasion, or turned their arms against him. They formed a strong and insurmountable barrier against a general despotism in the state; but they were themselves, by means of their warlike retainers, the tyrants of every little district, and prevented the establishment of order, or any regular applications of law. They took the advantage of weak reigns or minorities, to push their encroachments on the sovereign; or having made the monarchy elective, they by successive treaties and stipulations, at every election, limited or undermined the monarchical power. The prerogatives of the prince have been, in some instances, as in that of the German empire in particular, reduced to a mere title; and the national union itself preserved in the observance only of a few insignificant formalities.

Where the contest of the sovereign, and of his vassals, under hereditary and ample prerogatives annexed to the crown, had a different issue, the feudal lordships were gradually stripped of their powers, the nobles were reduced to the state of subjects, and obliged to hold their honors, and exercise their jurisdictions, in a dependence on the prince. It was his supposed interest to reduce them to a state of equal subjection with the people, and to extend his own authority, by rescuing the laborer and the dependent from the oppressions of their immediate superiors.

In this project the princes of Europe have variously succeeded. While they protected the people, and thereby encouraged the practice of commercial and lucrative arts, they paved the way for despotism in the state; and with the same policy by which they relieved the subject from many oppressions, they increased the powers of the crown.

But where the people had by the constitution a representative in the government, and a head, under which they could avail themselves of the wealth they acquired, and of the sense of their personal importance, this policy turned against the crown; it formed a new power to restrain the prerogative, to establish the government of law, and to exhibit a spectacle new in the history of mankind; monarchy mixed with republic, and extensive territory, governed, during some ages, without military force.

Such were the steps by which the nations of Europe have arrived at their present establishments: in some instances, they have come to the possession of legal constitutions; in others, to the exercise of a mitigated despotism; or continue to struggle with the tendency which they severally have to these different extremes.

...

## Section VI: Of Civil Liberty

If war, either for depredation or defense, were the principal object of nations, every tribe would, from its earliest state, aim at the condition of a Tartar horde; and in all its successes would hasten to the grandeur of a Tartar empire. The military leader would supersede the civil magistrate; and preparations to fly with all their possessions, or to pursue with all their forces, would, in every society, make the sum of their public arrangements.

He who first on the banks of the Volga, or the Jenisca, had taught the Scythian to mount the horse, to move his cottage on wheels, to harass his enemy alike by his attacks and his flights, to handle at full speed the lance and the bow, and when beat from the field, to leave his arrows in the wind to meet his pursuer; he who had taught his countrymen to use the same animal for every purpose of the dairy, the shambles, and the field; would be esteemed the founder of his nation; or, like Ceres and Bacchus among the Greeks, would be invested with the honors of a god, as the reward of his useful inventions. Amidst such institutions, the names and achievements of Hercules and Jason might have been transmitted to posterity; but those of Lycurgus or Solon, the heroes of political society, could have gained no reputation, either fabulous or real, in the records of fame.

Every tribe of warlike barbarians may entertain among themselves the strongest sentiments of affection and honor, while they carry to the rest of mankind the aspect of banditti and robbers. They may be indifferent to interest, and superior to danger; but our sense of humanity, our regard to the rights of nations, our admiration of civil wisdom and justice, even our effeminacy itself, make us turn away with contempt, or with horror, from a scene which exhibits so few of our good qualities, and which serve so much to reproach our weakness.

It is in conducting the affairs of civil society, that mankind find the exercise of their best talents, as well as the object of their best affections. It is in being grafted on the advantages of civil society, that the art of war is brought to perfection; that the resources of armies, and the complicated springs to be touched in their conduct, are best understood. The most celebrated warriors were also citizens; opposed to a Roman, or a Greek, the chieftain of Thrace, of Germany, or Gaul, was a novice. The native of Pella learned the principles of his art from Epaminondas and Pelopidas.

If nations, as hath been observed in the preceding section [section V, Of National Defense and Conquest], must adjust their policy on the prospect of war from abroad, they are equally bound to provide for the attainment of peace at home. But there is no peace in the absence of justice. It may subsist with divisions, disputes, and contrary opinions; but not with the commission of wrongs. The injurious, and the injured, are, as implied in the very meaning of the terms, in a state of hostility.

Where men enjoy peace, they owe it either to their mutual regards and affections, or to the restraints of law. Those are the happiest states which procure peace to their members by the first of these methods, but it is sufficiently uncommon to procure it even by the second. The first would withhold the occasions of war and of competition, the second adjusts the pretensions of men by stipulations and treaties. Sparta taught her citizens not to regard interest; other free nations secure the interest of their members, and consider this as a principal part of their rights.

Law is the treaty to which members of the same community have agreed, and under which the magistrate and the subject continue to enjoy their rights, and to maintain the peace of society. The desire of lucre is the great motive to injuries: law therefore has a principal reference to property. It would ascertain the different methods by which property may be acquired, as by prescription, conveyance, and succession; and it makes the necessary provisions for rendering the possession of property secure.

Beside avarice, there are other motives from which men are unjust; such are pride, malice, envy, and revenge. The law would eradicate the principles themselves, or at least prevent their effects.

From whatever motive wrongs are committed, there are different particulars in which the injured may suffer. He may suffer in his goods, in his person, or in the freedom of his conduct. Nature has made him master of every action which is not injurious to others. The laws of his particular society entitle him perhaps to a determinate station, and bestow on him a certain share in the government of his country. An injury, therefore, which in this respect puts him under any unjust restraint, may be called an infringement of his political rights.

Where the citizen is supposed to have rights of property and of station, and is protected in the exercise of them, he is said to be free; and the very restraints by which he is hindered from the commission of crimes, are a part of his liberty. No person is free, where any person is suffered to do wrong with impunity. Even the despotic prince on his throne, is not an exception to this general rule. He himself is a slave, the moment he pretends that force should decide any contest. The disregard he throws on the rights of his people recoils on himself; and in the general uncertainty of all conditions, there is no tenure more precarious than his own.

From the different particulars to which men refer, in speaking of liberty, whether to the safety of the person and the goods, the dignity of rank, or the participation of political importance, as well as from the different methods by which their rights are secured, they are led to differ in the interpretation of the term; and every people is apt to imagine, that its signification is to be found only among themselves.

Some having thought, that the unequal distribution of wealth is unjust, required a new division of property, as the foundation of freedom. This scheme is suited to democratic government; and in such only it has been admitted with any degree of effect.

New settlements, like that of the people of Israel, and singular establishments, like those of Sparta and Crete, have furnished examples of its actual execution; but in most other states, even the democratic spirit could attain no more than to prolong the struggle for Agrarian laws; to procure, on occasion, the expunging of debts; and to keep the people in mind, under all the distinctions of fortune, that they still had a claim to equality.

The citizen at Rome, at Athens, and in many republics, contended for himself, and his order. The Agrarian law was moved and debated for ages: it served to awaken the mind; it nourished the spirit of equality, and furnished a field on which to exert its force; but was never established with any of its other and more formal effects.

Many of the establishments which serve to defend the weak from oppression, contribute, by securing the possession of property, to favor its unequal division, and to increase the ascendant of those from whom the abuses of power may be feared. Those abuses were felt very early both at Athens and Rome.

It appears to be, in a particular manner, the object of sumptuary laws, and of the equal division of wealth, to prevent the gratification of vanity, to check the ostentation of superior fortune, and, by this means, to weaken the desire of riches, and to preserve in the breast of the citizen, that moderation and equity which ought to regulate his conduct.

This end is never perfectly attained in any state where the unequal division of property is admitted, and where fortune is allowed to bestow distinction and rank. It is indeed difficult, by any methods whatever, to shut up this source of corruption. Of all the nations whose history is known with certainty, the design itself, and the manner of executing it, appear to have been understood in Sparta alone.

There property was indeed acknowledged by law; but in consequence of certain regulations and practices, the most effectual, it seems, that mankind have hitherto found out, the manners that prevail among simple nations before the establishment of property, were in some measure preserved; the passion for riches was, during many ages, suppressed; and the citizen was made to consider himself as the property of his country, not as the owner of a private estate.

It was held ignominious either to buy or to sell the patrimony of a citizen. Slaves were, in every family, entrusted with the care of its effects, and freemen were strangers to lucrative arts; justice was established on a contempt of the ordinary allurement to crimes; and the preservatives of civil liberty applied by the state, were the dispositions that were made to prevail in the hearts of its members.

The individual was relieved from every solicitude that could arise on the head of his fortune; he was educated, and he was employed for life in the service of the public; he was fed at a place of common resort, to which he could carry no distinction but that of his talents and his virtues; his children were the wards and the pupils of the state; he himself was taught to be a parent, and a director to the youth of his country, not the anxious father of a separate family.

This people, we are told, bestowed some care in adorning their persons, and were known from afar by the red or the purple they wore; but could not make their equipage, their buildings, or their furniture, a subject of fancy, or of what we call *taste*. The carpenter and the house-builder were restricted to the use of the axe and the saw: their workmanship must have been simple, and probably, in respect to its form, continued for ages the same. The ingenuity of the artist was employed in cultivating his own nature, not in adorning the habitations of his fellow-citizens.

On this plan, they had senators, magistrates, leaders of armies, and ministers of state; but no men of fortune. Like the heroes of Homer, they distributed honors by the measure of the cup and the platter. A citizen, who, in his political capacity, was the arbiter of Greece, thought himself honored by receiving a double portion of plain entertainment at supper. He was active, penetrating, brave, disinterested, and generous; but his estate, his table, and his furniture, might, in our esteem, have marred the luster of all his virtues. Neighboring nations, however, applied for commanders to this nursery of statesmen and warriors, as we apply for the practitioners of every art to the countries in which they excel; for cooks to France, and for musicians to Italy.

After all, we are, perhaps, not sufficiently instructed in the nature of the Spartan laws and institutions, to understand in what manner all the ends of this singular state were obtained; but the admiration paid to its people, and the constant reference of contemporary historians to their avowed superiority, will not allow us to question the facts. "When I observed", says Xenophon, "that this nation, though not the most populous, was the most powerful state of Greece, I was seized with wonder, and with an earnest desire to know by what arts it attained its pre-eminence; but when I came to the knowledge of its institutions, my wonder ceased. — As one man excels another, and as he who is at pains to cultivate his mind, must surpass the person who neglects it; so the Spartans should excel every nation, being the only state in which virtue is studied as the object of government."

The subjects of property, considered with a view to subsistence, or even to enjoyment, have little effect in corrupting mankind, or in awakening the spirit of competition and of jealousy. Considered with a view to distinction and honor, where fortune constitutes rank, they excite the most vehement passions, and absorb all the sentiments of the human soul; they reconcile avarice and meanness with ambition and vanity; and lead men through the practice of sordid and mercenary arts to the possession of a supposed elevation and dignity.

Where this source of corruption, on the contrary, is effectually stopped, the citizen is dutiful, and the magistrate upright; any form of government may be wisely administered; places of trust are likely to be well supplied; and by whatever rule office and power are bestowed, it is likely that all the capacity and force that subsists in the state will come to be employed in its service. For on this supposition, experience and abilities are the only guides and the only titles to public confidence; and if citizens be ranged into separate classes, they become mutual checks by the difference of their opinions, not by the opposition of their interested designs.

We may easily account for the censures bestowed on the government of Sparta, by those who considered it merely on the side of its forms. It was not calculated to prevent the practice of crimes, by balancing against each other the selfish and partial dispositions of men; but to inspire the virtues of the soul, to procure innocence by the absence of criminal inclinations, and to derive its internal peace from the indifference of its members to the ordinary motives of strife and disorder. It were trifling to seek for its analogy to any other constitution of state, in which its principal characteristic and distinguishing feature is not to be found. The collegiate sovereignty, the senate, and the ephori, had their counterparts in other republics, and a resemblance has been found in particular to the government of Carthage. But what affinity of consequence can be found between a state whose sole object was virtue, and another whose principal object was wealth; between a people whose associated kings, being lodged in the same cottage, had no fortune but their daily food; and a commercial republic, in which a proper estate was required as a necessary qualification for the higher offices of state?

Other petty commonwealths expelled kings, when they became jealous of their designs, or after having experienced their tyranny; here the hereditary succession of kings was preserved. Other states were afraid of the intrigues and cabals of their members in competition for dignities; here solicitation was required as the only condition upon which a place in the senate was obtained. A supreme inquisitorial power was, in the persons of the ephori, safely committed to a few men, who were drawn by lot, and without distinction, from every order of the people. And if a contrast to this, as well as to many other articles of the Spartan policy, be required, it may be found in the general history of mankind.

But Sparta, under every supposed error of its form, prospered for ages, by the integrity of its manners, and by the character of its citizens. When that integrity was broken, this people did not languish in the weakness of nations sunk in effeminacy. They fell into the stream by which other states had been carried in the torrent of violent passions, and in the outrage of barbarous times. They ran the career of other nations, after that of ancient Sparta was finished: they built walls, and began to improve their possessions, after they ceased to improve their people; and on this new plan, in their struggle for political life, they survived the system of states that perished under the Macedonian dominion: they lived to act with another which arose in the Achaean league;

and were the last community of Greece that became a village in the
empire of Rome.

If it should be thought we have dwelt too long on the history of this
singular people, it may be remembered, in excuse, that they alone, in the
language of Xenophon, made virtue an object of state.

We must be contented to derive our freedom from a different source;
to expect justice from the limits which are set to the powers of the magistrate, and to rely for protection on the laws which are made to secure the
estate, and the person of the subject. We live in societies, where men
must be rich, in order to be great; where pleasure itself is often pursued
from vanity; where the desire of a supposed happiness serves to inflame
the worst of passions, and is itself the foundation of misery; where public justice, like fetters applied to the body, may, without inspiring the
sentiments of candor and equity, prevent the actual commission of
crimes.

Mankind come under this description the moment they are seized
with their passions for riches and power. But their description in every
instance is mixed: in the best there is an alloy of evil; in the worst a mixture of good. Without any establishments to preserve their manners,
besides penal laws, and the restraints of police, they derive, from instinctive feelings, a love of integrity and candor, and, from the very contagion
of society itself, an esteem for what is honorable and praise-worthy.
They derive, from their union, and joint opposition to foreign enemies, a
zeal for their own community, and courage to maintain its rights. If the
frequent neglect of virtue as a political object, tend to discredit the
understandings of men, its luster, and its frequency, as a spontaneous
offspring of the heart, will restore the honors of our nature.

In every casual and mixed state of the national manners, the safety of
every individual, and his political consequence, depends much on himself, but more on the party to which he is joined. For this reason, all who
feel a common interest, are apt to unite in parties; and, as far as that interest requires, mutually support each other.

Where the citizens of any free community are of different orders, each
order has a peculiar set of claims and pretensions: relatively to the other
members of the state, it is a party; relatively to the differences of interest
among its own members, it may admit of numberless subdivisions. But
in every state there are two interests very readily apprehended; that of a
prince and his adherents, that of a nobility, or of any temporary faction,
opposed to the people.

Where the sovereign power is reserved by the collective body, it
appears unnecessary to think of additional establishments for securing
the rights of the citizen, But it is difficult, if not impossible, for the collective body to exercise this power in a manner that supersedes the necessity of every other political caution.

If popular assemblies assume every function of government; and if, in
the same tumultuous manner in which they can, with great propriety,

express their feelings, the sense of their rights, and their animosity to foreign or domestic enemies, they pretend to deliberate on points of national conduct, or to decide questions of equity and justice; the public is exposed to manifold inconveniences; and popular governments would, of all others, be the most subject to errors in administration, and to weakness in the execution of public measures.

To avoid these disadvantages, the people are always contented to delegate part of their powers. They establish a senate to debate, and to prepare, if not to determine, questions that are brought to the collective body for a final resolution. They commit the executive power to some council of this sort, or to a magistrate who presides in their meetings. Under the use of this necessary and common expedient, even while democratic forms are most carefully guarded, there is one party of the few, another of the many. One attacks, the other defends; and they are both ready to assume in their turns. But though, in reality, a great danger to liberty arises on the part of the people themselves, who, in times of corruption, are easily made the instruments of usurpation and tyranny; yet, in the ordinary aspect of government, the executive carries an air of superiority, and the rights of the people seem always exposed to encroachment.

Though on the day that the Roman people assembled in their tribes, the senators mixed with the crowd, and the consul was no more than the servant of the multitude; yet, when this awful meeting was dissolved, the senators met to prescribe business for their sovereign, and the consul went armed with the axe and the rods, to teach every Roman, in his separate capacity, the submission which he owed to the state.

Thus, even where the collective body is sovereign, they are assembled only occasionally; and though on such occasions they determine every question relative to their rights and their interests as a people, and can assert their freedom with irresistible force, yet they do not think themselves, nor are they in reality, safe, without a more constant and more uniform power operating in their favor.

The multitude is everywhere strong; but requires, for the safety of its members, when separate as well as when assembled, a head to direct and to employ its strength. For this purpose, the ephori, we are told, were established at Sparta, the council of a hundred at Carthage, and the tribunes at Rome. So prepared, the popular party has, in many instances, been able to cope with its adversaries, and has even trampled on the powers, whether aristocratic or monarchical, with which it would have been otherwise unequally matched. The state, in such cases, commonly suffered by the delays, interruptions, and confusions, which popular leaders, from private envy, or a prevailing jealousy of the great, seldom failed to create in the proceedings of government.

Where the people, as in some larger communities, have only a share in the legislature, they cannot overwhelm the collateral powers, who having likewise a share, are in condition to defend themselves; where they act only by their representatives, their force may be uniformly employed. And they may make part in a constitution of government more lasting than any of those in which the people possessing or pretending to the entire legislature, are, when assembled, the tyrants, and, when dispersed, the slaves, of a distempered state. In governments properly mixed, the popular interest, finding a counterpoise in that of the prince or of the nobles, a balance is actually established between them, in which the public freedom and the public order are made to consist.

From some such casual arrangement of different interests, all the varieties of mixed government proceed; and on the degree of consideration which every separate interest can procure to itself, depends the equity of the laws they enact, and the necessity they are able to impose, of adhering strictly to the terms of law in its execution. States are accordingly unequally qualified to conduct the business of legislation, and unequally fortunate in the completeness, and regular observance, of their civil code.

In democratic establishments, citizens, feeling themselves possessed of the sovereignty, are not equally anxious, with the subject of other governments, to have their rights explained, or secured, by actual statute. They trust to personal vigor, to the support of party, and to the sense of the public.

If the collective body perform the office of judge, as well as of legislator, they seldom think of devising rules for their own direction, and are found more seldom to follow any determinate rule, after it is made. They dispense, at one time, with what they enacted at another; and in their judicative, perhaps even more than in their legislative, capacity, are guided by passions and partialities that arise from circumstances of the case before them.

But under the simplest governments of a different sort, whether aristocracy or monarchy, there is a necessity for law, and there are a variety of interests to be adjusted in framing every statute. The sovereign wishes to give stability and order to administration, by express and promulgated rules. The subject wishes to know the conditions and limits of his duty. He acquiesces, or he revolts, according as the terms on which he is made to live with the sovereign, or with his fellow-subjects, are, or are not, consistent with the sense of his rights.

Neither the monarch, nor the council of nobles, where either is possessed of the sovereignty, can pretend to govern, or to judge at discretion. No magistrate, whether temporary or hereditary, can with safety neglect that reputation for justice and equity, from which his authority, and the respect that is paid to his person, are in a great measure derived. Nations, however, have been fortunate in the tenor, and in the execution of their laws, in proportion as they have admitted every order of the people, by representation or otherwise, to an actual share of the legislature. Under establishments of this sort, law is literally a treaty, to which the parties concerned have agreed, and have given their opinion in settling its terms. The interests to be affected by a law, are likewise consulted in making it. Every class propounds an objection, suggests an addition or an amendment of its own. They proceed to adjust, by stature, every subject of controversy; and while they continue to enjoy their freedom, they continue to multiply laws, and to accumulate volumes, as if they could remove every possible ground of dispute, and were secure of their rights, merely by having put them in writing.

Rome and England, under their mixed governments, the one inclining to democracy, the other to monarchy, have proved the great legislators among nations. The first has left the foundation, and great part of the superstructure of its civil code, to the continent of Europe; the other, in its island, has carried the authority and government of law to a point of perfection, which they never before attained in the history of mankind.

Under such favorable establishments, known customs, the practice and decisions of courts, as well as positive statutes, acquire the authority of laws; and every proceeding is conducted by some fixed and determinate rule. The best and most effectual precautions are taken for the impartial application of rules to particular cases; and it is remarkable, that, in the two examples we have mentioned, a surprising coincidence is found in the singular methods of their jurisdiction. The people in both reserved in a manner the office of judgment to themselves, and brought the decision of civil rights, or of criminal questions, to the tribunal of peers, who, in judging of their fellow-citizens, prescribed a condition of life for themselves.

It is not in mere laws, after all, that we are to look for the securities to justice, but in the powers by which those laws have been obtained, and without whose constant support they must fall to disuse. Statutes serve to record the rights of a people, and speak the intention of parties to defend what the letter of the law has expressed; but without the vigor to maintain what is acknowledged as a right, the mere record, or the feeble intention, is of little avail.

A populace roused by oppression, or an order of men possessed of a temporary advantage, have obtained many charters, concessions, and stipulations, in favor of their claims; but where no adequate preparation was made to preserve them, the written articles were often forgotten, together with the occasion on which they were framed.

The history of England, and of every free country, abounds with the example of statutes enacted when the people or their representatives assembled, but never executed when the crown or the executive was left to itself. The most equitable laws on paper are consistent with the utmost despotism in administration, Even the form of trial by juries in England had its authority in law, while the proceedings of courts were arbitrary and oppressive.

We must admire, as the key-stone of civil liberty, the statute which forces the secrets of every prison to be revealed, the cause of every commitment to be declared, and the person of the accused to be produced, that he may claim his enlargement, or his trial, within a limited time. No wiser form was ever opposed to the abuses of power. But it requires a fabric no less than the whole political constitution of Great Britain, a spirit no less than the refractory and turbulent zeal of this fortunate people, to secure its effects.

If even the safety of the person, and the tenure of property, which may be so well defined in the words of a statute, depend, for their preservation, on the vigor and jealousy of a free people, and on the degree of consideration which every order of the state maintains for itself; it is still more evident, that what we have called the political freedom, or the right of the individual to act in his station for himself and the public, cannot be made to rest on any other foundation. The estate may be saved, and the person released, by the forms of a civil procedure; but the rights of the mind cannot be sustained by any other force but its own.

## PART IV
## Of the Consequences that result from the Advancement of Civil and Commercial Arts

### Section I: Of the Separation of Arts and Professions

It is evident, that, however urged by a sense of necessity, and a desire of convenience, or favored by any advantages of situation and policy, a people can make no great progress in cultivating the arts of life, until they have separated, and committed to different persons, the several tasks, which require a peculiar skill and attention. The savage, or the barbarian, who must build and plant, and fabricate for himself, prefers, in the interval of great alarms and fatigues, the enjoyments of sloth to the improvement of his fortune. He is, perhaps, by the diversity of his wants, discouraged from industry; or, by his divided attention, prevented from acquiring skill in the management of any particular subject.

The enjoyment of peace, however, and the prospect of being able to exchange one commodity for another, turns, by degrees, the hunter and the warrior into a tradesman and a merchant. The accidents which distribute the means of subsistence unequally, inclination, and favorable opportunities, assign the different occupations of men; and a sense of utility leads them, without end, to subdivide their professions.

The artist finds, that the more he can confine his attention to a particular part of any work, his productions are the more perfect, and grow under his hands in the greater quantities. Every undertaker in manufacture finds, that the more he can subdivide the tasks of his workmen, and the more hands he can employ on separate articles, the more are his expenses diminished, and his profits increased. The consumer too requires, in every kind of commodity, a workmanship more perfect than hands employed on a variety of subjects can produce; and the progress of commerce is but a continued subdivision of the mechanical arts.

Every craft may engross the whole of a man's attention, and has a mystery which must be studied or learned by a regular apprenticeship. Nations of tradesmen come to consist of members who, beyond their own particular trade, are ignorant of all human affairs, and who may contribute to the preservation and enlargement of their commonwealth, without making its interest an object of their regard or attention. Every individual is distinguished by his calling, and has a place to which he is fitted. The savage, who knows no distinction but that of his merit, of his sex, or of his species, and to whom his community is the sovereign object of affection, is astonished to find, that in a scene of this nature, his being a man does not qualify him for any station whatever: he flies to the woods with amazement, distaste, and aversion.

By the separation of arts and professions, the sources of wealth are laid open; every species of material is wrought up to the greatest perfection, and every commodity is produced in the greatest abundance. The state may estimate its profits and its revenues by the number of its people. It may procure, by its treasure, that national consideration and power, which the savage maintains at the expense of his blood.

The advantage gained in the inferior branches of manufacture by the separation of their parts, seem to be equaled by those which arise from a similar device in the higher departments of policy and war. The soldier is relieved from every care but that of his service; statesmen divide the business of civil government into shares; and the servants of the public, in every office, without being skilful in the affairs of state, may succeed, by observing forms which are already established on the experience of others. They are made, like the parts of an engine, to concur to a purpose, without any concert of their own; and, equally blind with the trader to any general combination, they unite with him, in furnishing to the state its resources, its conduct, and its force.

The artifices of the beaver, the ant, and the bee, are ascribed to the wisdom of nature. Those of polished nations are ascribed to themselves, and are supposed to indicate a capacity superior to that of rude minds. But the establishments of men, like those of every animal, are suggested by nature, and are the result of instinct, directed by the variety of situations in which mankind are placed. Those establishments arose from successive improvements that were made, without any sense of their general effect; and they bring human affairs to a state of complication, which the greatest reach of capacity with which human nature was ever adorned, could not have projected; nor even when the whole is carried into execution, can it be comprehended in its full extent.

Who could anticipate, or even enumerate, the separate occupations and professions by which the members of any commercial state are distinguished; the variety of devices which are practiced in separate cells, and which the artist, attentive to his own affair, has invented, to abridge or to facilitate his separate task? In coming to this mighty end, every generation, compared to its predecessors, may have appeared to be ingenious; compared to its followers, may have appeared to be dull; and human ingenuity, whatever heights it may have gained in a succession of ages, continues to move with an equal pace, and to creep in making the last as well as the first step of commercial or civil improvement.

It may even be doubted, whether the measure of national capacity increases with the advancement of arts. Many mechanical arts, indeed, require no capacity; they succeed best under a total suppression of sentiment and reason; and ignorance is the mother of industry as well as of superstition. Reflection and fancy are subject to err; but a habit of moving the hand, or the foot, is independent of either. Manufactures, accordingly, prosper most, where the mind is least consulted, and where the workshop may, without any great effort of imagination, be considered as an engine, the parts of which are men.

The forest has been felled by the savage without the use of the axe, and weights have been raised without the aid of the mechanical powers. The merit of the inventor, in every branch, probably deserves a preference to that of the performer; and he who invented a tool, or could work without its assistance, deserved the praise of ingenuity in a much higher degree than the mere artist, who, by its assistance, produced a superior work.

But if many parts in the practice of every art, and in the detail of every department, require no abilities, or actually tend to contract and to limit the views of the mind, there are others which lead to general reflections, and to enlargement of thought. Even in manufacture, the genius of the master, perhaps, is cultivated, while that of the inferior workman lies waste. The statesman may have a wide comprehension of human affairs, while the tools he employs are ignorant of the system in which they are themselves combined. The general officer may be a great proficient in the knowledge of war, while the soldier is confined to a few motions of the hand and the foot. The former may have gained, what the latter has lost; and being occupied in the conduct of disciplined armies, may practice on a larger scale, all the arts of preservation, of deception, and of stratagem, which the savage exerts in leading a small party, or merely in defending himself.

The practitioner of every art and profession may afford matter of general speculation to the man of science; and thinking itself, in this age of separations, may become a peculiar craft. In the bustle of civil pursuits and occupations, men appear in a variety of lights, and suggest matter of inquiry and fancy, by which conversation is enlivened, and greatly enlarged. The productions of ingenuity are brought to the market; and men are willing to pay for whatever has a tendency to inform or amuse. By this means the idle, as well as the busy, contribute to forward the progress of arts, and bestow on polished nations that air of superior ingenuity, under which they appear to have gained the ends that were pursued by the savage in his forest, knowledge, order, and wealth.

*Section III: Of the Manners of Polished and Commercial Nations*

Mankind, when in their rude state, have a great uniformity of manners; but when civilized, they are engaged in a variety of pursuits; they tread on a larger field, and separate to a greater distance. If they be guided, however, by similar dispositions, and by like suggestions of nature, they will probably, in the end, as well as in the beginning of their progress, continue to agree in many particulars; and while communities admit, in their members, that diversity of ranks and professions which we have already described, as the consequence or the foundation of commerce, they will resemble each other in many effects of this distribution, and of other circumstances in which they nearly concur.

Under every form of government, statesmen endeavor to remove the dangers by which they are threatened from abroad, and the disturbances which molest them at home. By this conduct, if successful, they in a few ages gain an ascendant for their country; establish a frontier at a distance from its capital; they find, in the mutual desires of tranquility, which come to possess mankind, and in those public establishments which tend to keep the peace of society, a respite from foreign wars, and a relief from domestic disorders. They learn to decide every contest without tumult, and to secure, by the authority of law, every citizen in the possession of his personal rights.

In this condition, to which thriving nations aspire, and which they in some measure attain, mankind having laid the basis of safety, proceed to erect a superstructure suitable to their views. The consequence is various in different states; even in different orders of men of the same community; and the effect to every individual corresponds with his station. It enables the statesman and the soldier to settle the forms of their different procedure; it enables the practitioner in every profession to pursue his separate advantage; it affords the man of pleasure a time for refinement, and the speculative, leisure for literary conversation or study.

In this scene, matters that have little reference to the active pursuits of mankind are made subjects of inquiry, and the exercise of sentiment and reason itself becomes a profession. The songs of the bard, the harangues of the statesman and the warrior, the tradition and the story of ancient times, are considered as the models, or the earliest production, of so many arts, which it becomes the object of different professions to copy or to improve. The works of fancy, like the subjects of natural history, are distinguished into classes and species; the rules of every particular kind are distinctly collected; and the library is stored, like the warehouse, with the finished manufacture of different arts, who, with the aids of the grammarian and the critic, aspire, each in his particular way, to instruct the head, or to move the heart.

Every nation is a motley assemblage of different characters, and contains, under any political form, some examples of that variety, which the humors, tempers, and apprehensions of men, so differently employed, are likely to furnish. Every profession has its point of honor, and its system of manners; the merchant his punctuality and fair dealing; the statesman his capacity and address; the man of society, his good breeding and wit. Every station has a carriage, a dress, a ceremonial, by which it is distinguished, and by which it suppresses the national character under that of the rank, or of the individual.

This description may be applied equally to Athens and Rome, to London and Paris. The rude or the simple observer would remark the variety he saw in the dwellings and in the occupations of different men, not in the aspect of different nations. He would find, in the streets of the same city, as great a diversity, as in the territory of a separate people. He could not pierce through the cloud that was gathered before him, nor see how the tradesman, mechanic, or scholar, of one country, should differ from those of another. But the native of every province can distinguish the foreigner; and when he himself travels, is struck with the aspect of a strange country, the moment he passes the bounds of his own. The air of the person, the tone of the voice, the idiom of language, and the strain of conversation, whether pathetic or languid, gay or severe, are no longer the same.

Many such differences may arise among polished nations, from the effects of climate, or from sources of fashion, that are still more unaccountable and obscure; but the principal distinctions on which we can rest, are derived from the part a people are obliged to act in their national capacity; from the objects placed in their view by the state; or from the constitution of government, which prescribing the terms of society to its subjects, has a great influence in forming their apprehensions and habits.

The Roman people, destined to acquire wealth by conquest, and by the spoil of provinces; the Carthaginians, intent on the returns of merchandise, and the produce of commercial settlements, must have filled the streets of their several capitals with men of a different disposition and aspect. The Roman laid hold of his sword when he wished to be great, and the state found her armies prepared in the dwellings of her people. The Carthaginian retired to his counter on a similar project; and, when the state was alarmed, or had resolved on a war, lent of his profits to purchase an army abroad.

The member of a republic, and the subject of a monarchy, must differ, because they have different parts assigned to them by the forms of their country: the one destined to live with his equals, or, by his personal talents and character, to contend for pre-eminence; the other, born to a determinate station, where any pretence to equality creates a confusion, and where naught but precedence is studied. Each, when the institutions of his country are mature, may find in the laws a protection to his personal rights; but those rights themselves are differently understood, and with a different set of opinions, give rise to a different temper of mind. The republican must act in the state, to sustain his pretensions; he must join a party, in order to be safe; he must form one, in order to be great. The subject of monarchy refers to his birth for the honor he claims; he waits on a court, to show his importance; and holds out the ensigns of dependence and favor, to gain him esteem with the public.

If national institutions, calculated for the preservation of liberty, instead of calling upon the citizen to act for himself, and to maintain his rights, should give a security, requiring, on his part, no personal attention or effort; this seeming perfection of government might weaken the bands of society, and, upon maxims of independence, separate and estrange the different ranks it was meant to reconcile. Neither the parties formed in republics, nor the courtly assemblies which meet in monarchical governments, could take place, where the sense of a mutual dependence should cease to summon their members together. The resorts for commerce might be frequented, and mere amusement might be pursued in the crowd, while the private dwelling became a retreat for reserve, averse to the trouble arising from regards and attentions, which it might be part of the political creed to believe of no consequence, and a point of honor to hold in contempt.

This humor is not likely to grow either in republics or monarchies: it belongs more properly to a mixture of both; where the administration of justice may be better secured; where the subject is tempted to look for equality, but where he finds only independence in its place; and where he learns, from a spirit of equality, to hate the very distinctions to which, on account of their real importance, he pays a remarkable deference.

In either of the separate forms of republic or monarchy, or in acting on the principles of either, men are obliged to court their fellow-citizens, and to employ parts and address to improve their fortunes, or even to be safe. They find in both a school for discernment and penetration; but in the one, are taught to overlook the merits of a private character, for the sake of abilities that have weight with the public; and in the other, to overlook great and respectable talents, for the sake of qualities engaging or pleasant in the scene of entertainment, and private society. They are obliged, in both, to adapt themselves with care to the fashion and manners of their country. They find no place for caprice or singular humors. The republican must be popular, and the courtier polite. The first must think himself well placed in every company; the other must choose his resorts, and desire to be distinguished only where the society itself is esteemed. With his inferiors, he takes an air of protection; and suffers, in his turn, the same air to be taken with himself. It did not, perhaps, require in a Spartan, who feared nothing but a failure in his duty, who loved nothing but his friend and the state, so constant a guard on himself to support his character, as it frequently does in the subject of a monarchy, to adjust his expense and his fortune to the desires of his vanity, and to appear in a rank as high as his birth, or ambition, can possibly reach.

There is no particular, in the mean time, in which we are more frequently unjust, than in applying to the individual the supposed character of his country; or more frequently misled, than in taking our notion of a people from the example of one, or a few of their members. It belonged to the constitution of Athens, to have produced a Cleon, and a Pericles; but all the Athenians were not, therefore, like Cleon, or Pericles. Themistocles and Aristides lived in the same age; the one advised what was profitable; the other told his country what was just.

---

## PART V
## Of the Decline of Nations

### *Section III*
### *Of Relaxations in the National Spirit incident to Polished Nations*

Improving nations, in the course of their advancement, have to struggle with foreign enemies, to whom they bear an extreme animosity, and with whom, in many conflicts, they contend for their existence as a people. In certain periods too, they feel in their domestic policy inconveniences and grievances, which beget an eager impatience; and they apprehend reformations and new establishments, from which they have sanguine hopes of national happiness. In early ages, every art is imperfect, and susceptible of many improvements. The first principles of every science are yet secrets to be discovered, and to be successively published with applause and triumph.

We may fancy to ourselves, that in ages of progress, the human race, like scouts gone abroad on the discovery of fertile lands, having the world open before them, are presented at every step with the appearance of novelty. They enter on every new ground with expectation and joy. They engage in every enterprise with the ardor of men, who believe they are going to arrive at national felicity, and permanent glory; and forget past disappointments amidst the hopes of future success. From mere ignorance, rude minds are intoxicated with every passion; and partial to their own condition, and to their own pursuits, they think that every scene is inferior to that in which they are placed. Roused alike by success, and by misfortune, they are sanguine, ardent, and precipitant; and leave to the more knowing ages which succeed them, monuments of imperfect skill, and of rude execution in every art; but they leave likewise the marks of a vigorous and ardent spirit, which their successors are not always qualified to sustain, or to imitate.

This may be admitted, perhaps, as a fair description of prosperous societies, at least during certain periods of their progress. The spirit with which they advance may be unequal, in different ages, and may have its paroxysms, and intermissions, arising from the inconstancy of human passions, and from the casual appearance or removal of occasions that excite them. But does this spirit, which for a time continues to carry on the project of civil and commercial arts, find a natural pause in the termination of its own pursuits? May the business of civil society be accomplished, and may the occasion of farther exertion be removed?

Do continued disappointments reduce sanguine hopes, and familiarity with objects blunt the edge of novelty? Does experience itself cool the ardor of the mind? May the society be again compared to the individual? And may it be suspected, although the vigor of a nation, like that of a natural body, does not waste by a physical decay, that yet it may sicken for want of exercise, and die in the close of its own exertions? May societies, in the completion of all their designs, like men in years, who disregard the amusements, and are insensible to the passions, of youth, become cold and indifferent to objects that used to animate in a ruder age? And may a polished community be compared to a man, who having executed his plan, built his house, and made his settlement; who having, in short, exhausted the charms of every subject, and wasted all his ardor, sinks into languor and listless indifference? If so, we have found at least another simile to our purpose. But it is probable, that here too, the resemblance is imperfect; and the inference that would follow, like that of most arguments drawn from analogy, tends rather to amuse the fancy, than to give any real information on the subject to which it refers.

The materials of human art are never entirely exhausted, and the applications of industry are never at an end. The national ardor is not, at any particular time, proportioned to the occasion there is for activity; nor curiosity, to the extent of subject that remains to be studied.

The ignorant and the artless, to whom objects of science are new, and who are worst furnished with the conveniences of life, instead of being more active, and more curious, are commonly more quiescent, and less inquisitive, than the knowing and the polished. When we compare the particulars which occupy mankind in their rude and in their polished condition, they will be found greatly multiplied and enlarged in the last. The questions we have put, however, deserve to be answered; and if, in the advanced ages of society, we do not find the objects of human pursuit removed, or greatly diminished, we may find them at least changed; and in estimating the national spirit, we may find a negligence in one part, but ill compensated by the growing attention which is paid to another.

It is true, in general, that in all our pursuits, there is a termination of trouble, and a point of repose to which we aspire. We would remove this inconvenience, or gain that advantage, that our labors may cease. When I have conquered Italy and Sicily, says Pyrrhus, I shall then enjoy my repose. This termination is proposed in our national as well as in our personal exertions; and in spite of frequent experience to the contrary, is considered at a distance as the height of felicity. But nature has wisely, in most particulars, baffled our project; and placed nowhere within our reach this visionary blessing of absolute ease. The attainment of one end is but the beginning of a new pursuit; and the discovery of one art is but a prolongation of the thread by which we are conducted to further inquiries, and only hope to escape from the labyrinth.

Among the occupations that may be enumerated, as tending to exercise the invention, and to cultivate the talents of men, are the pursuits of accommodation and wealth, including all the different contrivances which serve to increase manufactures, and to perfect the mechanical arts. But it must be owned, that as the materials of commerce may continue to be accumulated without any determinate limit, so the arts which are applied to improve them, may admit of perpetual refinements. No measure of fortune, or degree of skill, is found to diminish the supposed necessities of human life; refinement and plenty foster new desires, while they furnish the means, or practice the methods, to gratify them.

In the result of commercial arts, inequalities of fortune are greatly increased, and the majority of every people are obliged by necessity, or at least strongly incited by ambition and avarice, to employ every talent they possess. After a history of some thousand years employed in manufacture and commerce, the inhabitants of China are still the most laborious and industrious of any people on the surface of the earth.

Some part of this observation may be extended to the elegant and literary arts. They too have their materials, which cannot be exhausted, and proceed from desires which cannot be satiated. But the respect paid to literary merit is fluctuating, and matter of transient fashion. When learned productions accumulate, the acquisition of knowledge occupies the time that might be bestowed on invention. The object of mere learning is attained with moderate or inferior talents, and the growing list of pretenders diminishes the luster of the few who are eminent. When we only mean to learn what others have taught, it is probable, that even our knowledge will be less than that of our masters. Great names continue to be repeated with admiration, after we have ceased to examine the foundations of our praise. And new pretenders are rejected, not because they fall short of their predecessors, but because they do not excel them; or because, in reality, we have, without examination, taken for granted the merit of the first, and cannot judge of either.

After libraries are furnished, and every path of ingenuity is occupied, we are, in proportion to our admiration of what is already done, prepossessed against farther attempts. We become students and admirers, instead of rivals; and substitute the knowledge of books, instead of the inquisitive or animated spirit in which they were written.

The commercial and lucrative arts may continue to prosper, but they gain an ascendant at the expense of other pursuits. The desire of profit stifles the love of perfection. Interest cools the imagination, and hardens the heart; and, recommending employments in proportion as they are lucrative, and certain in their gains, it drives ingenuity, and ambition itself, to the counter and the workshop.

But apart from these considerations, the separation of professions, while it seems to promise improvement of skill, and is actually the cause why the productions of every art become more perfect as commerce advances; yet in its termination, and ultimate effects, serves, in some measure, to break the bands of society, to substitute form in place of ingenuity, and to withdraw individuals from the common scene of occupation, on which the sentiments of the heart, and the mind, are most happily employed.

Under the *distinction* of callings, by which the members of polished society are separated from each other, every individual is supposed to possess his species of talent, or his peculiar skill, in which the others are confessedly ignorant; and society is made to consist of parts, of which none is animated with the spirit of society itself. "We see in the same persons", said Pericles, "an equal attention to private and to public affairs; and in men who have turned to separate professions, a competent knowledge of what relates to the community; for we alone consider those who are inattentive to the state, as perfectly insignificant." This encomium on the Athenians, was probably offered under an apprehension, that the contrary was likely to be charged by their enemies, or might soon take place. It happened accordingly, that the business of state, as well as of war, came to be worse administered at Athens, when these, as well as other applications, became the objects of separate professions; and the history of this people abundantly showed, that men ceased to be citizens, even to be good poets and orators, in proportion as they came to be distinguished by the profession of these, and other separate crafts.

Animals less honored than we, have sagacity enough to procure their food, and to find the means of their solitary pleasures; but it is reserved for man to consult, to persuade, to oppose, to kindle in the society of his fellow-creatures, and to lose the sense of his personal interest or safety, in the ardor of his friendships and his oppositions.

When we are involved in any of the divisions into which mankind are separated, under the denominations of a country, a tribe, or an order of men any way affected by common interests, and guided by communicating passions, the mind recognizes its natural station; the sentiments of the heart, and the talents of the understanding, find their natural exercise. Wisdom, vigilance, fidelity, and fortitude, are the characters requisite in such a scene, and the qualities which it tends to improve.

In simple or barbarous ages, when nations are weak, and beset with enemies, the love of a country, of a party, or a faction, are the same. The public is a knot of friends, and its enemies are the rest of mankind. Death, or slavery, are the ordinary evils which they are concerned to ward off; victory and dominion, the objects to which they aspire. Under the sense of what they may suffer from foreign invasions, it is one object, in every prosperous society, to increase its force, and to extend its limits. In proportion as this object is gained, security increases. They who possess the interior districts, remote from the frontier, are unused to alarms from abroad. They who are placed on the extremities, remote from the seats of government, are unused to hear of political interests; and the public becomes an object perhaps too extensive, for the conceptions of either. They enjoy the protection of its laws, or of its armies; and they boast of its splendor, and its power; but the glowing sentiments of public affection, which, in small states, mingle with the tenderness of the parent and the lover, of the friend and the companion, merely by having their object enlarged, lose great part of their force.

The manners of rude nations require to be reformed. Their foreign quarrels, and domestic dissensions, are the operations of extreme and sanguinary passions. A state of greater tranquility hath many happy effects. But if nations pursue the plan of enlargement and pacification, till their members can no longer apprehend the common ties of society, nor be engaged by affection in the cause of their country, they must err on the opposite side, and by leaving too little to agitate the spirits of men, bring on ages of languor, if not of decay.

The members of a community may, in this manner, like the inhabitants of a conquered province, be made to lose the sense of every connection, but that of kindred or neighborhood; and have no common affairs to transact, but those of trade—connections, indeed, or transactions, in which probity and friendship may still take place, but in which the national spirit, whose ebbs and flows we are now considering, cannot be exerted.

What we observe, however, on the tendency of enlargement to loosen the bands of political union, cannot be applied to nations who, being originally narrow, never greatly extended their limits, nor to those who, in a rude state, had already the extension of a great kingdom.

In territories of considerable extent, subject to one government, and possessed of freedom, the national union, in rude ages, is extremely imperfect. Every district forms a separate party; and the descendents of different families are opposed to one another, under the denomination of tribes or of clans. They are seldom brought to act with a steady concert; their feuds and animosities give more frequently the appearance of so many nations at war, than of a people united by connections of policy. They acquire a spirit, however, in their private divisions, and in the midst of a disorder, otherwise hurtful, of which the force, on many occasions, redounds to the power of the state.

Whatever be the national extent, civil order, and regular government, are advantages of the greatest importance; but it does not follow, that every arrangement made to obtain these ends, and which may, in the making, exercise and cultivate the best qualities of men, is therefore of a nature to produce permanent effects, and to secure the preservation of that national spirit from which it arose.

We have reason to dread the political refinements of ordinary men, when we consider, that repose, or inaction itself, is in a great measure their object; and that they would frequently model their governments, not merely to prevent injustice and error, but to prevent agitation and bustle; and by the barriers they raise against the evil actions of men, would prevent them from acting at all. Every dispute of a free people, in the opinion of such politicians, amounts to disorder, and a breach of the national peace. What heart-burnings? What delay to affairs? What want of secrecy and dispatch? What defect of police? Men of superior genius sometimes seem to imagine, that the vulgar have no title to act, or to think. A great prince is pleased to ridicule the precaution by which judges in a free country are confined to the strict interpretation of law. We easily learn to contract our opinions of what men may, in consistence with public order, be safely permitted to do. The agitations of a republic, and the license of its members, strike the subjects of monarchy with aversion and disgust. The freedom with which the European is left to traverse the streets and the fields, would appear to a Chinese a sure prelude to confusion and anarchy. "Can men behold their superior and not tremble? Can they converse without a precise and written ceremonial? What hopes of peace, if the streets are not barricaded at an hour? What wild disorder, if men are permitted in any thing to do what they please?"

If the precautions which men thus take against each other be necessary to repress their crimes, and do not arise from a corrupt ambition, or from cruel jealousy in their rulers, the proceeding itself must be applauded, as the best remedy of which the vices of men will admit. The viper must be held at a distance, and the tiger chained. But if a rigorous policy, applied to enslave, not to restrain from crimes, has an actual tendency to corrupt the manners, and to extinguish the spirit of nations; if its severities be applied to terminate the agitations of a free people, not to remedy their corruptions; if forms be often applauded as salutary, because they tend merely to silence the voice of mankind, or be condemned as pernicious, because they allow this voice to be heard; we may expect that many of the boasted improvements of civil society, will be mere devices to lay the political spirit at rest, and will chain up the active virtues more than the restless disorders of men.

If to any people it be the avowed object of policy, in all its internal refinements, to secure the person and the property of the subject, without any regard to his political character, the constitution indeed may be free, but its members may likewise become unworthy of the freedom they possess, and unfit to preserve it. The effects of such a constitution may be to immerse all orders of men in their separate pursuits of pleasure, which they may now enjoy with little disturbance; or of gain, which they may preserve without any attention to the commonwealth.

If this be the end of political struggles, the design, when executed, in securing to the individual his estate, and the means of subsistence, may put an end to the exercise of those very virtues that were required in conducting its execution. A man who, in concert with his fellow-subjects, contends with usurpation in defense of his estate or his person, may find an exertion of great generosity, and of a vigorous spirit; but he who, under political establishments, supposed to be fully confirmed, betakes him, because he is safe, to the mere enjoyment of fortune, has in fact turned to a source of corruption the very advantages which the virtues of the other procured. Individuals, in certain ages, derive their protection chiefly from the strength of the party to which they adhere; but in times of corruption, they flatter themselves, that they may continue to derive from the public that safety which, in former ages, they must have owed to their own vigilance and spirit, to the warm attachment of their friends, and to the exercise of every talent which could render them respected, feared, or beloved. In one period, therefore, mere circumstances serve to excite the spirit, and to preserve the manners of men; in another, great wisdom and zeal for the good of mankind on the part of their leaders, are required for the same purposes.

Rome, it may be thought, did not die of a lethargy, nor perish by the remission of her political ardors at home. Her distemper appeared of a nature more violent and acute. Yet if the virtues of Cato and of Brutus found an exercise in the dying hour of the republic, the neutrality, and the cautious retirement of Atticus, found its security in the same tempestuous season; and the great body of the people lay undisturbed, below the current of a storm, by which the superior ranks of men were destroyed. In the minds of the people, the sense of a public was defaced; and even the animosity of faction had subsided: they only could share in the commotion, who were the soldiers of a legion, or the partisans of a leader. But this state fell not into obscurity for want of eminent men. If at the time of which we speak, we look only for a few names distinguished in the history of mankind, there is no period at which the list was more numerous. But those names became distinguished in the contest for dominion, not in the exercise of equal rights: the people were corrupted; the empire of the known world stood in need of a master.

Republican governments, in general, are in hazard of ruin from the ascendant of particular factions, and from the mutinous spirit of a populace, who being corrupted, are no longer fit to share in the administration of state. But under other establishments, where liberty may be more successfully attained if men are corrupted, the national vigor declines from the abuse of that very security which is procured by the supposed perfection of public order.

A distribution of power and office; an execution of law, by which mutual encroachments and molestations are brought to an end; by which the person and the property are, without friends, without cabal, without obligation, perfectly secured to individuals, does honor to the genius of a nation; and could not have been fully established, without those exertions of understanding and integrity, those trials of a resolute and vigorous spirit, which adorn the annals of a people, and leave to future ages a subject of just admiration and applause. But if we suppose that the end is attained, and that men no longer act, in the enjoyment of liberty, from liberal sentiments, or with a view to the preservation of public manners; if individuals think themselves secure without any attention or effort of their own; this boasted advantage may be found only to give them an opportunity of enjoying, at leisure, the conveniences and necessaries of life; or, in the language of Cato, teach them to value their houses, their villas, their statues, and their pictures, at a higher rate than they do the republic. They may be found to grow tired in secret of a free constitution, of which they never cease to boast in their conversation, and which they always neglect in their conduct.

The dangers to liberty are not the subject of our present consideration; but they can never be greater from any cause than they are from the supposed remissness of a people, to whose personal vigor every constitution, as it owed its establishment, so must continue to owe its preservation. Nor is this blessing ever less secure than it is in the possession of men who think that they enjoy it in safety, and who therefore consider the public only as it presents to their avarice a number of lucrative employments; for the sake of which they may sacrifice those very rights which render themselves objects of management or consideration.

From the tendency of these reflections, then, it should appear, that a national spirit is frequently transient, not on account of any incurable distemper in the nature of mankind, but on account of their voluntary neglects and corruptions. This spirit subsisted solely, perhaps, in the execution of a few projects, entered into for the acquisition of territory or wealth; it comes, like a useless weapon, to be laid aside after its end is attained.

Ordinary establishments terminate in a relaxation of vigor, and are ineffectual to the preservation of states; because they lead mankind to rely on their arts, instead of their virtues, and to mistake for an improvement of human nature, a mere accession of accommodation, or of riches. Institutions that fortify the mind, inspire courage, and promote national felicity, can never tend to national ruin.

Is it not possible, amidst our admiration of arts, to find some place for these? Let statesmen, who are entrusted with the government of nations, reply for themselves. It is their business to show, whether they climb into stations of eminence, merely to display a passion for interest, which they had better indulge in obscurity; and whether they have capacity to understand the happiness of a people, the conduct of whose affairs they are so willing to undertake.

---

**PART VI**
**Of Corruption And Political Slavery**

*Section III: Of the Corruption incident to Polished Nations*

Luxury and corruption are frequently coupled together, and even pass for synonymous terms. But in order to avoid any dispute about words, by the first we may understand that accumulation of wealth, and that refinement on the ways of enjoying it, which are the objects of industry, or the fruits of mechanic and commercial arts. And by the second a real weakness, or depravity of the human character, which may accompany any state of those arts, and be found under any external circumstances or condition whatsoever. It remains to inquire, what are the corruptions incident to polished nations, arrived at certain measures of luxury, and possessed of certain advantages, in which they are generally supposed to excel?

We need not have recourse to a parallel between the manners of entire nations, in the extremes of civilization and rudeness, in order to be satisfied, that the vices of men are not proportioned to their fortunes; or that the habits of avarice, or of sensuality, are not founded on any certain measures of wealth, or determinate kind of enjoyment. Where the situations of particular men are varied as much by their personal stations, as they can be by the state of national refinements, the same passions for interest, or pleasure, prevail in every condition. They arise from temperament, or an acquired admiration of property; not from any particular manner of life in which the parties are engaged, nor from any particular species of property, which may have occupied their cares and their wishes.

Temperance and moderation are, at least, as frequent among those whom we call the superior, as they are among the lower classes of men; and however we may affix the character of sobriety to mere cheapness of diet, and other accommodations with which any particular age, or rank of men, appear to be contented, it is well known, that costly materials are not necessary to constitute a debauch, nor profligacy less frequent under the thatched roof, than under the lofty ceiling. Men grow equally familiar with different conditions, receive equal pleasure, and are equally allured to sensuality, in the palace, and in the cave. Their acquiring in either habits of intemperance or sloth, depends on the remission of other pursuits, and on the distaste of the mind to other engagements. If the affections of the heart be awake, and the passions of love, admiration, or anger, be kindled, the costly furniture of the palace, as well as the homely accommodations of the cottage, are neglected. And men, when roused, reject their repose; or, when wearied, embrace it alike on the silken bed, or on the couch of straw.

We are not, however, from hence to conclude, that luxury, with all its concomitant circumstances, which either serve to favor its increase, or which, in the arrangements of civil society, follow it as consequences, can have no effect to the disadvantage of national manners. If that respite from public dangers and troubles which gives a leisure for the practice of commercial arts, be continued, or increased, into a disuse of national efforts; if the individual, not called to unite with his country, be left to pursue his private advantage; we may find him become effeminate, mercenary, and sensual; not because pleasures and profits are become more alluring, but because he has fewer calls to attend to other objects; and because he has more encouragement to study his personal advantages, and pursue his separate interests.

If the disparities of rank and fortune which are necessary to the pursuit or enjoyment of luxury introduce false grounds of precedence and estimation; if, on the mere considerations of being rich or poor, one order of men are, in their own apprehension, elevated, another debased; if one be criminally proud, another meanly dejected; and every rank in its place, like the tyrant, who thinks that nations are made for himself, be disposed to assume on the rights of mankind: although, upon the comparison, the higher order may be least corrupted; or from education, and a sense of personal dignity, have most good qualities remaining; yet the one becoming mercenary and servile; the other imperious and arrogant; both regardless of justice, and of merit; the whole mass is corrupted, and the manners of a society changed for the worse, in proportion as its members cease to act on principles of equality, independence, or freedom.

Upon this view, and considering the merits of men in the abstract, a mere change from the habits of a republic to those of a monarchy; from the love of equality, to the sense of a subordination founded on birth, titles, and fortune, is a species of corruption to mankind. But this degree of corruption is still consistent with the safety and prosperity of some nations; it admits of a vigorous courage, by which the rights of individuals, and of kingdoms, may be long preserved.

Under the form of monarchy, while yet in its vigor, superior fortune is, indeed, one mark by which the different orders of men are distinguished; but there are some other ingredients, without which wealth is not admitted as a foundation of precedence, and in favor of which it is often despised, and lavished away. Such are birth and titles, the reputation of courage, courtly manners, and a certain elevation of mind. If we suppose that these distinctions are forgotten, and nobility itself only to be known by the sumptuous retinue which money alone may procure; and by a lavish expense, which the more recent fortunes can generally best sustain; luxury must then be allowed to corrupt the monarchical as much as the republican state, and to introduce a fatal dissolution of manners, under which men of every condition, although they are eager to acquire, or to display their wealth, have no remains of real ambition. They have neither the elevation of nobles, nor the fidelity of subjects; they have changed into effeminate vanity, that sense of honor which gave rules to the personal courage; and into a servile baseness, that loyalty, which bound each in his place, to his immediate superior, and the whole to the throne.

Nations are most exposed to corruption from this quarter, when the mechanical arts, being greatly advanced, furnish numberless articles, to be applied in ornament to the person, in furniture, entertainment, or equipage; when such articles as the rich alone can procure are admired;

and when consideration, precedence, and rank, are accordingly made to depend on fortune.

In a more rude state of the arts, although wealth be unequally divided, the opulent can amass only the simple means of subsistence: They can only fill the granary, and furnish the stall; reap from more extended fields, and drive their herds over a larger pasture. To enjoy their magnificence, they must live in a crowd; and to secure their possessions, they must be surrounded with friends that espouse their quarrels. Their honors, as well as their safety, consist in the numbers who attend them; and their personal distinctions are taken from their liberality, and supposed elevation of mind. In this manner, the possession of riches serves only to make the owner assume a character of magnanimity, to become the guardian of numbers, or the public object of respect and affection. But when the bulky constituents of wealth, and of rustic magnificence, can be exchanged for refinements; and when the produce of the soil may be turned into equipage, and mere decoration; when the combination of many is no longer required for personal safety; the master may become the sole consumer of his own estate: he may refer the use of every subject to himself; he may employ the materials of generosity to feed a personal vanity, or to indulge a sickly and effeminate fancy, which has learned to enumerate the trappings of weakness or folly among the necessaries of life.

The Persian satrap, we are told, when he saw the King of Sparta at the place of their conference, stretched on the grass with his soldiers, blushed at the provision he had made for the accommodation of his own person: he ordered the furs and the carpets to be withdrawn; he felt his own inferiority; and recollected, that he was to treat with a man, not to vie with a pageant in costly attire and magnificence.

When, amidst circumstances that make no trial of the virtues or talents of men, we have been accustomed to the air of superiority, which people of fortune derive from their retinue, we are apt to lose every sense of distinction arising from merit, or even from abilities. We rate our fellow-citizens by the figure they are able to make; by their buildings, their dress, their equipage, and the train of their followers. All these circumstances make a part in our estimate of what is excellent; and if the master himself is known to be a pageant in the midst of his fortune, we nevertheless pay our court to his station, and look up with an envious, servile, or dejected mind, to what is, in itself, scarcely fit to amuse children; though, when it is worn as a badge of distinction, it inflames the ambition of those we call the great, and strikes the multitude with awe and respect.

We judge of entire nations by the productions of a few mechanical arts, and think we are talking of men, while we are boasting of their estates, their dress, and their palaces. The sense in which we apply the terms, great, and noble, high rank, and *high life*, show, that we have, on such occasions, transferred the idea of perfection from the character to the equipage; and that excellence itself is, in our esteem, a mere pageant, adorned at a great expense, by the labors of many workmen.

To those who overlook the subtle transitions of the imagination, it might appear, since wealth can do no more than furnish the means of subsistence, and purchase animal pleasures, that covetousness, and venality itself, should keep pace with our fears of want, or with our appetite for sensual enjoyments; and that where the appetite is satiated, and the fear of want is removed, the mind should be at ease on the subject of fortune. But they are not the mere pleasures that riches procure, nor the choice of viands which cover the board of the wealthy, that inflame the passions of the covetous and the mercenary. Nature is easily satisfied in all her enjoyments. It is an opinion of eminence, connected with fortune; it is a sense of debasement attending on poverty, which renders us blind to every advantage, but that of the rich; and insensible to every disgrace, but that of the poor. It is this unhappy apprehension that occasionally prepares us for the desertion of every duty, for a submission to every indignity, and for the commission of every crime that can be accomplished in safety.

Aurengzebe was not more renowned for sobriety in his private station, and in the conduct of a supposed dissimulation, by which he aspired to sovereign power, than he continued to be, even on the throne of Hindustan. Simple, abstinent, and severe in his diet, and other pleasures, he still led the life of a hermit, and occupied his time with a seemingly painful application to the affairs of a great empire. He quitted a station in which, if pleasure had been his object, he might have indulged his sensuality without reserve; he made his way to a scene of disquietude and care; he aimed at the summit of human greatness, in the possession of imperial fortune, not at the gratifications of animal appetite, or the enjoyment of ease. Superior to sensual pleasure, as well as to the feelings of nature, he dethroned his father, and he murdered his brothers, that he might roll on a carriage incrusted with diamond and pearl; that his elephants, his camels, and his horses, on the march, might form a line extending many leagues; might present a glittering harness to the sun; and loaded with treasure, usher to the view of an abject and admiring crowd, that awful majesty, in whose presence they were to strike the forehead on the ground, and be overwhelmed with the sense of his greatness, and with that of their own debasement.

As these are the objects which prompt the desire of dominion, and excite the ambitious to aim at the mastery of their fellow-creatures; so they inspire the ordinary race of men with a sense of infirmity and meanness, that prepares them to suffer indignities, and to become the property of persons, whom they consider as of a rank and a nature so much superior to their own.

The chains of perpetual slavery, accordingly, appear to be riveted in the East, no less by the pageantry which is made to accompany the possession of power, than they are by the fears of the sword, and the terrors of a military execution. In the West, as well as the East, we are willing to bow to the splendid equipage, and stand at an awful distance from the pomp of a princely estate. We too, may be terrified by the frowns, or won by the smiles, of those whose favor is riches and honor, and whose displeasure is poverty and neglect. We too may overlook the honors of the human soul, from an admiration of the pageantries that accompany fortune. The procession of elephants harnessed with gold might dazzle into slaves, the people who derive corruption and weakness from the effect of their own arts and contrivances, as well as those who inherit servility from their ancestors, and are enfeebled by their natural temperament, and the enervating charms of their soil, and their climate.

It appears, therefore, that although the mere use of materials which constitute luxury, may be distinguished from actual vice; yet nations under a high state of the commercial arts, are exposed to corruption, by their admitting wealth, unsupported by personal elevation and virtue, as the great foundation of distinction, and by having their attention turned on the side of interest, as the road to consideration and honor.

With this effect, luxury may serve to corrupt democratic states, by introducing a species of monarchical subordination, without that sense of high birth and hereditary honors which render the boundaries of rank fixed and determinate, and which teach men to act in their stations with force and propriety. It may prove the occasion of political corruption, even in monarchical governments, by drawing respect towards mere wealth; by casting a shade on the luster of personal qualities, or family distinctions; and by infecting all orders of men, with equal venality, servility, and cowardice.

### Section IV: The same subject continued

The increasing regard with which men appear, in the progress of commercial arts, to study their profit, or the delicacy with which they refine on their pleasures; even industry itself, or the habit of application to a tedious employment, in which no honors are won, may, perhaps, be considered as indications of a growing attention to interest, or of effeminacy, contracted in the enjoyment of ease and convenience. Every successive art, by which the individual is taught to improve on his fortune, is, in reality, an addition to his private engagements, and a new avocation of his mind from the public.

Corruption, however, does not arise from the abuse of commercial arts alone; it requires the aid of political situation; and is not produced by the objects that occupy a sordid and a mercenary spirit, without the aid of circumstances that enable men to indulge in safety any mean disposition they have acquired.

Providence has fitted mankind for the higher engagements which they are sometimes obliged to fulfill; and it is in the midst of such engagements that they are most likely to acquire or to preserve their virtues. The habits of a vigorous mind are formed in contending with difficulties, not in enjoying the repose of a pacific station; penetration and wisdom are the fruits of experience, not the lessons of retirement and leisure; ardor and generosity are the qualities of a mind roused and animated in the conduct of scenes that engage the heart, not the gifts of reflection or knowledge. The mere intermission of national and political efforts is, notwithstanding, sometimes mistaken for public good; and there is no mistake more likely to foster the vices, or to flatter the weakness, of feeble and interested men.

If the ordinary arts of policy, or rather, if a growing indifference to objects of a public nature, should prevail, and, under any free constitution, put an end to those disputes of party, and silence that noise of dissension, which generally accompany the exercise of freedom, we may venture to prognosticate corruption to the national manners, as well as remissness to the national spirit. The period is come, when, no engagement remaining on the part of the public, private interest, and animal pleasure, become the sovereign objects of care. When men, being relieved from the pressure of great occasions, bestow their attention on trifles; and having carried what they are pleased to call sensibility and delicacy, on the subject of ease or molestation, as far as real weakness or folly can go, have recourse to affectation, in order to enhance the pretended demands, and accumulate the anxieties, of a sickly fancy, and enfeebled mind.

In this condition, mankind generally flatter their own imbecility under the name of politeness. They are persuaded, that the celebrated ardor, generosity, and fortitude, of former ages, bordered on frenzy, or were the mere effects of necessity, on men who had not the means of enjoying their ease, or their pleasure. They congratulate themselves on having escaped the storm which required the exercise of such arduous virtues; and with that vanity which accompanies the human race in their meanest condition, they boast of a scene of affectation, of languor, or of folly, as the standard of human felicity, and as furnishing the most proper exercise of a rational nature.

It is none of the least menacing symptoms of an age prone to degeneracy, that the minds of men become perplexed in the discernment of merit, as much as the spirit becomes enfeebled in conduct, and the heart misled in the choice of its objects. The care of mere fortune is supposed to constitute wisdom; retirement from public affairs, and real indifference to mankind, receive the applauses of moderation and virtue.

Great fortitude, and elevation of mind, have not always, indeed, been employed in the attainment of valuable ends; but they are always respectable, and they are always necessary when we would act for the good of mankind, in any of the more arduous stations of life. While, therefore, we blame their misapplication, we should beware of depreciating their value. Men of a severe and sententious morality have not always sufficiently observed this caution; nor have they been duly aware of the corruptions they flattered, by the satire they employed against what is aspiring and prominent in the character of the human soul.

...

If men must go wrong, there is a choice of their very errors, as well as of their virtues. Ambition, the love of personal eminence, and the desire of fame, although they sometimes lead to the commission of crimes, yet always engage men in pursuits that require to be supported by some of the greatest qualities of the human soul; and if eminence is the principal object of pursuit, there is, at least, a probability, that those qualities may be studied on which a real elevation of mind is raised. But when public alarms have ceased, and contempt of glory is recommended as an article of wisdom, the sordid habits, and mercenary dispositions, to which, under a general indifference to national objects, the members of a polished or commercial state are exposed, must prove at once the most effectual suppression of every liberal sentiment, and the most fatal reverse of all those principles from which communities derive their hopes of preservation, and their strength.

It is noble to possess happiness and independence, either in retirement, or in public life. The characteristic of the happy, is to acquit themselves well in every condition; in the court, or in the village; in the senate, or in the private retreat. But if they affect any particular station, it is surely that in which their actions may be rendered most extensively useful. Our considering mere retirement, therefore, as a symptom of moderation, and of virtue, is either a remnant of that system, under which monks and anchorets, in former ages, have been canonized; or proceeds from a habit of thinking, which appears equally fraught with moral corruption, from our considering public life as a scene for the gratification of mere vanity, avarice, and ambition; never as furnishing the best opportunity for a just and a happy engagement of the mind and the heart.

Emulation, and the desire of power, are but sorry motives to public conduct; but if they have been, in any case, the principal inducements from which men have taken part in the service of their country, any diminution of their prevalence or force is a real corruption of national manners; and the pretended moderation assumed by the higher orders of men, has a fatal effect in the state. The disinterested love of the public, is a principle without which some constitutions of government cannot subsist. But when we consider how seldom this has appeared a reigning passion, we have little reason to impute the prosperity of preservation of nations, in every case, to its influence.

It is sufficient, perhaps, under one form of government, that men should be fond of their independence; that they should be ready to oppose usurpation, and to repel personal indignities. Under another, it is sufficient, that they should be tenacious of their rank, and of their honors; and instead of a zeal for the public, entertain a vigilant jealousy of the rights which pertain to themselves. When numbers of men retain a certain degree of elevation and fortitude, they are qualified to give a mutual check to their several errors, and are able to act in that variety of situations which the different constitutions of government have prepared for their members. But, under the disadvantages of a feeble spirit, however directed, and however informed, no national constitution is safe; nor can any degree of enlargement to which a state has arrived, secure its political welfare.

In states where property, distinction, and pleasure are thrown out as baits to the imagination, and incentives to passion, the public seems to rely for the preservation of its political life, on the degree of emulation and jealousy with which parties mutually oppose and restrain each other. The desires of preferment and profit in the breast of the citizen, are the motives from which he is excited to enter on public affairs, and are the considerations which direct his political conduct. The suppression, therefore, of ambition, of party-animosity, and of public envy, is probably, in every such case, not a reformation, but a symptom of weakness, and a prelude to more sordid pursuits, and ruinous amusements.

On the eve of such a revolution in manners, the higher ranks, in every mixed or monarchical government, have need to take care of themselves. Men of business, and of industry, in the inferior stations of life, retain their occupations, and are secured, by a kind of necessity, in the possession of those habits on which they rely for their quiet, and for the moderate enjoyments of life. But the higher orders of men, if they relinquish the state, if they cease to possess that courage and elevation of mind, and to exercise those talents which are employed in its defense, and its government, are, in reality, by the seeming advantages of their station, become the refuse of that society of which they once were the ornament; and from being the most respectable, and the most happy, of its members, are become the most wretched and corrupt. In their approach to this condition, and in the absence of every manly occupation, they feel a dissatisfaction and languor which they cannot explain: They pine in the midst of apparent enjoyments; or, by the variety and caprice of their different pursuits and amusements, exhibit a state of agitation, which, like the disquiet of sickness, is not a proof of enjoyment or pleasure, but of suffering and pain. The care of his buildings, his equipage, or his table, is chosen by one; literary amusement, or some frivolous study, by another. The sports of the country, and the diversions of the town; the gaming table, dogs, horses, and wine, are employed to fill up the blank of a listless and unprofitable life. They speak of human pursuits, as if the whole difficulty were to find something to do; they fix on some frivolous occupation, as if there was nothing that deserved to be done; they consider what tends to the good of their fellow creatures, as a disadvantage to themselves; they fly from every scene, in which any efforts of vigor are required, or in which they might be allured to perform any service to their country. We misapply our compassion in pitying the poor; it were much more justly applied to the rich, who become the first victims of that wretched insignificance, into which the members of every corrupted state, by the tendency of their weaknesses, and their vices, are in haste to plunge themselves.

It is in this condition, that the sensual invent all those refinements on pleasure, and devise those incentives to a satiated appetite, which tend to foster the corruptions of a dissolute age. The effects of brutal appetite, and the mere debauch, are more flagrant, and more violent, perhaps, in rude ages, than they are in the later periods of commerce and luxury, but that perpetual habit of searching for animal pleasure where it is not to be found, in the gratifications of an appetite that is cloyed, and among the ruins of an animal constitution, is not more fatal to the virtues of the soul, than it is even to the enjoyment of sloth, or of pleasure; it is not a more certain avocation from public affairs, or a surer prelude to national decay, than it is a disappointment to our hopes of private felicity.

In these reflections, it has been the object, not to ascertain a precise measure to which corruption has risen in any of the nations that have attained to eminence, or that have gone to decay; but to describe that remissness of spirit, that weakness of soul, that state of national debility, which is likely to end in political slavery; an evil which remains to be considered as the last object of caution, and beyond which there is no subject of disquisition in the perishing fortunes of nations.

# Institutes of Moral Philosophy

## 1769[1]

## INTRODUCTION

### Section I: Of Knowledge in general

All knowledge is either of particular facts, or of general rules. The knowledge of facts is prior to that of rules; and is the first requisite in the practice of arts, and in the conduct of affairs. A general rule is the expression of what is common, or is required to be common, in a number of particular cases. General rules are the result of observation, or will; and consequently are derived from mind. Practice, or conduct of any sort, though regulated by general rules, has a continual reference to particulars. In speculation, we endeavor to establish general rules. In practice, we study particular cases, or apply general rules to regulate our conduct.

### Section II: Of Science

A collection of facts, in description or narration, constitutes history. General rules, and their applications, to regulate or to explain particulars, constitute science. Any general rule collected from facts, is termed *a law of nature*. A general rule, when applied to explain or regulate particulars, is termed *a principle*; and explanation from principle is termed *theory*. The particulars to be explained are termed *phenomena*.

Method in science is of two kinds: analytic, and synthetic. Analytic method is that by which we proceed from observation of fact, to establish general rules. Synthetic method, is that by which we proceed from general rules to their particular applications. The first is the method of investigation. The second of communication, or of the enlargement of

---

[1]   *Institutes of Moral Philosophy: For the use of Students in the College of Edinburgh,*
      reprint of edition of 1769 (London: Routledge/Thoemmes Press, 1994).

science. Argument is of two kinds: *a priori*, and *a posteriori*. By an argument *a posteriori*, the law is proved from the fact.

## Section III: Of the laws of Nature

The laws of nature are either physical, or moral. A physical law is any general expression of a natural operation, as exemplified in a number of particular cases. In every operation, men are by nature disposed to apprehend an operating power or cause. Causes are of two kinds: efficient, and final. The efficient cause, is the energy or power producing an effect. The final cause, is the end or purpose for which an effect is produced. In supposing final causes, we suppose the existence of mind. Physical laws refer only to efficient causes; such therefore are the immediate objects of science.

A moral law is any general expression of what is good; and therefore fit to determine the choice of intelligent beings. A physical law exists so far only as it is the fact; a moral law exists in being obligatory.

The subject from which physical laws are collected, may be classed under four principal heads: mechanism, vegetation, animal life, and intelligence. It has not hitherto been made appear, although sometimes attempted, that the operations of any of these different natures are comprehended under the same laws to which the others are subjected. The phenomena of vegetation are not comprehended under any known law of mechanism, much less animal life or intelligence.

The subjects from which moral laws are collected are the sentiments and actions of intelligent natures. The immediate use of physical laws is theory. The immediate use of moral laws, is moral philosophy.

## Section IV: Of Theory

Theory consists in referring particular operations to the principles, or general laws, under which they are comprehended; or in referring particular effects to the causes from which they proceeded.

To point out any general rule or law of nature previously known, in which any particular fact is comprehended, is to account for that fact. Thus Sir Isaac Newton accounted for the planetary revolutions, by showing that they were comprehended in the laws of motion and gravitation. To pretend to explain phenomena, by showing that they may be comprehended in any supposition, or by applying to them, metaphorically, the language which is derived from any other subject, is illusory in science. Thus the vortex of Descartes, being a mere supposition, made no true explanation of the planetary system; and the terms, *idea, image*, or *picture*, of things, being terms merely metaphorical, cannot explain human knowledge or thought.

All phenomena not comprehended under any known law, are the proper materials of natural history. All facts that cannot be explained by any rule previously known, or better known than the facts themselves, may be termed ultimate facts. It is evident, that all theory must rest on ultimate facts. To require proof *a priori* for every fact were to suppose that human knowledge requires an infinite series of facts and explanations, which is impossible.

## Section V: Of Moral Philosophy

Moral philosophy is knowledge of what ought to be, or the application of rules that ought to determine the choice of voluntary agents. Before we can ascertain rules of morality for mankind, the history of man's nature, his dispositions, his specific enjoyments and sufferings, his condition and future prospects, should be known. Pneumatics, or the physical history of mind, is the foundation of moral philosophy.

## Section VI: Of Pneumatics

Pneumatics treats physically of mind of spirit. This science consists of two parts. The first treats of man; the second, of God. That part which treats of man, may contain the history of man's nature, and an explanation or theory of the principal phenomena of human life. That which treats of God, contains the proofs of his existence, attributes, and government.

The history of man contains either such facts as occur on a general view of the species, or such as occur to the individual, in recollecting what passes in his own mind. The first may be termed, *the history of the species*; the second, that *of the individual*. In the theory of human nature are solved questions relating to the characters of men, to the nature and future prospects of the human soul.

---

### PART III
### Of the Knowledge of God

### Chapter I: Of the Being of God

#### Of the Universality of this Belief

The belief of the existence of God has been universal. The cavils of skeptics do not derogate from the universality of this belief, no more than like cavils derogate from the universality of the perception men have of the existence of matter; for this likewise has been questioned.

This belief does not imply any adequate notion of the Supreme Being. Men, for the most part, have entertained notions on this subject, unworthy even of human reason. But the belief that an artist, or author, exists, is consistent with mean and improper notions of his capacity and intentions. The belief that Homer composed the *Iliad*, is compatible with inadequate notions of that poet's genius. The belief that books read at school were composed by men is consistent with a notion that even the classics were written for the use of children.

## Of the Foundations of this Belief

The belief of God being universal, cannot depend on circumstances peculiar to any age or nation, but must be the result of human nature, or the suggestion of circumstances that occur in every place and age.

In the nature of man, there is a perception of causes from the appearance of effects, and of design from the concurrence of means to an end. Skeptics have not denied the reality of these perceptions; they have rather complained of them, as the foundation of general and vulgar errors.

But natural perceptions are the foundations of all our knowledge. This is the foundation of what we know from sensation, from testimony, and from interpretation. In any of these cases, we can assign no reason for our belief, but that we are so disposed by our nature. No argument is required to prove, nor can argument have any effect to refute, where nature has determined that we shall continue to believe. No one can refrain believing, that the eye was made to see, the ear to hear; that the wing was made for the air, the fin for the water, the foot for the ground; and so forth.

The perception of an end or intention in the works of men comprehends the belief of an artist. The perception of end or intention in the works of nature comprehends the belief of God. Nature presents final causes wherever our knowledge extends. Final causes may be considered as the language in which the existence of God is revealed to man. In this language the sign is natural, and the interpretation instinctive.

## Chapter II: Of the Attributes of God

### Of these Attributes in general

The attributes of God are characters of the Supreme Being suggested by his works. They may be referred to five heads: Unity, Power, Wisdom, Goodness, and Justice.

### The Unity of God

The perception of final causes implies the belief only of one God. The notion of a plurality of gods is a corruption. Different nations separately formed their notions of the Deity. On comparing these notions, they did not endeavor to reconcile them to the belief of one supreme being; they formed a list composed of many gods, having their different attributes and separate provinces in nature.

## Of Power

Power is the attribute of the first cause; and in the creator of all things, cannot be circumscribed by any thing that exists.

## Of Wisdom

Wisdom is the attribute of intelligence; and the belief of wisdom in the author of nature is implied in the belief of final causes. The wisdom of God comprehends the knowledge of every nature, of the mutual relations and dependencies of different natures, and of what is best for each, and for the whole.

## The Goodness of God

This is the attribute of the creator and preserver of all things. The proofs of goodness are,

1.    The creating of sensitive and rational beings;

2.    The measures of good which they are made to enjoy;

3.    The order established for the preservation [of the whole].

Without the first [1], there would be no object on which goodness could exert itself. And the numbers of such objects, as well as the enjoyments they are made to receive, are proofs of goodness in the first cause.

2. What their numbers or enjoyments [are], cannot be known to us; but the order and tendency of what we know leads to the belief of universal good.

The lot of man is mixed, but his nature likewise is fitted to a mixed scene. He complains of evil in his external circumstances, or in his own nature and conduct. The first subject of complaint is termed *physical evil*; the second, *moral*.

His complaints of physical evil are not symptoms of absolute evil in nature, but the symptoms of an active nature in himself properly placed, and having proper excitements to exert its power. A scene in which there were no apparent evils to be corrected, or, what is equivalent, no accession of good to be gained, would be a scene of inaction, adverse to the nature of man. Or, in other words, a being that perceived no evil, or had no want, could have no principle of activity.

Man, by being employed as an active power in the order of nature, is not made to forgo his own happiness. His happiness does not depend on the measure of convenience he enjoys, but on the part he acts; not on his safety, but on the degree of courage he possesses; not on what he gains for himself or others, but on the degree of ardor and affection he exerts.

Complaints of moral evil are the symptoms of a progressive or improving nature. A being that perceived no moral evil, or no defect, could have no principle of improvement. To remove the complaints of moral evil, it is necessary that men were either freed of all imperfections, or rendered insensible of the imperfections they have. The first is impossible: men must have the imperfections of created nature. What is the least possible measure of these imperfections, we know not. But man, imperfect as he is, is not a blemish in nature. He has a pungent sense of his own errors and defects. This is the source of his complaints, and of his improvements, and is a beauty in his nature.

He is a voluntary agent, destined to act under the following wise restraint: that his hurtful dispositions are painful to himself, and his beneficial dispositions are pleasant. The suffering, as well as the enjoyment, in this case, is a proof of beneficence in the power that inflicts it.

3. Every part, in the order of nature, is calculated for the preservation of the whole. Things the most remote are made to concur to the same salutary purposes. The order of the planetary system is calculated for the preservation of every being that occupies any part of this system. The pains, as well as the pleasures, of living and sensitive creatures, tend to their preservation. The order of nature is preserved by succession, not by perpetuity of life; and while the individual is perishing, the species of every animal is safe, and the system of nature is secured from decay.

## Of the Justice of God

Justice is the result of wisdom and goodness. Justice is goodness impartial and universal, rendering every part subservient to the good of the whole, and calculating the whole for the preservation of its parts; but precluding every part from any enjoyment in what is pernicious to the whole. The pains and pleasures incident to man's nature are distributed agreeably to this rule of justice. For to sum up the whole, benevolence is always pleasant, malice is always painful.

## Chapter III: Of the belief of the Immortality of the Human Soul, as founded in Principles of Religion

Contrary to the appearances at death, the human soul has been generally supposed to survive its separation from the body, and to be reserved to a future state of rewards and punishments. This apprehension is agreeable to the most rational notions of the goodness and justice of God. That goodness which disposed the Almighty to create, may likewise dispose him forever to preserve his intelligent creatures.

There is a continual creation of rational as well as animal natures. But animal natures are certainly extinguished; why not rational? The first is necessary. The world would be overstocked with animals, if generations did not die to make way for each other. But the world of spirits may, without inconvenience, increase forever.

The desire of immortality is instinctive, and is a reasonable intimation of what is intended by the author of this desire. The progress of man's intelligent nature may be continued beyond the attainments of this life. The government of God is righteous; but man's instinctive desire of distributive justice is not fulfilled in this life. Hence the universal belief, that wicked men are to receive additional punishments, and good men additional rewards, in a future state.

...

# History of the Progress and Termination of the Roman Republic

*1783*[1]

## BOOK III

### Chapter IV: Character of the Times; Philosophy

It may appear strange, that any age or nation should have furnished the example of a project conceived in so much guilt, or of characters so atrocious as those under which the accomplices of Catiline are described by the eloquent orator and historian [Cicero], from whose writings the circumstances of the late conspiracy are collected. The scene, however, in this republic, was such as to have no parallel, either in the past or in the subsequent history of mankind. There was less government, and more to be governed, than has been exhibited in any other instance. The people of Italy were become masters of the known world; it was impossible they could ever meet in a fair and adequate convention. They were represented by partial meetings; or occasional tumults in the city of Rome; and to take the sense of the people on any subject was to raise a riot. Individuals were vested with powers almost discretionary in the provinces, or continually aspired to such situations. The nominal assemblies of the people were often led by profligate persons, impatient of government, in haste to govern. Ruined in their fortunes by private prodigality, or by the public expense in soliciting honors; tempted to repair their ruins by oppression and extortion where they were entrusted with command, or

[1]  *The History of the Progress and Termination of the Roman Republic* (New York: J.C. Derby, 1856), as reprinted by The Scholarly Publishing Office, University of Michigan.

by desperate attempts against the government of their country if disappointed in their hopes. Not only were many of the prevailing practices disorderly, but the law itself was erroneous; adopted indeed at first by a virtuous people, because it secured the persons and the rights of individuals, but now anxiously preserved by their posterity, because it gave a license to their crimes.

The provinces were to be retained by the forces of Italy; the Italians themselves by the ascendant of the capital; and in this capital all was confusion and anarchy, except where the senate, by its authority and the wisdom of its counsels, prevailed. It was expedient for the people to restrain the abuses of aristocratic power; but when the sovereignty was exercised in the name of the collective body of the Roman people, the anarchy and confusion that prevailed at Rome spread from one extremity of her dominion to the other. The provinces were oppressed, not upon a regular plan to aggrandize the state, but at the pleasure of individuals, to enrich a few of the most outrageous and profligate citizens. The people were often assembled to erect arbitrary powers, under the pretence of popular government. The public interests and the order of the state were in perpetual struggle with the pretensions of single and of profligate men. In such a situation there were many temptations to be wicked; and in such a situation, likewise, minds that were turned to integrity and honor had a proportionate spring to their exertions and pursuits. The range of the human character was great and extensive, and men were not likely to trifle within narrow bounds; they were destined to be good or to be wicked in the highest measure, and, by their struggles, to exhibit a scene interesting and instructive beyond any other in the history of mankind.

Among the causes that helped to carry the characters of men in this age to such distant extremes, may be reckoned the philosophy of the Greeks, which was lately come into fashion, and which was much affected by the higher ranks of men in the state. Literature being, by the difficulty and expense of multiplying copies of books, confined to persons having wealth and power, it was considered as a distinction of rank, and was received not only as a useful, but as a fashionable accomplishment. The lessons of the school were considered as the elements of every liberal and active profession, and they were practiced at the bar, in the field, in the senate, and everywhere in the conduct of real affairs. Philosophy was considered as an ornament, as well as a real foundation of strength, ability, and wisdom in the practice of life. Men of the world, instead of being ashamed of their sect, affected to employ its language on every important occasion, and to be governed by its rules so much as to assume, in compliance with particular systems, distinctions of manners and even of dress. They embraced their forms in philosophy, as the sectaries in modern times have embraced theirs in religion; and probably in the one case honored their choice by the sincerity of their faith and the regularity of their practice, much in the same degree as they have done in the other.

In these latter times of the Roman republic the sect of Epicurus appears to have prevailed; and what Fabricius wished, on hearing the tenets of this Philosophy, for the enemies of Rome, had now befallen her citizens. Men were glutted with national prosperity; they thought that they were born to enjoy what their fathers had won, and saw not the use of those austere and arduous virtues by which the state had increased to its present greatness. The votaries of this sect ascribed the formation of the world to chance, and denied the existence of Providence. They resolved the distinctions of right and wrong, of honor and dishonor, into mere appellations of pleasure and pain. Every man's pleasure was to himself the supreme rule of estimation and of action. All good was private. The public was a mere imposture, that might be successfully employed, perhaps to defraud the ignorant of their private enjoyments, while it furnished the conveniences of the wise. To persons so instructed, the care of families and of states, with whatever else broke in upon the enjoyments of pleasure and ease, must appear among the follies of human life. And a sect under these imputations might he considered as patrons of licentiousness, both in morality and religion, and declared enemies to mankind. Yet the Epicureans, when urged in argument by their opponents, made some concessions in religion, and many more in morality. They admitted the existence of gods, but supposed those beings of too exalted a nature to have any concern in human affairs. They owned that, although the value of virtue was to be measured by the pleasure it gave, yet true pleasure was to be found in virtue alone; and that it might be enjoyed in the highest degree even in the midst of bodily pain. Notwithstanding this decision on the side of morality, the ordinary language of this sect, representing virtue as a mere prudent choice among the pleasures to which men are variously addicted, served to suppress the specific sentiments of conscience and elevation of mind, and to change the reproaches of criminality, profligacy, or vileness, by which even bad men are restrained from iniquity, into mere imputations of mistake, or variations of taste.

Other sects, particularly that of the Stoics, maintained, almost in every particular, the reverse of these tenets. They maintained the reality of Providence, and of a common interest of goodness and of justice, for which Providence was exerted, and in which all rational creatures were deeply concerned. They allowed, that in the nature of things there are many grounds upon which we prefer or reject the objects that present themselves to us, but that the choice which we make, not the event of our efforts, decides our happiness or our misery; that right and wrong are the most important and the only grounds upon which we can at all times safely proceed in our choice, and that, in comparison to this difference, every thing else is of no account; that a just man will ever act as if there was nothing good but what is right, and nothing evil but what is wrong;

that the Epicureans mistook human nature when they supposed all its principles resolvable into appetites for pleasure, or aversions to pain; that honor and dishonor, excellence and defect, were considerations which not only led to much nobler ends, but which were of much greater power in commanding the human will; the love of pleasure was groveling and vile, was the source of dissipation and of sloth; the love of excellence and honor, was aspiring and noble, and led to the greatest exertions and the highest attainments of our nature. They maintained that there is no private good separate from the public good; that the same qualities of the understanding and the heart, wisdom, benevolence, and courage, which are good for the individual, are so likewise for the public; that these blessings every man may possess, independent of fortune or the will of other men; and that whoever does possess them has nothing to hope, and nothing to fear, and can have but one sort of emotion, that of satisfaction and joy; that his affections, and the maxims of his station, as a creature of God, and as a member of society, lead him to act for the good of mankind; and that for himself he has nothing more to desire, than the happiness of acting this part. These, they said, were the tenets of reason leading to perfection, which ought to be the aim of every person who means to preserve his integrity, or to consult his happiness, and towards which every one may advance, although no one has actually reached it.

Other sects affected to find a middle way between these extremes, and attempted, in speculation, to render their doctrines more plausible; that is, more agreeable to common opinions then either; but were, in fact, of no farther moment in human life than as they approached to the one or to the other of these opposite systems.

# Principles of Moral and Political Science

## 1792[1]

---

**VOLUME 1**

### Introduction

Most subjects in nature may be considered under two aspects: under that of their actual state, and under that of a specific excellence, or defect, of which they are susceptible.

Under the first, they are subjects of mere description, or statement of fact. Under the second, they are objects of estimation or contempt, of praise or censure.

In respect to what men have actually done or exhibited, human nature is a subject of history and physical science. Considered in respect to the different measures of good and evil, of which men are susceptible, the same nature is a subject of discipline and moral science.

In treating of Man, as a subject of history, we collect facts, and endeavor to conceive his nature as it actually is, or has actually been, apart from any notion of ideal perfection, or defect.

In treating of him as a subject of moral science, we endeavor to understand what he ought to be; without being limited, in our conception, to the measure of attainment or failure, exhibited in the case of any particular person or society of men.

To have an object or purpose, and to employ means for the attainment of it, is the distinctive condition of mind or intelligent being. The first implies will and choice; the second implies energy and power. For man, therefore, to know his province, and to be qualified for his station, requires equally that he should be acquainted with the foundations of both.

---

[1]  *Principles of Moral and Political Science, reprint of edition of 1792* (New York: AMS Press, 1973).

Animals have power, consisting in muscular strength; and, in this respect, man is inferior to many of the brutes, but his dominion in nature is derived from a different source—from his superior skill, and the authority of a mind over-ruling and wise.

The power of the husbandman consists in the knowledge of soils and manures; that of the physician in his knowledge of the animal economy, diet, and food. The power of the engineer consists in his knowledge of the laws of motion, to which the structure of his works should be fitted. And it may be said of mankind in general, that an extension of knowledge is an accession of power.

Where subjects are within the reach of man, and may be disposed of at pleasure, knowledge of the laws of nature, or of the forms according to which nature herself proceeds, in respect to such subjects, will enable the artist, in every branch, to have the operation of nature repeated to his respective effect or purpose.

The chemist, by his knowledge of a menstruum, can have the hardest substance of metal dissolved, or reduced into a fluid state; as Archimedes, by his knowledge of the lever, we are told, could have ships suspended in the air, with all their lading and crews.

To man there is a subject of study, and a material of art, of more immediate concern than the soil from which he raises his food, or the mechanical resistance which he may wish to overcome: His own mind is a province of more importance, and more entirely subjected to his government.

It is somewhere mentioned by Mr. [Joseph] Addison, as a notion among the statuaries, that in every block of marble, there is an exquisite figure, if the sculptor be qualified only to remove the superfluous matter. This manner of expressing the fitness of marble to be employed in statuary, may, perhaps with less indulgence of fancy, be applied to mind. Here there is a godlike form of understanding and of will, that may be found by every person who is desirous to find it, and who is resolute to clear away the erroneous matter under which it is concealed and disfigured. Here also, we may presume that knowledge is power; and that, whoever is successful in the study of his own nature, as he may lay the foundations of a happy choice in the exercise of his will, so he may lay the foundations of power also, in applying the laws of his nature to the command of himself.

The subject, even to those who give it no attention, is ever present and familiar; and, for this reason, perhaps, the less understood.

The mind is qualified by nature to recognize itself; but, on account of this little use which is commonly made of this qualification, it is aptly enough compared to the eye, that perceives every object besides itself. In most men, indeed, intelligence appears to be little more than a principle of life, or a species of organ employed in the perception of external things, but incapable of stating itself as a subject of reflection or study. It is thus that the vulgar, by disuse, or by the habit of attending only to what is presented to their senses, lose or impair the powers of reflection; and even men of science, excited by the desire of knowledge, become intimate with the laws of every nature but their own; and the more they pursue other objects of study, the more they are confirmed in the habit of neglecting themselves, insomuch that, in a period of many pretensions to science, it became the first office of moral wisdom practiced by Socrates, to recall the attention of mankind from the heavens to the earth, or from the consideration of things remote to the near and immediate concerns of human life.

The only condition on which we can receive information of this matter is, that we attend to the facts of which we are conscious in ourselves; and whoever pretends to tell us of anything new, or that is not of our own minds, has mistaken his subject, or would mislead us from it.

Questions may be stated, and a method proposed; but he alone who can recur to himself with proper reflection can make any advance in such studies. And although, in the following pages there may appear a continual effort to state the argument, as well as to arrange the matter in question; yet the author is sensible that method is the principal aid he can give, and that, to succeed in the study of mind, every reader must perform the work for himself.

A principal difficulty, indeed, in entering upon the study of our own nature, may arise from the familiarity of the subject, and from a presumption that we are already possessed of full information. The mind is conscious of itself, and the learner of moral wisdom is himself the witness to be cited in evidence of the truth. He must be content to recollect what everyone knows; to value a fact rather for its consequence than its novelty; and even to value it the more for its being notorious and common. It is from the ordinary course of things that the laws of nature are collected; and it is upon the same ordinary course that the artist must rely for the conduct of his art, and success of his operations. In so much that, although things new and strange may amuse the imagination; yet the affectation of novelty is often misplaced in science of any kind, but nowhere so much as in the study of mind; concerning which, the facts, if fairly stated, cannot be new to the mind itself.

In determining the course which man ought to run, we must observe the steps he is qualified to make, and guess at the termination of his progress, from the beginning of it, or from the direction in which he sets out.

As the study of human nature may refer to the actual state, or to the improvable capacity, of man, it is evident, that, the subjects being connected, we cannot proceed in the second, but upon the foundations which are laid in the first. Our knowledge of what any nature ought to be, must be derived from our knowledge of its faculties and powers; and the attainment to be aimed at must be of the kind which these faculties and powers are fitted to produce. From the horse we cannot expect the flight of the eagle, nor from the eagle the firm pace and strength of the horse.

It is too common, in treating of human affairs, to indulge some bias to panegyric or satire. The last may gratify our spleen as the first, by raising the pretensions of a nature in which we partake, may flatter our vanity. But, though either may proceed from an allowable disposition, the one from partiality to our kind, the other from indignation at vice; yet they are surely misplaced, and ought to be avoided in disquisitions of science, where the object is to ascertain fact and reality, and in our judgment neither to overrate, nor depreciate the subject; but to cultivate the good of which it is susceptible, and to restrain the evil to which it is exposed.

In this, with all the intimacy of every individual with himself he has much to learn, not only in the habit of which the vulgar are so little possessed, the habit of observing what passes in their own minds, but likewise in the habit of turning what they know of themselves to account.

There is also much to be learned from the system of things, in the midst of which mankind are placed, and from the varieties of aspect under which the species has appeared in different ages and nations. So far, without being disqualified to recollect our own feelings and thoughts, we may indulge the habit of looking abroad for objects of observation; or, in doing so, may rather be incited to study the intimate principles of our own nature, which have appeared with so many signal effects in the history of mankind.

For this reason it is thought proper, in the choice of our method, to look abroad into the general order of things, and to contemplate the place as well as the description of man, while we endeavor to fix the distinction of good and evil relative to his nature; a distinction which may be collected from his situation relative to other beings, as well as from the description of what he is in himself.

The author, in some of the statements which follow, may be thought partial to the Stoic philosophy, but is not conscious of having warped the truth to suit with any system whatever. His notions were taken up, where certainly truth might be learned, however little it were formed into system by those from whom it was collected.

The Stoics conceived human life under the image of a game at which the entertainment and merit of the players consisted in playing attentively and well, whether the stake was great or small. This game the author has had occasion to see played in camps, on board of ships, and in presence of an enemy, with the same or greater ease than is always to be found in the most secure situations. And his thoughts were long employed to account for this appearance, before he adverted to the illustration which is given by Epictetus, in the above allusion to a game of chance or of skill.

If his inquiries led him to agree with the tenets that were held by a sect of philosophers about two thousand years ago, he is the more confirmed in his notion; notwithstanding the name of this sect has become, in the gentility of modern times, proverbial for stupidity.

Cicero in his mere speculations was an academic, and professed indiscriminate skepticism, but when he came to instruct his son in the duties of morality, he seized on the principles of the Stoic philosophy, as the most applicable to the conduct of human life. From this source also the better part of the Roman law was derived; and, to such decided distinction of right and wrong, jurisprudence must ever recur; as, in framing its rules regard must be had to justice alone, whether the matter be of great or small account.

Even in modern times, and at the distance of many ages, notwithstanding the vulgar contempt, this sect has been revered by those who were acquainted with its real spirit, Lord Shaftesbury, Montesquieu, Mr. [James] Harris, Mr. Hutcheson, and many others. And surely one of the first lessons that ought to be learned by youth, however others may be past the time of learning it, is — neither to admire nor to contemn what they do not know.

There is not perhaps in this collection any leading thought, or principle of moment, that may not be found in the writings of others; and, if the author knew where, he might have been as well employed in pointing them out as in composing this book. But the latter is perhaps the easier task of the two; and, as the concurrence of many in the same thoughts is not a presumption of their falsehood, it is no reason why they should be omitted here. The object is not novelty, but benefit to the student. The author will not neglect citing those who have gone before him, as often as his is sensible of having borrowed his thoughts, or as often as he recollects at the moment, that the student can with advantage be referred to other instructors.

The work consists of two parts: The first relating to the fact, or matter of description, and statement, in the history of man's progressive nature. The second to the principles of right, or the foundations of judgment and choice, whether in matters of personal quality, law, manners, or political establishments.

The object, in these different parts respectively, is to ascertain the foundations of power and of choice in human nature.

In entering on the first part, it appeared not unlikely to furnish striking and instructive views of the subject, to contemplate man as a mere part in this system of living natures; and to indulge the mind in pursuing analogies which extend to him even from the lower orders of being, as well as to view him in his points of elevation and contrast.

For this reason are stated, as in the first chapter of the following part, the distinction of natures living and active; and, among these, the distinction of animals associating and political; which lead, by a thread of analogy, to man, distinguished as he is by intelligence and the powers of observation and choice; and more specially by his destination to know himself, to perceive, in the frame of nature, intelligence superior to his own, and to become his own master in the attainment of qualities that constitute the perfection of his being.

As the history of mind, with the laws of man's progressive nature, are to him primary objects of knowledge, and the foundations of that power which he is to exercise over himself, these are principal objects of consideration, and furnish the subjects of the second and third chapters. With respect to these matters, however, the facts are presented not as discoveries, but as the data from which to infer the judgments and conclusions of the second part, relating to the foundations of choice, or what men ought to wish for himself, for his country, and for mankind.

The author is sensible that a work of this sort, to be properly executed, ought to be calculated, not for any particular class of readers, but for mankind. And, although he cannot flatter himself with the thoughts of having attained this high point of perfection, he is willing to hope, that, as his defects of one sort may be forgiven by the learned; so his allusions to abstruse points of science, in treating the history of mind, or his quotations from ancient languages, may, without any prejudice to the general strain of his argument, be passed over by readers, to whom such allusions or quotations are not familiar. And he hopes that there may be enough besides entitled to the candor, or within the competence, of everyone who may be disposed to peruse his work.

### Part I, Chapter II
### Of Mind or the Characteristics of Intelligence

*Section III: Of the Actual Sources of Knowledge and Measures of Evidence*

The sources of knowledge may be referred to four titles, viz. consciousness, perception, testimony, and inference.

The two first may be termed primary or immediate, because from them we receive the first elements of our conception, and obtain information by immediate recourse to the subject of knowledge.

In the third and fourth instances, knowledge may be termed derived or secondary, because it is obtained by some medium interposed, or by means different from that of mere attention to the subject itself.

If the original sources of information were shut up, the knowledge they are fitted to yield, could not be supplied in any other way. If a person, for instance, were not himself conscious of a given passion or affection, whether fear or love, he could not have any conception of such mental qualities; and, it is well known, that persons having no perception of colour or sound, remain through life without any such conceptions; whereas, want of testimony, from which to receive information, or want of data, from which to infer it, may be mutually supplied one by the other; if not by more immediate acquaintance with the subject, in personal observation or perception.

Consciousness is the first and most essential attribute of the mind. It is expressed in what the grammarians term the first personal pronoun *I*, or *Ego*, and is stated in every sentence of which that pronoun is the subject. In multiplying such sentences, the conscious mind seems to give an account of itself; and, in doing so, may either enumerate particulars, or proceed to generalize, investigating the laws of its own nature, in a process perfectly similar to what is followed in treating any other subject of observation, of history, or science.

Mind, considered in respect to its powers of communication of expression is a subject of those sciences, which are termed grammar and rhetoric. Considered in respect to its faculties of perception, inquiry, and discernment of truth, it is the subject of logic; considered in respect to the principles of choice, its discernment of good and evil, and its capacity of enjoyment and suffering, it is the subject of moral wisdom. And, when articles of all these different kinds are collected merely as characteristics of its nature, it is the subject of pneumatology, or the description and natural history of mind.

The knowledge obtained by reflection, from consciousness, is, of all others, the most intimate and sure. It consists in a conviction of reality that sets every cavil and dispute at defiance, or does not admit of a question, whether that of which we are conscious may not be otherwise than as we are conscious of it. In other matters, even in matters of perception, there is an information, and a subject of information, that may be separately stated; but, in this instance, the subject and information it brings, the thought or affection, and the consciousness of thought or affection, are inseparable. Here the evidence of reality remains unshaken and unattempted by the boldest assaults of skepticism. The very statement of doubt is a dogmatic assumption of personal existence and thought.

In metaphysics, or mathematics, are stated some axioms, of which the truth is not only real but necessary; and in this they differ from the facts of which we are conscious, which, however irrefragably established by that evidence, are in the nature of things contingent, or might have been otherwise.

In the mean time, it may be questioned, whether many, if not all the axioms having the evidence of necessary truth, be not some species of disguised tautology, in which a subject repeated in the form of a predicate is affirmed of itself. Thus the tautological axiom of whatever *is is*, may be disguised in the following expressions: *It is impossible for the same thing to be and not to be. Of contradictory propositions, the one must be true, the other false.* Things equal to *the same thing* must be equal to *one another.* Take equal things from equal things, the *remainders will be equal.* To these we may join the axiom, That every effect must have a cause. For we affirm in the predicate no more than what we assume in the subject — that an effect, which ever implies some one thing that is produced by another, is so produced. Change the term to existence, and it is not equally necessary that every existence should have a cause prior to itself.

In perception, we have cognizance of objects distinct or apart from ourselves, and learn that we are but a part in the system of nature.

We perceive in our frame certain animal organs of smell, of taste, hearing, seeing, and touch, which being sensibly affected, give the perceptions of external objects.

The whole of any one object is not originally perceivable by the sensation of any one organ, although in the sequel of our experience, we need no more to inform us of an object than some one of the perceptions by which it is known. Although we neither smell, taste, hear, or see the solid dimension of a body, yet, having examined by the touch what we smell, taste, hear, or see, we are from thenceforward, by any one or more of those senses, apprised of bodies existing in the solid dimensions of length, breadth, and thickness. We are apprised of a fruit by its smell, or visible appearance, and know what we should feel if we touched it. The subject of a first perception is often traced to a second; this to a third, a fourth, and so on, as far as we have any experience or knowledge in the system of nature. Thus, the fragrance of the air in a summer's evening is traced to the exhalation of odours from the woods after a shower; and odor itself is traced to the evaporation of volatile substances that replenish the air we inspire at the nostrils. A rattling noise is traced to a carriage that is passing in the street; and sound itself is traced to a tremulous motion produced in the air. Superficial figures having length and breath, with a certain distribution of light and shade, may be traced either to a picture on a plain surface, or to the solid dimension of a body placed before any ground that serves to mark its contour. A circle or a triangle, properly shaded, may be traced either to a picture on canvas, or to a solid sphere, a cone, or a pyramid, according to the outline within which the distribution of light and shade is made. Polygons fitly diversified with light and shade, may be traced to pictures of solids, whether regular or irregular, and under any combination of surfaces. Solid bodies, indeed, for the most part, may, by the eye, unassisted with any other organ, be distinguished from pictures, however artfully drawn; but, if there should be any doubt, respecting any such visible appearance, the reality of a solid dimension may be fully ascertained by the touch; and, from the organ of touch, perhaps, it is, that we are enabled to trace the visible appearance of bodies, to solid dimensions of any sort.

Throughout a certain class of objects in nature, the feeling, or touch, is our surest and last resort for information. As we cannot either smell, taste, nor hear, the solid dimensions of bodies; a being restricted to the use of these organs would have no conception of extended or impenetrable matter. Body is perceived by the touch to be solid and inert, or resisting to change of state. What, in respect to one degree of pressure to the touch is hard; in respect to another, is soft. But the ultimate result of perception, in tangible bodies, is, that matter compressed to the utmost will be extended and exclusively occupy space. And, although some are of opinion, that even solidity itself might be traced to somewhat else, as sound is traced to a tremulous motion in the air; yet, to be entirely unknown, is, in respect to us, the same thing as not to exist.

There are, indeed, subjects of perception in nature, which we cannot trace even to this ultimate point of reality. Light is perceived by the sight, but not by the touch. Heat is perceived by the touch, but not through the means of its inertia or solid resistance. The attractive powers of gravitation and magnetism are perceived by their effects; electricity is perceived by its light, and by the sound or effect of its explosions.

Things connected in nature are perceived, or perhaps rather inferred, one from another. Their connection, as Dr. Reid has observed, gives to them mutually the effect of signs; and they may be presented in any order one by another: Thus, charcoal and ashes are the signs of recent fire, as the flames that rise from combustible substances are the signs of materials about to be reduced to ashes. Even corporeal appearances are the signs of mind. That animal frame in man, with many of its functions, serves to express the operations of intellectual faculties. Order, or the combination of means in nature to the attainment of ends, is the sign of intelligent power.

In many of these instances, perception approaches to the nature of inference, and is rather a derived and secondary than a primary and immediate source of information. The measure of its evidence varies, perhaps even declines in force, as it passes from the first description of a primary source to that of a derived and conjectural means of information. Even under the first description the evidence of perception is unequal in different instances. In some we receive it with caution, and grope our way amidst sensible appearances, that we may not be deceived; in others the evidence of perception is unquestionable. But whether doubtful or certain, it is the only light with which we are furnished towards the discernment of reality in external things. Hence all we know of the earth and the heavens, of the sun, planets, and fixed stars, of the air, the sea, and the land, of minerals, plants, and animals, of property, of profit and loss, of men and other men's minds, of our country, of superiors, inferiors, or equals, of friends and strangers, of parent and child, of justice or injustice — in short, of the whole world apart from ourselves. And whoever rejects this evidence is reduced to think himself sole in the predicament of existence; so much that, if his mind be not already in a state of insanity, he is far gone in the way to incur it.

A person, indeed, may doubt whether body be such an existence as he apprehends it; but no one who knows the import of his own words, can deny its reality.

Under the highest measures of conviction, which attend our perception of external things, truth does not appear to be necessary; and the reality may be different from the appearance that is perceived by us. What the maxim of wisdom, with respect to perception, may be, we shall have occasion to inquire, in considering the laws of evidence.

By testimony, we receive information of what others have perceived or known. In this form, we are willing both to give and to receive communication of knowledge. This is a part of our social nature of much importance in this place; and still more where we have occasion to state the moral obligations of faith and veracity, in the dealings and conversations of men.

Great part of what we know is derived from this source; as to it may be referred all that we learn from books, from history, or conversation. It may be of consequence, however, in rating the value of such information, to observe, that testimony can present us only with new combinations, of which the particulars themselves, or constituent parts, before we can be made to understand the description or enumeration in which they are conveyed, must have been previously known by consciousness or perception. The combination may be new, but must consist of particulars already conceived. Seas of milk and ships of amber are objects new and strange, but sea, milk, ship, and amber, must have been previously conceived, to make way for such fictions. Where the previous conception of elements is wanting, it were vain to think of conveying information of a subject, by enumerating the particulars of which it is composed. This were to speak in words which are not understood. The traveler may inform us of a land, mountainous or plain, wooded or clear, stocked with animals of a particular description, inhabited by men of a particular figure, stature, and form. He may even feign any combination of thing, but as his accounts are communicated in words, or in the names of particulars so combined, the meaning, as well as the name must have been previously known, for us to conceive the assemblage under which they are presented. This fact is material, and should be attended to in ascribing to their different sources the benefits to be derived from books or information, on the other. A treatise on color, read to the blind, would to him be void of meaning; or, in search of a meaning, perhaps be referred to some conception of sound. Could the deaf be told of sound, he would probably recur to some conception of color or mental affection, of which he is conscious. And it is thus, probably, that, while we read of subjects of which the constituent parts are unknown to us, we substitute somewhat else instead of that to which our reading relates, and, in fact, receive no real or useful information on the subject. A person, who had never seen troops in the field, will not learn from the *Commentaries* of Cesar, or the Memoirs of Turenne.

Testimony, in the courts of law, is a principal source of information, and that on which the title of evidence is specially bestowed; insomuch, that the term, witness and evidence, are promiscuously applied. Even when circumstances are admitted in proof, those circumstances are taken from the testimony of witnesses.

We presume the witness to speak truth, as we presume the mirror to reflect the image that was cast upon it. But the evidence of testimony is so far inferior to that of perception, as it brings the additional defects which lie open to doubt, with respect to the competence of the witness, his capacity of observation, or his caution to avoid being himself deceived; his veracity, the inducements he may have to deceive, or his ability to resist them.

The terms credible, doubtful, or incredible, seem peculiarly applicable to this species of evidence; and belief, or disbelief, are its specific effects. The circumstances that enforce the credit of a witness, his known veracity, his want of any temptation to depart from it, or his declaration being the reverse of what his temptations would lead him to make, as they carry the evidence of testimony to its highest measure, may amount in their effect to entire conviction.

Circumstances, that make for or against the credit of a witness, may be so balanced as to make belief hang in suspense, or circumstances unfavorable to his credit may so preponderate as to quite overthrow it.

Belief and assent, which are due to a credible testimony, express the degree of confidence with which we rest on a probable opinion; but are inadequate to express the effect of consciousness or perception. In these the evidence and conviction are inseparable. Although we may say that we know a truth, of which we are conscious, or which we perceive; yet, to say that we are conscious of it, or that we perceive it, is enough, and amounts to conviction or knowledge. Inquiries, therefore, into the cause of belief, in matters of consciousness, or evident perception, appear to be misplaced, and only insinuate a question, where nature has refused to admit of a doubt.[2]

Under the fourth title, or that of inference, there remains to be considered yet another road to the attainment of knowledge. In this we collect, from facts or circumstances previously admitted, some farther information which would of itself, or otherwise, be wanting.

Under the fourth title, or that of inference, there remains to be considered yet another road to the attainment of knowledge. In this we collect, from facts or circumstances previously admitted, some farther information which would of itself, or otherwise, be wanting.

The facts or circumstances admitted may be founded in consciousness, perception, testimony, or even previous argument, and are termed the data or premises, while that which is inferred from them, is termed the conclusion; and the evidence will be proportioned to that of the premises, and to the connection which leads to infer the conclusion. The evidence of inference or argument, therefore, will partake in that of consciousness, perception, or testimony, according as the premises are derived from one or the other of these sources. It will decline as that of the premises declines; and, even where these are certain, will become

---

[2] We must not say, with the skeptic [Ferguson refers here to David Hume], that nature has given us ideas or impressions of things, and left us to collect the reality of an object from thence: She has given us perception; and this is at once a knowledge of its object.

doubtful, in proportion as the connection between the premises and the conclusion may be questioned.

Things are connected in nature as cause and effect, as general and particular, or as ordinary concomitants; and, on these varieties of connection, inference of various evidence is founded. From a given cause we infer an effect; or, from a given effect, we infer a cause: From the weight of the atmosphere, we infer what shall be the height of a column of a given fluid in the barometer; or, from that height, at a particular time, we infer the actual pressure or weight of the atmosphere in its state then present.

From a general law of nature, or from a generic description, we infer the fact in particular instances, or we class individuals under the genera to which they belong. From a sufficient number of facts, we infer a law of nature; or, from the agreement of many individuals in one set of qualities, we infer or we collect a generic description.

From one or any part of the circumstances, that are usually observed together, we infer the whole; or, from the general appearance of an object, infer some particular part. The mathematician reasons from his own definition; the lawyer, from the statute or practice of his country; the metaphysician, from his primary conception of being and its attributes; the physiologist either, by some adequate enumeration of facts, investigates a law of nature, or, to explain a particular phenomenon, applies a law of nature he had previously conceived or established.

## Section IV: Of the Laws or Canons of Evidence

Among the felicities incident to human nature, next to a temper correct and resolute, we may reckon a judgment undisturbed in the discernment of truth. These advantages are indeed connected together: The temper is supported by just conceptions of things; and, if our conceptions are mistaken or embarrassed, we must suffer proportionally, in respect to every circumstance in the condition of mind.

The proper use of discernment, in relation to what we admit as truth, may indeed be considered as an article of wisdom, and a branch of the moral science; but, as we have this interest at stake, no less when we reason than when we act, it may not be improper to touch upon it in this place, or immediately in the sequel of the facts, now stated, respecting the sources of knowledge.

The errors to which we are exposed, in the admission or in the rejection of evidence, may be on either extreme, of indiscriminate credulity, on the one hand, or indiscriminate skepticism on the other. With the credulous, every appearance and every report passes undistinguished and unquestioned. With the skeptic, every doctrine is a subject of cavil, and the despair of knowledge is substituted for caution in the selection of truth.

To guard against the first of these errors, we are to distinguish what is consistent with the order of nature, and to require, in support of every tenet, the evidence with which it should naturally be attended if true.

We are not to believe, upon the attestation of others, what, if true, we ourselves ought to be conscious of, or should have perceived. We are not to believe, upon the report of one witness, what, if true, many others should be equally ready to attest.

Affecting to secure the foundations of knowledge, some have set out with a maxim, that no tenet or fact is to be admitted without evidence. This is undoubtedly true; but the meaning of evidence must be explained before the maxim can be safely applied.

If, by the term evidence, we mean a sufficient cause of knowledge, consciousness and perception are of all others the preferable grounds of assent or conviction. But, if the term evidence be restricted to any particular cause of belief, such as testimony, or argument, the maxim ought to be rejected; for many thing are to be admitted as true, which cannot receive confirmation either from testimony or argument.

Whatever we are conscious of, or whatever we perceive, has an evidence prior to argument or testimony; and it is indeed from premises so known, that we are enabled, in the construction of argument, to infer the most certain conclusions. But, as testimony has usurped the name of evidence in the courts of law, argument or inference has usurped it no less in the discussions of science. And the maxim, that no proposition is to be received without evidence, is supposed to imply the necessity of argument in support of every truth.

Hence Descartes thought it necessary to state an argument in proof of his own existence, before he would proceed, upon that supposition, to treat of anything else. This limited application of the term evidence, more than we are apt to imagine, may be the cause of that skepticism which disputes the assent, if not to matters of consciousness, at least to those of perception, or any other of the most evident facts.

It is obvious, that the force of an argument partly consists in the evidence of premises or of truths previously known, or better known than the conclusion inferred from them. And, for this reason, whatever is already equally or better known, than any premises from which we can propose to infer it, cannot be established by argument. The skeptic, therefore, who requires argument in support of every assumption, must begin to doubt precisely at the point at which the truth is most certainly known.

It is probably in this limited sense of the term, that the skeptic requires evidence, before he admits the perceptions of sense. In deciding on the truth of perception, indeed, we have sometimes to examine the information of one sense by those of another; and, where observation is doubtful, in one or a few instances, we repeat the same observation in many, and bring every competent organ of sense to our aid. But, when we have done so much, or when our perception is already clear and determinate, we have no farther resource, and have not any previous data on which to establish the faith of what we perceive.

While we admit the maxim, that no information is to be received without the evidence it must have had if true, we must also admit the converse; that, in matters within our cognizance, and on which a decision is required of us, information, supported by all the evidence it could have had if true, ought to be sustained as sufficient to command our belief. What we ourselves cannot have perceived must be admitted on the credible report of others. What has not passed in the presence of witnesses, must be admitted, or rejected, on the credit of the circumstances which serve to evince or disprove it. To reject such information, were to shut up the mind against the admission of knowledge, and to reject the guide which nature had furnished for our direction through life.

Skepticism, no doubt, by restraining credulity, may guard against one species of error, but, carried to extreme, would discourage the search of truth, suspend the progress of knowledge, and become a species of palsy of all the mental powers, whether of speculation or of action.

The skeptic, indeed, sometimes affects to distinguish the provinces of speculation and of action. While, in speculation, he questions the evidence of sense; in practice, he admits it with the most perfect confidence. But speculations in science are surely of little account, if they have not any relation to subjects of actual choice and pursuit; and if they do not prepare the mind for the discernment of matters, relating to which there is actual occasion to decide, and to act, in the conduct of human life.

Upon the whole, we may venture to sum up the law of assent or dissent, respecting either extreme of credulity or skepticism, in the following terms, "That, as it were absurd to believe without evidence, or to affect knowledge where nature has not furnished any means of information; so it were equally absurd and ruinous in its consequences to reject, in any matter of importance, the only means of information which nature has furnished."

## Part I, Chapter III
## Of Man's Progressive Nature

*Section II: Of the Principles of Progression in Human Nature*

Among the principles of progression in human nature, may be reckoned, first of all, what is common to man with other beings endowed with life: the vegetating and animal powers by which the organized body waxes in stature and in strength.

These powers are known to us only by their effects, operating in the midst of organs and combinations of matter, subject to waste, and requiring supply. The living forms are in a continual state of fluctuation and change. The supply of one period exceeding the waste, and that of another period falling short of it, they advance and recede. They are, at the same time, exposed to disturbance and interruption from external causes; and affected in their course by inequalities of health or disease. But the powers of life, with which they are endowed in the most uninterrupted possession of health, wear out; or incur a decline and a final extinction.

Thus the principle of life, by which organized matter for a while is animated, itself ceases to act; and the materials on which it operated depart from their organization, and become inert.

With these are connected, in the human frame, a power of intelligence, conscious of itself, and of its gradual enlargement. This important circumstance is not otherwise known than as a fact, or as the particular phenomenon of a general law, common to all living and active natures: *That a faculty, or organ, which is properly exerted, gets accession of strength or mass; whilst that which is overstrained, or neglected goes to decay.*

The improvement of human faculties, therefore, is likely to depend on the propriety of their exercises; and the progress of the species itself will, without their intending it, keep pace with the ordinary pursuits, in which successive generations are engaged.

Under the general title of exercises, may be enumerated the various pursuits, into which mankind are led by the wants and necessities they have to supply, the inconveniences that have to remove, or the advantages which are placed in their view, as the spur which nature applies to excite and to direct their exertions.

The pursuits of human life, are, in part, occasioned by the exigencies of mere animal nature, and have for object the supplies of necessity, accommodation, or pleasure.

The supply which is provided for any, or all of these purposes consists of many separate articles, which, variously distributed in the form of property, render commerce and exchange a mutual convenience to the parties concerned, a consequence which may justify our distinguishing the expedients which are employed in the procuring or disposing of these articles, under the general title of commercial arts.

The active pursuits of man result also from the exigencies of human society, or its need of establishments, to restrain disorders, and to procure the benefits of which it is susceptible.

The provisions required for the safety and better government of men in society, may be termed the political arts.

Men are also engaged in the pursuits of knowledge, and in multiplying intellectual attainments; no less an exigency of the mind, than the means of subsistence and accommodation, are an exigency of mere animal life.

To penetrate the order established in nature; to emulate this order in works of design and invention; to unfold the principles of estimation, and realize the conceptions of excellence and beauty, in works to be executed by human art, or in the character and mind of the artist himself, is the peculiar province of man; and in his conduct, with respect to it, gives occasion to the most improving exertion of his faculties.

These exercises of intelligence, whether found in pursuits of knowledge, or elegant design, or moral improvement, may be stated under their respective titles, of investigation and theory, of fine arts, and moral philosophy.

To the end for which any, or all of these arts are practiced, the principle of ambition applies itself. This is defined in our dictionary,[3] the desire of something better than is possessed at present, and prevents acquiescence in any precise measure of attainment already made. In the pursuits of wealth, it is the desire of more property than is possessed at present. In civilization, it is the desire of establishments more complete, and more effectual for the peace and good order of society. In the pursuits of science, it is the desire of more knowledge. In the fine arts, it is the desire of more finished productions. And in philosophy, it is the desire of schemes more correct and accomplished, applicable to the character, action, and institutions of men.

In each of these pursuits, or applications of mind, we may farther remark, that the operation does not pass away in mere transient exertion; or, like the shadow of a cloud on the plain, leaves not a track behind. Continued practice is productive of habit, or facility of doing again what has been done; some acquired inclination, and some accession of power, which serve to give the mind a possession of the inclination or will it has for any time entertained, and of the faculty it has brought into use.

Habit is the well-known effect of continuance in any employment or course of life. Like every other law, which may be said to stand prominent on the surface of nature, it is familiar to everyone; and, like the laws of gravitation and motion, is made the most ordinary foundation of method, in whatsoever we do. Hence, we go to learn a calling, by continued endeavors to attain it; and repeat a performance, at which we are at first awkward, in order to become more dexterous or expert in the practice of it.

Such then, in general, we may consider as the principles of progression in the human mind; but the law of nature, as it operates in each, yet merits a more ample discussion. That of ambition and habit, in particular, though the last in this enumeration, may very properly have the first place; as they enter into the consideration of every pursuit and attainment, of whom they are the fruit or the incitement, the active engagements of men being prompted by ambition, and, in fact, to be estimated very much by the habits they furnish and leave behind.

Habit is known to be that, by which the good or bad actions of men remain with them, and become part of their characters. But how far a person may avail himself of this law, in choosing not only what he shall do at any particular time, but also what he shall at all times be inclined to

---

[3]  [Samuel Johnson's *Dictionary of the English Language*, 1755.]

do, has not perhaps, been sufficiently tried; and the importance of the question may justify a detail of the subject, however little recommended by novelty or entitled to the praise of discovery. It is indeed dwelt upon here, not as a matter new to the observation of anyone, but as a matter which ought to be attended to, as much as it is known.

### Section III: Of Habit in general

Habit is a source of inclination, but is not numbered among the original propensities of human nature because it is not that by which we are at first inclined to act, but a disposition which results from our having already acted. It is the acquired relation of a person to the state in which he has repeatedly been: as the relation of a tradesman to his calling; of a statesman to the detail of affairs; or of a warrior to the operations of war. In all of which the adept is distinguished from the novice by a difference of inclination or choice, by superior skill, power, and facility of performance.

The fact is familiar, and may be assumed as a law of nature common to men, and to animals of every description, *That whatever the living nature is able to perform without impairing its organs is persisted in, will produce a habit.* In this habit, as mankind experience it, there is implied sometimes a gradual diminution of pain, which accompanies first attempts; a promptitude, gradually acquired, in surmounting difficulties; accessions of power and strength, in producing effects; and a propensity or disposition, even without reflection or design, to be doing that to which the person acting has been sometimes accustomed.

In subjects of desirable attainment, habit is matter of felicity and commendation. In matters idle or unnecessary, it is reckoned a misfortune or a blemish.

There is somewhat analogous to this law of nature in the vegetable and mechanical kingdoms, as well as in the animal or in the rational. The twig that is turned from its position, and forced away from the natural direction of its growth, will continue to vegetate in its new direction, or will come round and become bent, in order to recover at every shoot the natural direction from which it was diverted. Even bodies destitute of organization, have an elastic power, by which they recover from any change that has been made in their figure, or in the relative position of their parts. As soon as the external pressure is withdrawn, they suddenly revert to their ordinary state; but, under the effects of violence continued for any time, they are observed to become in manner less reluctant to a state into which at first they were forced; and in which, if retained during the time that is necessary for this effect, they become quiescent, adopt a new figure, and exert their elastic power, as before, in preserving or recovering the state they had acquired. Thus the bow, that has been too long bent, at first becomes weak, or if kept so long in that position as to acquire a new shape, its elasticity operates in retaining a curvature contrary to that which it originally had. And it may be figuratively said to have acquired a new habit.

An animal will move spontaneously, not only in the track to which he has an original propensity or instinctive direction, but also in any track into which he has been forced, provided he has been made to move in it, during the period of time which is necessary for that purpose.

## Section IV: Of Habits of Thinking

As the conception entertained in the present time is, to every person while he continues to entertain it, the standard of truth and reality, it were difficult to persuade him, that his present conviction, in any instance, is the mere effect of continued representation, whether made to him in the ordinary course of things, in accidental coincidences, or in the received opinions and notions of other men.

This subject has been touched in a former section, though without any inclination to skepticism, or doubt of the conceptions which are attended with the genuine evidence of truth.

Nature, in providing the means of information, has warranted for truth and reality whatever she uniformly or generally presents in the order of her works. But what we rashly infer from singular instances, or what is obtruded in vulgar opinions, may be ill grounded and false; and yet men, in being repeatedly made to conceive an object in the same way, come to mistake their own habit of conception for an evidence of truth. Whence is it else, that the subjects of monarchy have one opinion respecting the expedience of political establishments, and the members of democracy a different one? Whence is it that the creed of the vulgar is so different in Asia, from what it is in Europe?

There are topics, no doubt, from which the enquiring mind may derive evidence of truth in these matters; but to these topics the vulgar seldom resort, and are generally the most bigoted to their tenets, the less they recur to the ground on which they rest. The habit of unquestioned belief is, in fact, more powerful than evidence, to make the implicit believer not only reject any new information, but meet the attempt to convince him with surprise and detestation.

There are habits of thinking peculiar to nations, to different ages, and even to individuals of the same nation and age, taken up at first without evidence, and often tenaciously retained without being questioned. In Greece, it was thought dishonorable to lose the shield in battle, or turn the back upon an enemy; in Scythia, flight was thought an ordinary stratagem in war. In Greece, music and dancing were reckoned accomplishments; at Rome, they were reckoned disgraceful. Our ancestors conceived the military character, as that which distinguished the lord or the gentleman. In their opinion, to be noble and military was the same. Ask a gentleman of the continent of Europe what it is to be noble? He will answer, it is to be descended through a certain number of generations of noble ancestors. Cannot merit compensate the want of birth? The answer is, that merit may recommend a gentleman in his rank, but no merit can ever title a peasant or a burgher to the reception that is due to a gentleman. Ask him to discuss the evidence of these opinions: He will reject the proposal with contempt. The citizen in a democratic government, on the contrary, cannot conceive how a man that is born free should be inferior to another, who does not excel him in parts, integrity, or in service performed to his country.

The authority of government itself, under every political establishment, rests on the habits of thinking which prevail among the people. In monarchy, the subject has a respectful conception of royalty; and every one in his place has respect for the rank that is immediately over him. In aristocratic government, this respect is by the many, entertained for a few. And in republics, which admit every order of the people to some share in the government of their country, the object of respect is conceived in the state itself, and in the law by which it is governed. Sovereignty, in all these instances, is entrusted with force, and the arms of the community are wielded by some species of executive power that may be obliged, on occasion, to employ them against the disorderly. Even violence is effectual to support the authority of government, so long as the bulk of the people agree in opinion with their rulers, and think that the force of the state is properly applied. But, when the body of the people are of a different opinion, or conceive the use of force to be an act of injustice, they themselves being conscious of a superior force, are not overawed, but rather exasperated, by its application, and made to unite in their own defense.

In ordinary times, the pretensions of sovereignty are received with implicit faith. Unnecessary applications, whether of force, or even of argument, in support of those pretensions, do but endanger the shaking of a habit of thinking, which might otherwise remain unmoved.

If the force is to be employed against the sense of a majority, this majority too, has force which, when brought to the trial, must be found the greatest, or, if reason is to be consulted, the reason of the majority, under the influence of any opinion, is always on their own side. James I of England would never cease convincing his subjects, that he had a right to their personal services, and to their property, but they had, at least, began to think otherwise; and he, by keeping the subject in view, entailed an argument on his posterity, which ended in the downfall of his house.

Erroneous opinions are termed mistakes or prejudices. A mistake may be of any date, but if recent, for the most part, easily gives way to better information. Prejudice implies opinion of a certain standing, or longer duration. The prejudices of childhood are sometimes corrected by the experience of manhood or youth. But otherwise, the longer a notion has remained unquestioned, the more firm its possession of the mind. For this reason national prejudices are, of all others, the most firmly retained; they are early inculcated, and remain unquestioned under the authority of numbers, or of the prevailing opinion, which individuals can seldom resist.

The distinction of Greek and Barbarian, within the pass of Thermopylae, was an expression of self-estimation in the Greek, and of contempt to the rest of mankind. The Athenians, we are told, believed their city to be the centre of Greece, and Greece to be the centre of the world. Round these centers, other parts of the earth were conceived as no more than skirts and appendages. A like opinion is said to be exemplified in the geography and self-estimation of the Chinese.

Many a Muslim would be greatly surprised, or receive the information with contempt, if they were told, that there may be persons, in a nation of Christians, no less entitled to consideration, or no less worthy or esteem than the most renowned of the faithful.

From such facts, relating to the effects of habit, the principal lessons to be taken are; first, respecting ourselves, to abate of our confidence in notions long entertained, except in so far as they are supported by evidence; and next, to prevent our thinking unfavorably of the understanding or sincerity of those who differ from ourselves in habits of thinking, which they may not have had sufficient occasion to question; and to remember, that although such habits render men obstinate in mistaken notions of things, they also render them steady to the truth, which they may have been so happy as to have once perceived; and that habit prevents the wavering and fluctuation of mind, which might otherwise arise from too easy reception of one opinion or notion of things for another.

It is wisely appointed into the order of nature, that the course of events to a certain degree is regular, and that occasions return at their ordinary periods. In what concerns the mind, there is a certain stability of thought, no less a part in the order of intellectual being. It is secured to the wise, not only by the permanence of those appearances on which they rest a well-grounded assent. It is confirmed, also, by... habit, which gives to opinion its continued possession of the mind, without always recurring to the evidence on which it was originally founded.

In matters of mere discretion, or small moment, such as are, for the most part, the ordinary constituents of good or ill manners; the properties of language and dress; the routine of hours for meals, for business, or play; the place of distinction in company; or the choice of innocent and arbitrary rites; it is better that the members of society should be of one mind, though perhaps with little foundation of evidence or reason, than that every one should, under pretence of thinking for himself, be at variance with his neighbor in matters of trifling account.

The authority of prevailing opinions makes at least one bond of society; and it is more fit that the people should move together, though not in the best way that might be devised for them, than that they should disband and separate into different ways, where no one might find, in the way he had chosen for himself, anything to compensate his separation from the rest of his kind.

The volume of nature is open for the information of mankind. If, in matters of importance, the sagacious are well informed, they may lead the opinions of others. And it is beneficently provided, that opinions once formed, and continued into habit, should give to human affairs, in every country, and in every age, a certain stability or regularity, to which every person, in the choice of his own conduct, may accommodate himself.

As uniformity, or the coincidence of many, in particular way of thinking, proceeds from communication, and is preserved by habit, it were absurd to employ any other method, to obtain or preserve unanimity. The use of force in particular, to dictate opinion, is preposterous and ineffectual: It tends to give importance to trifles, to awaken suspicions of a design to tyrannize, and arms the mind with obstinacy or enthusiasms, to retain what was slightly adopted, to reject what is violently offered, and what, if the mind were left to itself, would be easily changed for any other apprehension of things that is more prevailing or common.

### Section V: *Of Habit, as it affects the Inclinations of Men; and their Capacity of Enjoyment or Suffering*

It is a well-known effect of habit, to reconcile men to what was once disagreeable, or to disable them from bearing what was once supportable: Thus a manner of life, in respect to diet, accommodation, or dress, to which we are at first repugnant may, by use, be rendered agreeable, or even necessary, to our satisfaction. A person, accustomed to the life of a mariner may become reconciled, and even attached, to the sea. The converse also is true. A person, long disused to what was once agreeable, may lose his relish for it, and even contract a dislike to it. A person, long disused to the exercises of the field and the open air, may feel himself distressed upon being obliged to go abroad.

It is commonly observed, that some articles, such as spiritous liquors, and intoxicating drugs, tobacco, or opium, which the vulgar, in different parts of the world, are most apt to debauch, are however, in the first use of them, unpleasant or harsh to the taste.

We have not any sufficient reason to believe that men, of remote ages and nations, differ from one another otherwise than by habits acquired in a different manner of life: But how differently are they affected by external causes? And what a difference do they exhibit in their choice of food, accommodations, and pleasures? The train-oil, or putrid fish, which is a feast in Labrador or Kamchatka, would be little else than poison to a European stomach.

Or if men, in situations so remote from one another, should be supposed to be of a different race, or to have incurred, from a difference of climate or situation, a change in the construction of their organs. Variet-

ies, almost equally striking, are observable, in the habits contracted in
different ranks of life, by men of the same country and age. The peasant
is at ease in his cottage, under a roof, and in the midst of accommodations that would extremely discontent or displease a person accustomed
to other conveniences.

In such instances, no doubt, men are affected by their habit of thinking, no less than by the use of what they are accustomed to enjoy or to
bear. In the ranks of society, distinguished by their respective accommodations, the inferior fondly aspires to that which would raise him to the
level of his superior. *State* itself, or the appearance of greatness, is the
charm that gives, to the apparatus of luxury, its principal value. Men,
whose fortunes indulge them in the possession of every convenience,
and in the enjoyment of every pleasure, can nevertheless forego them
with ease, in the hardships of hunting or war, where the privation is not
supposed to degrade, or any way to affect their station. Such hardships,
incurred in the capacity of a beggar, or supposed to proceed from want
of means to live more at their ease, would occasion extreme distress and
dejection of mind. "The tradesman at Paris", says the author
[Louis-Sébastien Mercier] of the *Tableau de Paris*, "goes forth, on certain
holidays, to purchase a fowl for his supper; and in this he consults his
vanity no less than his palate, for he proposes to fare like a gentleman."
But such effects of association in the mind, no less than the effects of a
continued use in the bodily organs, are to be ascribed to habit alone.

A task, which at first is severe and laborious, becomes easy, and even
agreeable, through use. In youth, we are ever bent on pleasure or amusement, and at first averse to the application or restraint of business, but, as
there is ever some degree of active exertion in what we term amusement
or pastime, we often slide, by a habit of application, from the one to the
other. The habit of business, when once it is acquired, is from experience,
well known to supplant the taste for amusement; and to render us indifferent to what, before we had acquired such habit, we considered as
pleasure.

In manhood, what does not engage some serious passion, and has no
other recommendation but that of pastime, appears insipid or frivolous;
and, when the powers of action have been employed in scenes of difficulty or moment, we cannot stoop to employ them in matters of a less
serious, or even less hazardous, nature. The mariner has no enjoyment in
the tranquility of a life on shore; the warrior is not amused with concerns
that do not affect his safety or his honor; the mathematician has no
delight in problems which are too easily solved; nor the lawyer, in cases
that do not admit of dispute.

The varieties of sentiment, which men incur through habit, whether of
association or mere practice and use, are evident in their judgment of
manners and action, no less than in their feeling of circumstances that
affect their own condition. What, in the manners of one country, is oblig-
ing and a favor, in another would be felt as an offence: As death is accept-

able to the superannuated huntsman in the neighborhood of Hudson's Bay, to bestow it is reckoned a favor; and the office devolves on a son or a grandson, who, being supposed to have received the highest obligations, are thus destined to repay it by the last act of piety to his parent.

In the contemplation of these, and such varieties affecting the manners of nations, we are apt to enquire, whether any thing be so fixed in the nature of man, as that habit or custom cannot change or remove it?

It is well known that external expressions, whether of moral sentiment, or devotion, in the manners or religious observances of men, are, like the words of their language, mere arbitrary signs, which custom accordingly may alter. But the sentiments themselves, whether of benevolence towards men, or devotion to God, retain their distinctive quality under all the variations of external expression. If our question, therefore, refer to qualities of the mind, and the distribution of enjoyment and suffering, from the good or ill qualities of which the mind is susceptible, we may decidedly answer, in the affirmative, that the laws are fixed, and that no continuance of situation, and no repetition of act, can alter them. Fear and malice, in all the shapes they assume, whether of jealousy, envy, or revenge, are ever constituents of suffering or of misery. Benevolence and fortitude are ever agreeable and constituent of happiness. No continuance of practice can render fear or malice a state of enjoyment; no habit of thinking can change their effects. Some, through the continued repetition of crimes, may have the conscience *seared as with a hot iron*; and the wicked may have a momentary triumph in the gratification of malice. But no charm can change malice itself, or fear, into pleasure, nor does a happy temper of mind pall on the sense, or lose its effect by continued enjoyment.

If habit should produce any change in these important respects, it must be by substituting one affection or temper of the mind for another, candor for malice, and courage for timidity, not by altering the effect while the same temper remains. Of such changes men no doubt are susceptible; and it is an object of supreme concern that they should be made for the better, and not for the worse.

…

### Section VIII: Of Ambition, or the Desire
### of something higher than is possessed at present

Different circumstances in the condition of man render him susceptible of various attainments, or contribute to forward his progress; and, on this account, were enumerated among the principles of progression in human nature. But *Ambition*, in the sense given to it as above, is the specific principle of advancement uniformly directed to this end, and not satiated with any given measure of gratification: It continues to urge its pursuit after the highest attainments are made, no less than it did when farthest removed from its end.

This passion is observed to operate in the concerns of mere animal life; in the provision of subsistence, of accommodation, and ornament; in the progress of society, and in the choice of its institutions. It operates in the attainments of knowledge, and in every aim at perfection, whether in executing works of genius, or in the honorable part which the worthy desire to support through life.

Personal qualities, however, we must suppose to be its genuine object, as these are the real constituents of eminence or true elevation. And perfection in the nature of man being never actually attained, will account for the peculiar form of this instinct, which, even where it mistakes its object, and seems to find a limit beyond which it is vain to urge its pursuits, as in the provision to be made for the accommodation of animal life; yet even in this article, it ever aims at somewhat higher and better than is possessed at present. The miser, after he has got all he can use, continues to hoard without end what he is determined not to use.

Ambition is, upon this account, also peculiar to man. He alone, among the animals, seems to conceive the distinction of perfection and defect, and refers to it in many of his most vehement sentiments and passions, such as esteem, admiration, respect, veneration, and love, on the one hand; contempt, detestation, and scorn, on the other.

In respect to whatever object these sentiments are felt, we may presume that the distinction of excellence and defect is either realized in the object itself, as it is in the character and disposition of the human mind; or, if the object be in its own nature indifferent, as in compositions of mere matter and form, we may suppose that the notion of perfection or defect is associated with it in the mind, and gives occasion to the opposite sentiments of admiration or disgust with which the object is received or beheld.

There is a real excellence or defect in all the examples of personal merit or demerit, in all the examples of justice or injustice in the manners or institutions of men, and in the degrees in which minds are possessed of genius, or defective in point of ability.

Excellence and defect, on the other hand, are associated merely in our conception, with circumstances of birth or fortune, insomuch that men entertain esteem for persons of one condition, and contempt for those of another, upon the mere difference of estate or of family. Whole nations admire the possession of wealth in themselves, and take rank from the accommodations they possess. Not satisfied with the gratifications which riches afford, they boast of them as matters of estimation also, and assume a rate of elevation, which the real degradation of manners and spirit but too often belies.

The national pursuit of such objects, indeed, are urged to indefinite extent, rather by the interest and ambition of individuals than by the policy of states; and communities become rich, not from the impulse of public institutions, but rather from the ambition of their separate members, who wish to provide for themselves what is considered as a constituent of superiority in the distinctions of rank.

Such is the operation of ambition in the pursuits of wealth. But, as excellence is more frequently associated with power than with riches, ambition is commonly more understood to be a love of dominion, than of wealth. Crassus was eminent for riches, but was reckoned ambitious so far only as he made wealth subservient to power. Ambition is reckoned the characteristic of Cesar because, although indifferent to riches, he aimed at dominion over his equals, and could not be satisfied with any condition below that of sovereign of his country. Sylla, though not correct in his notion of greatness, still rose above this idea, and contemned the sovereignty among fools as much as he would have done their applause or esteem.

The circumstances which lead the mind, in forming these associations, whether analogy or prevailing opinion, are various; and power is certainly more easily mistaken for comparative elevation than either family or wealth. Power is even sometimes founded on the best qualities of human nature—wisdom, goodness, and fortitude. But, being obtained also by cunning or brutal force, being always distinguishable from merit or real worth, it may lead to the most pernicious and fatal effects. Or, as it implies subjection in some, as well as dominion in others, it is in human life a principal source of contention, war, and injustice.

Apart from the ruinous effects of violence in the pursuits of dominion, it is ungenerous to desire that others should be at our mercy, or subject to our caprice; and this desire is sure to make itself enemies, and to meet with resistance, whether from competitors in the same line of pretension or from others who disdain subjection, and contend for their rights.

If Cato and Antoninus were ambitious in aiming at the highest measures of personal worth, or, as it is described in the Caesars of Julian, in aspiring to a resemblance of the supreme God, how must the ambition of Cesar appear, in wishing only to reduce his fellow citizens and equals to hold their lives and fortune at his discretion.

As we may hope, that intelligent beings, sooner or later, in the present or some future state, are destined to perceive the true path of ambition; this principle, we acknowledge, is, beneficently, made one of the most powerful motives of action in human nature. Even in its present, too frequently erroneous course, it serves to engage men in never-ceasing pursuits and exertions which, though aimed at a mistaken end, nevertheless occasion the improvement of faculties, so intensely applied—insomuch that we may venture to state this passion, even in its most signal aberrations, as a material principle in the progressive nature of man; operating in all his pursuits; and denying him, even in search of a supply of his animal wants, that repose which nature, as often as an appetite is fully gratified, seems to allow throughout every other part of the animal kingdom.

Man is born naked, defenseless, and exposed to greater hardships than any other species of animal; and though he is qualified to drag a precarious existence under these disadvantages, yet as we find him, in the situation of his greatest defect, urged by motives to supply it, no way short of necessity, so we find him, by a continued application of this motive, which we term ambition, still urged to proceed in every subsequent state of his progress.

His society, also, prior to any manner of political establishment, we may imagine exposed to extreme disorder; and there, also, we may fancy the spur of necessity no less applied than in the urgency of his mere animal wants. From these motives, accordingly, we admit the arts of human life, whether commercial or political, to have originated, and suppose that the consideration of necessity must have operated prior to that of convenience, and both prior to the love of mere decoration and ornament.

The wants of men, indeed, are of different kinds, and may be unequally urgent; but the movements, performed for the supply of very different wants, appear to be simultaneous, and bring at once into practice the rudiments of every art, without any such order as we might suppose to arise from their comparative degree of importance, or the urgency of occasions on which they are practiced.

The convenient and ornamental in their several forms, however rude, are studied in the same age with the necessary; and the same person, who subsists from meal to meal on the precarious returns of the chase, is, in the intervals of his necessity, no less studious of ornament in his person, his dress, and the fabric of his habitation, his weapons, or arms, than he was earnest procuring his food. He studies the distinction of ingenious thought and ardent emotion in the song which he recites, or in the talk which he holds in the assembly of his tribe. He conceives an honor to be pursued, and a dignity of character to be preserved, in which his ambition is not surpassed, even by those who are most effectually relieved from the distractions that tend the inferior cares and necessities of animal life.

Without meaning, therefore, in any degree to insinuate that the pursuits of external accommodation, or the rudiments of commercial arts, had a priority in the order of time, to those of political institution or mental attainment, we may separate these particulars, and place them in the order that appears most convenient for our own discussion. Or beginning with commercial arts, we may proceed to consider the political occupations of men before we state the mental attainments which mankind are actually making, whilst they are engaged in those other pursuits.

The human mind, in whatever manner it be employed, if its faculties are brought into exercise, ever receives some increment of power and some modification of habit; so that, without intending to operate upon itself, it nevertheless partakes of the effect that is produced, and receives an addition to the stock of personal qualities in the midst of attentions that were bestowed on a different subject.

Such in general is the fortune of nations. They do not propose to improve the character of their people in point of wisdom or virtue, but the people, nevertheless, receive instruction and habits of civilization, in the midst of labors bestowed in procuring their subsistence, accommodation, or safety.

## VOLUME II

### Part II, Chapter I
### Of the Specific Good Incident to Human Nature

*Section III: Of Beauty and Deformity, Excellence and Defect*

In the rational nature of man, there are principles which do not terminate merely in sensibility to pleasure and pain, or in mere active exertions, but consist in a kind of censorial inspection, over the general tenor of enjoyments and actions, serving to distinguish, among pleasures, the elegant and beautiful from the inelegant and deformed; and, among specimens of existence, the perfect or excellent, from the defective or imperfect. Such is the discriminating power of intelligence, by which the qualities of things are estimated, by which unequal measures of worth are conceived, and the gradations of excellence assigned in the scale of being.

In the exercise of these reflex and censorial powers, there is great enjoyment and suffering, according as the objects of them are happily or miserably distributed to ourselves or others. *Disgust, indignation, remorse,* and *shame,* are among the pains of which they render us susceptible; *delight, esteem, approbation, confidence, love,* and *peace of mind* and *of conscience,* are among their gratifications, or happy effects.

In the discernment of external objects, there arises a sentiment, which may be expressed in terms of praise or blame, of estimation or contempt, and which frequently constitutes, or sensibly modifies, the general affection of the mind, in respect to the distinction of good and evil. For, as good is pleasant, so, also in many instances, is it estimable; as evil is painful, so also is it, in many instances, vile and contemptible.

Of these sentiments, the specific occasions or objects are termed beauty and deformity, excellence and defect.

To perceive beauty or excellence, is to admire or esteem. And, lest these expressions, which are applicable to subjects of the highest nature, should appear too strong, when applied to matters of inferior consideration, in which some degree of beauty nevertheless may be admitted, let it be remembered, that it is the species of sentiment, not any measure of the emotion, or degree of merit in its object, which we are now about to consider.

Admiration and esteem, like benevolence and love, are agreeable sentiments; so much, that, to admire or esteem and to be pleased with an object, are expressions often mutually substituted one for the other.

We are pleased with beauty and excellence; we are displeased with deformity and defect. But all that pleases is not beautiful or excellent; nor all that displeases, deformed or defective. We know not, however, frequently, how otherwise to express the pleasure we take in any subject, than by pronouncing it excellent or beautiful; nor how to express the displeasure we feel, otherwise than by pronouncing the cause of it, ugly or defective. The wonderful organ of human language does not always serve the purpose of discrimination, even where it is of the most real importance to state the subjects of consideration apart.

We may, nevertheless, endeavor, in this place to consider beauty and excellence, as distinguishable from other causes of pleasure, by the specific accompaniment of esteem or preference to which, even if no one should admire, we conceive the object entitled; and to consider deformity and defect as distinguishable from other causes of pain by a peculiar sentiment of disapprobation or contempt, of which we conceive them to be proper objects even if the world should not perceive the defect or the deformity.

These specific sentiments, differing either in respect to the occasion on which they arise, or the degrees of intensity with which they are felt, have, in every language, a variety of appellations or names. In our language, *approbation* and *disapprobation, esteem* or admiration, opposed to *indifference, disgust,* or *contempt,* make a part of the terms by which we express them.

The ingenious author of some *Essays on the Nature and Principles of Taste* (Mr. [Archibald] Alison), has observed, that material subjects give sensation and perception of reality, but no emotion or sentiment of beauty or deformity, except so far as they are associated with some object of affection, whether character or disposition of mind, cheerfulness or melancholy, wisdom, goodness, or power.

> If a subject please, in consequence of its being associated with some object of esteem, the delight it affords is properly enough classed with the species of sentiment which we are now considering; but if it be associated only with utility, safety, or joy, it may please in consequence of this association. But the compound so made up is not any more a subject of admiration or esteem, than is the pleasurable circumstance by which it is recommended.

Attempts have been made to resolve this principle of esteem or admiration into some of the other principles or forms of proceeding, equally familiar in the operations of the human mind; and consequently, to account for the use of these terms, without the necessity of supposing that there is in nature any distinction of excellence, or in us any distinctive faculty by which it is known. And it should follow, from any theory of this sort, that, in reality, we mistake for esteem some other operation or affection of mind: but, in such substitutions of one species of affection for another, it does not appear that any advantage is gained. We neither can resolve the sentiment of admiration or esteem into anything better known than itself, nor the good qualities of mind, into any thing that, being more in our power, may show us a readier way to the improvement of our nature.

We shall, therefore, be contented with giving to the sentiments which beauty or excellence occasions, some one of their ordinary names of preference, whether delight, approbation, or esteem. The subjects of beauty and excellence themselves, in the meantime though thus agreeing in the class of sentiments to which they give occasion, seem to be disjoined in nature; or by us, at least, to be conceived apart. Beauty is sometimes said to cover defects; and excellent qualities are said to be concealed under apparent deformities. Beauty frequently strikes, from the first and more obvious aspect of things; excellence is to be collected by observation of their essential qualities. Every person that enters a room presents at once the beauty of which he is possessed. His excellence, in the meantime, or essential good qualities are to be known only upon farther acquaintance. These epithets, however, in proportion as the subjects of them come to be understood, gradually approach in their applications, and seem at last to unite in the same thing. When apparent beauty is found to conceal defects, it ceases to be admired, or even incurs contempt. When apparent deformities are found to conceal essential good qualities, we not only cease to contemn, but, from a principle of retributive justice, are the more inclined in the sequel to admire that we at first overlooked the value of our object, whether person or thing. So that the progress of intelligence in the discernment of excellence and beauty seems to terminate in a point, which unites these epithets into one general ground of preference; and which, in that case, we shall perhaps be more inclined to express in the terms of perfection and excellence, than in that of elegance or beauty, which still carry a reference to first and external appearances.

In the system of nature, there is a beauty that belongs to the mechanical, to the vegetable, the animal, and intellectual kingdoms.

In the mechanical kingdom, the principal, if not the sole constituent of beauty, as the *Pere Buffier* has well observed, *is order*; or, as the same author farther explains this term, the *apt combination of parts, whether simultaneous or successive, for the attainment of a beneficent purpose.*

Mere matter, though perceivable by sense, is in itself indifferent to any affection of the mind, except so far as some object of affection is associated with it. With an apt combination of parts for a beneficent purpose, are associated the supreme objects of admiration, love, and respect, viz. *wisdom, goodness,* and *power.* The association is not casual, or derived from mere analogy or likeness, but from the essential and inseparable relation of cause and effect.

The system of nature is sublime in respect to the might of its author. It is beautiful, with respect to the regular fitness of parts for the attainment of their ends, and in respect to the beneficent purpose which they are fitted to serve. The latter circumstance, above all, is essential to their beauty.

The fruits of continual exertion, without the regularity that proceeds from a well-concerted design, as in the meaningless activity of children and restless animals, overturning and displacing whatever comes in their way, produces disorder, confusion, and extreme deformity. The regular tradesman shudders at their being admitted into his workshop.

A design at the same time may be perceptible, but, if directed by folly or malice, it is an object of disgust or of reprobation, not of admiration or esteem. The figures of birds, beasts, cones, or pyramids, cut out of an evergreen, in the antiquated garden, have marks of design; but frivolous, and contemptible. The piece of statuary, of which we are told, in the bull of Phalaris, or in the Apiga or spouse of Nubis, may have been exquisite in the workmanship, but the design was hideous or cruel. And, as the mere indication of mind is ambiguous, the indication of perfidy and malice is horrid; beneficence alone, directed by wisdom, is supremely beautiful.

In the material system of nature, the beneficent purpose of its author is manifest in the accommodations provided for beings distinguished by their organization, or beings endowed with life. These, in our terrestrial world, are plants, animals, and men. The elements are disposed to promote the vegetation of plants, and these to furnish their subsistence and place of abode to animals; and the whole to furnish the materials of supply, and the subjects of thought and contemplation to the living and intelligent nature of man.

In the living kingdom of animals, the same beneficent purpose, while it extends to the general system, partly terminates also in the animal himself. He is made that he may be gratified, as well as that he may gratify others; and both are essential to the excellence and beauty of his frame. For this his organization is admired, and the prosperous state of that organization is so much valued, under the denomination of health.

With respect to man, also, the beneficent purpose of nature, so far as we are yet qualified to discern it, terminates in himself, not in the individual considered apart, but in the subserviency of many to the common cause of the whole. The individual is made that he may be gratified, but his chief gratification is made to consist in beneficence, or a participation in the welfare of mankind. He is an active power in nature, which cannot suspend its exertions, without incurring a state of weariness, suffering, and disgust. He is a beneficent power in nature, to whom benevolence is pleasure, malevolence is pain, and who cannot willingly forsake the paths of beneficence, without incurring the chastisement of remorse. His beauty and excellence is a participation, however faintly obtained, of that wisdom and goodness which constitute the splendor and majesty of the works of God.

To perceive beauty, in any material subject, is to perceive indications of wisdom and goodness; and, if we are asked, why wisdom and goodness should be admired? we may answer, For a reason like to that for which pleasure is coveted: because [it is] in itself desirable and good. While other things are desired or esteemed on account of the pleasure they give, or the excellence they constitute, pleasure and excellence are themselves desired or esteemed, on their own account.

In the scale of natures susceptible of excellence or perfection intelligence is supreme, and wisdom and goodness are the supreme perfections of intelligent being. Their presence, when suggested by the order of nature, awakening the sentiments of admiration, are termed beautiful, but, in the mind itself to which they belong, are more properly termed its excellence, perfection, or merit. Folly and malice, on the other hand, may, in a figurative stile, be termed the deformities of mind, but are more properly referred to the predicaments of defect, guilt, and demerit.

From the whole, there is reason to believe, that beauty when real may be resolved into excellence and, that deformity may be resolved into defect—the one an essential distinction of good, and the other of evil, [and] that both, or either, can have existence in mind alone. So that, in this question, man is doubly interested: He is concerned in the existence of excellence or beauty, as presenting him with an agreeable object of contemplation and love, but more especially as constituting an admirable state or condition of nature, attainable by himself.

In the human figure, there is one beauty of form in the structure of its organs, or in the found state or configuration of the whole person, indicating exquisite design, wisdom, and goodness of the Maker. There is another beauty, consisting in the aspect and expression of the mind, that occupies and actuates this created frame, indicating good sense, equanimity, and benevolence of temper.

In both, it is the beauty of mind that strikes through the form of a work, or the aspect of a person: The wisdom and goodness of the Creator, in the one; or the good meaning and temper of his creature, in the other.

Where one of these beauties exists, in any degree, the other may be sensibly wanting. Thus, we are familiar with instances, in which personal defects are compensated with a favorable expression and benevolence of aspect; or instances in which natural advantages are deformed by an aspect of vanity, malice, or folly.

The ancient artists, in the features of Medusa, though a Fury, feigned to themselves the most perfect form; or supposed her countenance to be cast in the most exquisite mold of natural beauty, but of an aspect, derived from the temper within, so terrific and hideous, as to appall the most daring, and even to turn those on whom she looked into stone.

Mind, we have reason to believe, predominates in nature; so that, in a comparative survey of all that exists, whatever is not mind would be as nothing.

It is heat, we are told, that gives spring and agitation to the mechanical world. Remove this ingredient, and all matter would freeze into one solid mass, and become the formless repository of inertia, darkness, and death.

In the fame manner, and with still greater confidence, may we not say, it is mind that strikes out from the forms of body, in the lovely aspects of excellence and beauty? And it is the diversity of operating minds, in such forms of matter, that gives the distinction of beauty and deformity to subjects otherwise, in their own nature, indifferent.

What were millions, and myriads of millions of corpuscular particles assembled in the body of the sun, without the benignant power that renders him the source of heat and of light to surrounding worlds? What were these worlds without the beneficent impulse that gives them motion, and retains them in their orbits, at a proper distance from the source of light and of heat? And what could avail their motions, without this combination of elements on their globes that fit them for the residence of living natures?

The same thing, multiplied through innumerable systems, owes its magnificence to the greatness of might and of thought, that acts in the formation and conduct of such boundless scenes of existence.

The distinction of excellence and defect, so obvious to man in the contemplation of his own nature, and so easily transferred by association to any of his works or external circumstances, is the radical principle of elevation or progression in the human mind, to which there is ever presented, as an object of desire, something higher and better than is possessed at present. This principle, in all its forms, proceeds upon some preconceived notion of absolute or comparative excellence, in respect to which the mind is never disposed to acquiesce in its present attainment. Birth, fortune, power, and other constituents of rank, are the circumstances in which the vulgar of every condition strive to excel one another. The dwelling, the furniture, the equipage, and the table of the rich, flatter his vanity more than his sense of pleasure and stir the emulation more than the appetite of those who admire his condition.

Whoever would govern mankind, if he can command their conception of what is excellent, or lead them to associate honor with the task he would have them to perform, will find no farther difficulty, in procuring from them every sacrifice of pleasure, interest, or safety. This, as we have formerly observed, is the honest man's integrity, and the gentleman's honor, which neither will forego to preserve his fortune or his life. It is the soldier's glory, which renders danger and hardship agreeable; it is the martyr's crown which renders extreme suffering, and the prospect of death, an occasion of triumph and joy.

On a subject of so great importance, and of such powerful effects in human life, it behooves us to examine our opinions, and to be well founded in the conceptions, to which we thus surrender and deliver up all the other powers of our nature. If there be an excellence or beauty, specific to man, we may presume that, in the contemplation and possession of it, his supreme good, the most agreeable state of his nature, and the happiest course of his life is likely to consist.

### Section IV: Of Virtue and Vice

When, in the manner of [the] last section, we have resolved the excellence and beauty of this created frame into the wisdom and goodness of God, and return from this contemplation of nature to consider, what is the specific excellence of man, we must recognize in him at once a constitution or form received from his Maker, and together with the gifts of intelligence and free will, a personage and character to be ascribed to himself. In respect to either, he is distinguished in nothing so much as in this power and disposition to perceive with delight, an intelligent and beneficent author in the system of things around him. Were he thus to judge of any human production, his perception of beauty in the work would argue some participation in the genius of its author. May we not therefore, conceive, that his admiration of what appears in the universe of God implies some qualification to participate in the godlike principles of beneficence and wisdom. In this system, of which he is a part, the measures of providence are taken, and the design is carried into execution; he too is destined to act. But when we consider the magnitude of this system, and in how many ways, of which he cannot trace any tendency to the purpose of universal good, he himself may be affected, his concurrence in the design is likely to be merely passive, or so far only as to make him bear with complacency what the general order requires, rather than to call upon him for any active exertion directed to a purpose so far extended beyond his comprehension.

Even when we confider the world of men and animals, how far extended beyond the reach of any active interposition of the individual for its general good, we must suppose that the character of goodness, applicable to man, in respect to this object also, consists in pious resignation to the will of God; or, at most in perfect good will to mankind, in every instance in which the active power of an individual can apply. Fortunately for him, when he acts in particular instances, for his friend, his neighbor, his country, or for any of the human race, there occurs, an occasion to practice and to promote that mutual affection, fidelity, justice, and humanity, which in fact are a common blessing to mankind; insomuch, that for him to adopt and to communicate the effect of these characters, is to act for the good of his fellow-creatures, and, so far he becomes an able and a willing instrument in the hand of God for the beneficent ends of his providence.

The merit of this character, however, is more a subject of consciousness, or intuitive judgment, than of discussion or reasoning; and they who are, in common life, most decided in their choice of good actions, proceed upon the ground of their affections and sentiments, more than upon any information derived by investigation or research. In attempts at science, however, we must descend to particulars, and endeavor to collect, by induction from the phenomena of that nature we are considering, what may be its destination, and what the standard by which its worth is to be estimated.

Among subjects organized, we have already observed that man is distinguished as living and active; among the living and active he is distinguished as intelligent, or endowed with powers of discernment, apprised of the distinction of good and evil, and invested with freedom of choice. Among the gregarious animals, he is distinguished as associating and political, and conscious of his station as a member in the community of his fellow creatures. The order of nature itself is in a certain degree manifest to him; he is fitted to hold communication with its Author, to apprehend His will and to become a willing instrument in promoting the ends of government.

In striving to conceive the destination of such a being, we may with great confidence reject the idea of its being limited to preservation of mere animal life, or even, as Epicurus assumed, to the possession of mere pleasing thoughts or sensations of any sort. There is an active character to be sustained, and a part to be filled up; first, in the community of men, who are partners in the joint cause of humanity and justice. There is a world of still and living nature, in the midst of which this active being must acquit himself, with sensibility in respect to some, and with circumspection and care respecting the whole. There is a commanding order of things to which he must accommodate himself, which he is required to study, and concerned to know, and to which, even where it exceeds his comprehension, he must with submission surrender his will.

To fill up such a part are required *skill, discernment,* or knowledge, *fit disposition, application,* and *force.* Hence the four cardinal virtues, celebrated in the schools of philosophy, *Wisdom, Justice, Temperance,* and *Fortitude.*

*Wisdom* is the virtue of intelligence, or a just discernment of the considerations on which we are to rely for happiness, and the undisturbed possession of the faculties which are given for the government of life. Man, in his character of intelligent being, is active in a form, and to an extent, greatly superior to any of the other animals. Every quality of his nature is an energy, not a quiescent mode of existence; and, whatever be the limits within which he is destined to exert his faculties, within the same limits, and in the same form of active exertion, are to be found his excellencies and defects, his enjoyments and sufferings.

The lot of man is not, like that of the other animals, at once completely furnished by nature; he is invested with powers, and left to employ them for his own advantage, or that of his fellow creatures. He merits the praise of wisdom, or he incurs the imputation of folly, according to the use which he makes of his intelligent faculties; and in this, perhaps, gives the first striking specimen of the excellence or defect, of which he is susceptible. His powers of conception, when well employed, lay the foundations of wisdom; when misapplied or neglected, lay the foundations of folly; and so far present him to his fellow creatures, as an object either of esteem and respect, or of contempt and derision.

With the exception of a few determinate instincts, such as direct him on particular occasions to the means of self preservation, or such as connect the individual with his kind, man, we have observed, is left to follow the dictates of his own observation, discernment and experience. In nonage or infancy, indeed, he is committed to the discretion of his parent; but, in the more advanced periods of life, he is committed to his own. His instincts and appetites are seldom to him, as they are to the other animals, determinate guides in the application of means to the attainment of his end, or seldom secure him in the proper choice and measure of his gratification. When urged by hunger, though in the midst of plenty, if the fruit or species of food presented to him be new or untried, but must proceed with caution in the use of it, and examine well before he ventures to taste—much more before he ventures to feed on viands unknown, though of the fairest appearance.

Although his gratifications, like those of the other animals when the purpose of nature is served, frequently determine or pall on the sense, and satiety, even in his case, might be sufficient to guard him against excess; yet he is, by an error of his imagination, frequently led to exceed even these limits, and to seek for pleasure, where it is not any longer to be found, in the object of a satiated appetite. In him, therefore, the defects of instinct must be supplied by reflection; and, he is to be taught, by experience and observation alone, to distinguish the real sources of permanent happiness.

As to man, therefore, the errors of his own imagination, as well as the defects of his instinct, are occasions of evil, they are to be supplied or corrected by the proper use of his intelligent powers. And it may be asked, Are we to consider the intelligence of man as a mere substitute for the correctness of choice to which the other animals are formed by nature, and to estimate its value, by its apparent destination to do for him what instinct, and the want of imagination, have done for the brutes? This were to suppose him destined to attain, by a tedious and uncertain process, that of which other animals are at once possessed by the suggestion of a specific propensity. The bee, without any other direction than this, constructs his cell upon a model which the most perfect science of mechanism cannot improve, and possesses that skill, from the first, which in the human species, many ages and successive trials are required to obtain.

Animals, in general, whatever be their destination, are enabled to fulfill it at once. They acquiesce in their state, or enjoy its advantages, without any sense of its wants or defects. Man, at his outset, being worse provided than any other animal, is accordingly not disposed to acquiesce in his primary state. The wants or defects of his first condition seem, in the exercise of his faculties to press him with all the force of necessity. But, after his first wants or defects are supplied, fancy succeeds to necessity, and whatever supply he may have gained, or accommodation provided for himself, he is still urged with a desire of somewhat beyond the present attainment, and is as little disposed to acquiesce in the highest, as in the lowest state of his animal accommodation. The spur of impatience to better himself, which, in his rudest condition appears necessary to his preservation, continued on to his state of highest attainment, seems to form in him a principle of progression, of indefinite or endless extent. He is made intelligent, not merely that he may be able to procure a supply to his animal wants, but his animal wants appear to be multiplied, and his fancy rendered insatiable, that he may find an early scope for the exercise of his intellectual powers, and, by the indefinite pursuit of their ends, make that progress in knowledge, which constitutes so essential a part in the excellence or perfection of which his mind is susceptible.

We may thus collect the specific excellence of any nature, from its capacity, and from the direction of its progress; and that of man, in particular, from his capacity of receiving information, of improving in discernment and penetration, and from the progress he is qualified to make in these particulars. In him, the mere continuance of life is a course of observation, and repeated occasion, on which to exercise those faculties of the mind, which improve in being employed.

Man becomes powerful in the system of nature, in proportion as he becomes knowing or wise: And the species, in this particular, seems well apprised of the standard by which to ascertain its own merits or defects. Signal ability and understanding are admired, comparative incapacity, and dullness are despised. And there is, therefore, in respect to him no difficulty in collecting the grounds of esteem or contempt, whether we consider *a priori* what is suited to his destination, or attend to the reception which his qualities meet with in the estimation of his kind.

Philosophers have thought, that every subject of commendation, to which human nature is competent; every virtue and every constituent of happiness, might be comprised under the title of wisdom, or the excellence of intelligent being; that, on the contrary every subject of dispraise or contempt, every vice and every character of misery, might be comprised under the title of folly. But, it is not necessary, nor perhaps even expedient, thus to force the attributes of human nature, under single appellations, however comprehensive or general. Although it is both wise and profitable to love our fellow creatures, we can no more become affectionate to our friend, in the mere search of wisdom, than we can in search of our interest. Our constitution must have the ingredient of benevolence, in order that a mind well informed may improve upon this principle of nature, and learn to direct it aright.

"There are good qualities", say the Duke de la Rochefoucauld, "which degenerate into faults when they are natural, and others which are never perfect when they are acquired. It is necessary, for instance, that we should become by reflection sparing of our money and of our confidence; on the contrary, we should by nature be furnished with benevolence and valor." The understanding at the outset has its perfection to acquire; the heart is good by the inspiration of nature.

But, in whatever terms we propose to express the standard of estimation relative to man, whether *wisdom, virtue,* or *goodness of heart,* there are various conditions required to the performance of his part, and which must occur in every statement of qualities, that constitute the specific excellence or perfection of his nature. He is formed for society, and is excellent in the degree in which he possesses the qualifications of an associate and a friend. He is excellent, in the degree in which he loves his fellow creatures; he is defective, in the degree in which he hates them, or is indifferent to their welfare. Benevolence, therefore, is a principal excellence of human nature; and malice an article of extreme vileness or defect. These are the great sources of merit and demerit, of justice and beneficence, on the one hand; of wrong, iniquity, and cruelty, on the other—a distinction, to the reality of which mankind in all ages have borne the strongest testimony. To which, on the one hand, they have paid the highest tribute of esteem and of love; and, on which, on the other, they have poured forth the highest measures of contempt and detestation.

With respect to *Temperance,* it is a beautiful part, we may again observe, in the economy of animal life, that things pernicious a painful, and things salutary are pleasant; that even things salutary and pleasant, in the proper use of them become painful, in the abuse, or when carried to excess. Under this constitution of nature, the mere animals are safely directed through life, but man's animal frame is either originally less perfect in this respect or disturbed by the operations of a fancy, which lead him to look for enjoyments beyond the foundations which nature has laid.

By nature, the gratifications of appetite are occasional, and do not occupy any improper portion of time; but the voluptuary conceives them as a source of continued enjoyment. And sensuality is a distemper of the imagination, not a disorder in the balance which nature has established between the animal and the rational part of man's constitution. The voluptuary does not enjoy more than the abstemious, but he employs more of his time in vain attempts to restore a satiated appetite, and to render that continual, which nature has ordained to be occasional and temporary.

As great inequalities of character and estimation result from the different degrees in which men avoid the habits of debauchery on the one hand, or gain the habits of a just application to the better pursuits of a rational nature, on the other, there is, in this particular, much room for wisdom, and much danger from folly. In this, as in many other instances, man is destined by nature to govern himself, or to make the best of materials which become pernicious, if he abuse or neglect them, and which, to secure the proper use of them, require his utmost attention and care.

This virtue, among the active qualifications of man, may be referred to the title of application; for the pursuit, which the temperate withholds from the mere objects of animal gratification may be applied to the better and more worthy objects of human life. Sensuality, indeed, for the most part, is selfish and more solicitous about the gratifications of appetite, than about the concerns of other men; and temperance being an exemption, at least from this principle of selfishness, lays open the mind of man to those incitements of benevolence and candor, from which the disinterested are prepared to act. Temperance, therefore, in this point of view also, may be reckoned among the primary excellencies of human nature; intemperance or sensuality may be reckoned among its most real defects.

With respect to *Fortitude*, the fourth in the enumeration of cardinal virtues, we may observe that, in every active nature, besides the disposition, the application, and the measure of skill, in respect to which such natures may be unequally estimated, there is a measure of force also required to support their active exertions, and a measure of weakness sufficient to frustrate the purpose of nature, or to betray the confidence that may be placed in the highest measures of skill and of good disposition.

Force of mind has a peculiar reference to the state of man, to the difficulties, hardships, and dangers, in the midst of which he is destined to act. In the support of what is honorable and just, he has sometimes occasion to suffer what is inconvenient or painful to his animal frame. In espousing the cause of the just, he may incur the animosity and opposition of the wicked. In performing the offices of beneficence to others, he may encounter with hardship or danger to himself.

But this circumstance, which seems to restrain or limit his activity, serves rather to whet his spirit, and increase his ardor in the performance of worthy actions. The difficulty he surmounts becomes an evidence of the disposition which he approves, and actually endears the object for whose sake he exposes himself. Hence it is, that ingenuous minds are confirmed in the love of virtue, in proportion as it becomes a principle of elevation, of heroism, or magnanimity. These, it is scarcely necessary to observe, are primary topics of praise, and principal excellencies of human nature while pusillanimity and cowardice are amongst the lowest subjects of contempt.

From these particulars, then, we may collect that the excellence of a man includes the following particulars: *Wisdom*, or skill to choose, and to accomplish what he ought to attempt; a *benevolent affection*, which wisdom is fitted to direct; an *application of mind*, which inferior considerations cannot divert from its purpose; and a *force*, which opposition, difficult, or danger, cannot dismay. And, as the excellent man is wise, beneficent, courageous, and temperate, the defective, on the contrary, is foolish, malicious, cowardly, and sensual. The wise choose, among their ends, what is best; among the means they employ what is most effectual. The benevolent are committed to their best affections; the courageous are exempted from the suffering and the weakness of fear; the temperate reserve their faculties, and their time, for the best and worthiest occupations of their nature; and, if from this statement of the excellence to which human nature is competent, we look back to what has been already observed on the subject of pleasure and pain, we shall have reason to conclude, that the Author of nature has not only made that most agreeable which is most salutary, but that more especially constituent of happiness, which, in the estimate of human qualities, is also most excellent, or most highly esteemed.

To be conscious of excellence, from the very nature of approbation and esteem, is a state of enjoyment; and, to be conscious of vileness or defect, a state of suffering. Or, if these sentiments could be suppressed, still, the constituents of man's specific excellence, *Wisdom, Justice, Temperance*, and *Fortitude*, apart from any reflections they may bring, are in themselves, either an exemption from pain, or accession of pleasure. And providence seems to intend, that this distinction, which is the source of elevation, integrity, and goodness, in the mind of man, should be the guide by which he is most securely led to the highest enjoyments, to which his nature is competent. The excellence and beauty he admires may become an attribute of his own mind; and, whether in reflection or action, constitute the most agreeable state of his nature.

If we thus figure to ourselves an active intelligent being in the best state of which he is susceptible, this, in respect to him is to be virtuous. Or, if we should be disposed to consider even the excellent mind, in respect to its external relations and effects rather than in respect to its own constitution, we may observe, that the wise, the courageous, the temperate, and the benevolent, are of all others most likely to stand well-affected to their fellow creatures, to the universe, and to the Creator of the world; that none are so likely to recognize the providence and moral government of God, or to settle religion itself on its best foundations of integrity and goodness. But before we proceed to state the conclusion of this argument, in any general expression of the supreme good to which human nature is competent, it is proper to take into our account also, what may occur on the subject of prosperity, or of those external advantages in which the gifts of fortune consist.

## Part II, Chapter II
## Of the Fundamental Law of Morality, its Immediate
## Applications and Sanctions

*SECTION III: Of the Difficulty which has arisen in accounting for
Moral Approbation*

If, according to the result of our enquiries on the subject of good and evil, what is required as the excellence or virtue of human nature, also constitute happiness; and if vice, on the contrary, is to be dreaded as the constituent of misery, there cannot be any doubt of the choice to be made.

But virtue, even to those who are far from considering it as happiness, is still matter of esteem and respect, and vice, even where the vicious are conceived to possess the good things of this life, is reprobated and condemned; insomuch, that virtue is approved even by those who depart from it, and vice is disapproved even where it is embraced.

This sentiment, therefore, is of a peculiar nature, not a specimen of mere desire and aversion, directed to a particular object, but a censorial act in the mind of man, having cognizance of a *right* or a *wrong* in the measure or tendency of his own desires or aversions, even when they have most entirely determined his will.

Doctor Clarke [Samuel Clarke, *A Discourse Concerning the Unchangeable Obligations of Natural Religion*, 1705], and some others, considering virtue as the fitness of man's character and practice to his own frame, and to his place in the system of nature, and, considering reason or understanding itself as competent to observe the fitness of things, have assumed human reason as the principle of moral discernment.

This system is nearly the same with that which, making virtue to conflict in the conformity of will to truth, makes reason also the arbiter of right and wrong, as of truth and error.

But these systems have been rejected, as unfit to explain the phenomenon of moral approbation, which, being itself an affection or sentiment of the mind, must be derived from a principle to be sought for among the considerations that influence the will, not among the perceptions of mere intelligence, which go no farther than to remark the existence of things.

Upon this ground, men of speculation have had recourse to various considerations of *utility* (private or public), of *sympathy*, and of *moral sense* to account for the approbation or disapprobation of actions which they themselves or others perform.

The investigation and application of any one of these principles, joined to the refutation of others, has amounted to treatises and led to discussions of great length. But the utmost that can be done in this place and in a mere summary state of so much argument, is to enumerate a few of the principal theories, and endeavor to extricate the mind from the perplexity, which so many discordant accounts of the same subject may occasion.

In the mean time, the *Regulae Philosophandi*, or canons of reason, as they are prescribed in other examples of physical investigation, must be sustained in this.[4]

*I. We are not to assign, as the cause of any appearance, what is not itself known as a fact in nature.*

Upon this principle, we reject hypothesis, or the mere *supposition* of a cause, of whose existence we have not any previous knowledge, as the vortex of Descartes is rejected in accounting for the planetary revolutions.

On this rule, it is probable that none of our theorists will trespass; for, although some have proposed to account for intelligence itself on the supposition of some occult configuration of the motion of material atoms, constituting reflection and thought, yet, as the mind, when so constituted, ever acts upon some consideration known to itself, it is impossible to think of explaining an act of the mind, in any particular instance, without recurring to some one or other of the considerations, on which the mind is generally known to proceed.

*II. We are not to deduce effects from causes, which, though real are unfit to produce the effect.*

In the *connection of cause and effect*, in contradistinction to a mere fortuitous contiguity of circumstances, there is supposed continual or inseparable accompaniment of one with the other. wherever the cause exists, there must the effect exist also. And the converse. They are ever to be found together, and in the same proportions.

Upon these principles, actual *utility*, whether private of public, will not account for the phenomenon of moral approbation.

For, apart at least from any *private utility*, it must be acknowledged that men approve of virtue, as it was exhibited in scenes long since past, and on occasions in which they could not possibly have any private or interested concern.

The sentiment of approbation, therefore, is certainly not proportioned to the private benefit actually received from the action approved, by the person who approves.

*Utility*, as it concerns mankind indiscriminately, and without any limitation of persons and times, is certainly more likely to account for this phenomenon.

Virtue is no doubt of a nature to be useful to mankind; but if, under the title of *utility*, as is probable, we refer to the external effects of virtue, we

---

[4]     See [Isaac] Newton's *Principia*, book iii.

shall not find moral approbation keep pace with the actual measure of benefit mankind received from this or any other cause.

There are many examples of great utility, in which no subject of moral approbation is conceived. Land is fertile; a tree is fruitful; a steer performs much useful labor; yet, in these there is no subject of moral esteem. The supposed cause, contrary to rule, is found to exist in many such instances, without producing the effect it is brought to explain.

In answer to this objection, it used to be admitted, by the author [presumably David Hume] of this system, "that moral approbation does not extend to matters of mere physical utility; or is limited to mind, and its active exertions." This limitation, accordingly, may be admitted. But actual utility, even in affections of mind, does not always amount to a subject of moral approbation. What [is] more useful in nature, than the disposition of every man to preserve himself, for, on this the safety of the whole depends. Yet its most reasonable effects are merely tolerated, seldom applauded as virtue, and often reprobated as selfishness and vice.

This effect, also, of moral approbation is sometimes found without the actual utility which is supposed to be its cause.

The mere attempts of a virtuous man to serve his friend, or his country, is an object of moral esteem, not only where he may have failed in his purpose, but even where the event may have been calamitous to himself, or to others. The person who dies with his friend, in attempting to save him; the person who sinks under the ruins of his country, in striving to preserve it, is no less an object of moral approbation, than the most successful adventurer in either cause. And, if success, for the most part, give luster to enterprise, the tender melancholy that arises from a tragic event, is well known also to enforce the love of virtue, without regard to utility, of which the idea is excluded by the want of success.

It appears plain from these instances, that moral approbation though limited to the exertions of mind, yet does not accompany every useful exertion; nor even where it applies, does it require any actually useful effect. The will alone is sufficient to procure it. This, in other words, is to admit that benevolence, not actual utility, is the object of moral approbation. And, concerning this, most parties may be agreed. Even Mr. [Francis] Hutcheson, who assumed a moral sense, as being a specific faculty, required to distinguish between moral good and evil, considered *benevolence*, nevertheless, as the essence of moral good, or that quality which mankind, by their sense of right and wrong, are enabled to distinguish as good.

The benevolent will concur, one with another, in every thing that is for the benefit of mankind; but, in accounting for moral approbation, we must still return to the consideration of that peculiar sentiment of estimation, of which virtue is the object. And the whole mist end in a confession, that virtue, of which a principal part is benevolence, is estimable in itself, not merely as the means of obtaining any other end.

If, in the term *utility*, we include whatever is beneficial, or tends to the benefit of mankind, then is virtue itself, or its constituents of *wisdom, goodness, temperance*, and *fortitude*, the greatest good of which human nature is susceptible. And we only risk misleading the mind from its principal object, by substituting utility for the more proper expression of a blessing important to the person whose character it is, more than even to those on whom any of its external effects are bestowed.

It were preposterous to express the value of happiness, by calling it useful. Or, if a person who is happy in himself thereby disposed to be useful to others, it were preposterous say, that the happiness of one person is valuable only so far as is useful to another.

Virtue is, no doubt, supremely useful, even in the ordinary sense of this term. Justice, liberality, and charity, appear in acts of beneficence, and render those who are inclined to practice them, the guardians and friends of their fellow creatures. Even what we term acts of prudence, fortitude, or temperance, though seeming to terminate in the welfare of the person acting, are in fact preservatives of good order, and contribute to the welfare of mankind. The benevolent man is the more serviceable to his fellow creatures, that he is in himself prudent, pernicious, or unserviceable.

This tendency of virtue has been set forth in colours of glowing and superior eloquence.[5]

The external effects of virtue are acknowledged; but we cannot suppose that the sentiment of love, or respect, of which virtue is the object, is resolvable into a mere consideration of convenience or profit; nor can we overlook its value in constituting the worth and felicity of those by whom it is possessed, for the sake of a convenience it may procure to others, who, without any merit of their own, may wish to derive benefit from the external effect of merit in other men.

Upon this principle of utility, the distinction of right and wrong appears to be resolved into a mere difference of tendency, or external effect in the actions of men. In another ingenious attempt to explain the same phenomenon, the approbation of virtue is resolved into *sympathy*, or what may, for ought we know, be a kind of accidental humor in those who approve or condemn a supposed virtuous or vicious action.

*Sympathy*, in common language, is limited to *commiseration* or *pity*, but, has of late, by men of speculation [Adam Smith in his *Theory of Moral Sentiments*], been extended to sentiments of *congratulation* also. It may be supposed either merely instinctive, and a contagion of sentiment, as when without any knowledge of a cause, we laugh with those who laugh, become gay with the joyful, or sad with the melancholy. Or it may be supposed to proceed from a conception of the occasion or cause, whether joyful, provoking, or melancholy, that is the motive of action, or

---

[5]   See Hume's Moral Essays [Presumably, Ferguson is referring to *An Enquiry Concerning the Principles of Morals*, 1751].

object of passion. And it appears to be in this last sense, that *sympathy is* assumed as the principle of moral approbation.

When the observer feels, in a certain degree, the passion or motive by which another is actuated, upon a supposition that the same thing had happened to himself, this participation of sentiment is supposed to constitute approbation. Thus, when a person complains or exults, if the observer, upon a state of the case, partake in his sorrow or his joy, it is said, that *he cannot but approve of it.*

If the joy or grief exceed what the observer can go along with, it is condemned as weakness or levity; if it fall short of what the observer is disposed to feel, it is condemned as insensibility; if nearly what he himself would feel in a similar case, it is esteem or respected as proper; and so on of every other passion of sentiment appearing in the conduct of human life.

It may be difficult, in this account of the matter, to fix where the moral quality resides, whether in the person observed, in the observer, or in neither separately, but in the mere concurrence of one with another.

This last, indeed, or a mutual sympathy, may imply that two parties are satisfied with one another; but, in the sense of all mankind besides, their agreement may be wrong. And, if the action of one person needs the sympathy of another to justify it, we are still to enquire in what manner is that sympathy itself evinced to be right.

This theory proceeds upon an assumption, that to partake any passion or sentiment, or to be conscious that we ourselves should, in like circumstances, be so affected, is to approve of the motive to action, and to approve of its effects. But it is acknowledged, on all hands, that approbation or disapprobation is a specific sentiment, not a species or degree of any other sentiment; that it concerns the right or wrong of other passions, whether original or sympathetic, and therefore enabling the mind, on occasion, to pronounce of sympathy itself, whether it be proper or improper.

If, in judging of this theory, we recur to the maxims of reason already cited [Newton's *Regulae Philosophandi*], we shall find them violated in this, no less in the assumption of utility, for a principle of moral approbation. That is, the effect will be found without the supposed cause, and the cause will be found without its supposed effect. In respect to acts of uncommon bravery, we admire the more for being conscious that we ourselves could not have done so much. Although we are conscious that, in extreme indigence, we ourselves must have asked for relief, yet we do not admire a beggar. Although we are conscious that with money we ourselves should have bought an estate, yet we do not admire the purchaser. Although we sympathize very feelingly with the admirer of a fine woman, we do not mistake his passion for virtue, any more than we mistake for generosity the choice made by him who bought an estate. There is sympathy, as well as utility, without approbation; and there is approbation without either; for we sometimes have an idea of what we ought to have done, or to have felt, as very different from the part which we actually take in the feelings of other men. And it is remarkable that sympathy should be then only equivalent to approbation, when we sympathise with the benevolent, the disinterested, the courageous, and the just.

But, if it should be acknowledged, that, to partake in the sentiment of another is to approve, and not to partake is to disapprove of his conduct, it remains, upon this system, to be stated, by what sympathy it is that we judge of ourselves.

If, by the actual participation of others in our sentiments and actions, it should follow, that, in actions concealed from the world, there should be no conscience of right or wrong; or that, in actions submitted to vulgar judgment, we should be in great danger of error: the multitude is often ill-informed, and otherwise ill-qualified to judge of merit. And this indeed is so far acknowledged, in forming the theory in question, that virtue is not referred to the test of actual sympathy, but to the test of a sympathy, imagined and selected in the case of a well-informed and impartial observer.

Here too there is a masterly tone of expression [Smith's *Theory of Moral Sentiments*], and, if eloquence were the test of truth, no want of evidence to obtain belief. But, in this reference to a supposed well informed and impartial observer, there is an implied confession, that there is some previous standard of estimation, by which to select the judge of our actions; and this standard, by which to select an impartial and well informed spectator, to whose judgment we refer, or by which we are enabled to judge of sympathy itself, as well as of every other action or passion, is that principle of moral approbation, of which we are now in search.

This is not merely a question of fact, as in other examples of physical theory: For we do not enquire what men actually do in any number of instances, but what they ought to do in every instance. What is the principle of moral discernment on which they may safely proceed, whether in judging of other, or in choosing for themselves?

Sympathy is no doubt a part in the social nature of man. Individuals mutually bestow, and delight to receive it, but, like every other natural disposition, it is susceptible of abuse, and by no means a safe or an adequate principle of estimation. As the presumptuous appreciate others by their own standard, the weak and dependent rise or fall in their own esteem, according to the value that is put upon them by others; but neither one nor the other, surely, should be set up as the models of perfection to mankind.

It is difficult to name the power by which man is enabled to distinguish between right and wrong, without recurring to the generic appellation of some of his other faculties, as *sense, perception,* or *judgment.* This power has accordingly been termed a moral sense, or a sense of moral good or evil; and the name has led to an hypothesis or supposition, that as nature, in the case of different animals, has superadded to the other principles of sensitive life, some peculiar faculty of *seeing, smell,* or *feeling,* as in the lynx's eye, the hound's nostril, or the spider's touch, as to other qualities of the loadstone, are joined the magnetic polarity and the affinity to iron. So, to the mind of man, over and above the powers cognitive and active, the Maker has given a power judicative, respecting the merit or demerit of character, and approving or disapproving even the dispositions, from which the moral conduct proceeds.

Lord Shaftesbury sometimes uses the term moral sense, as expressive of a conscious discernment of moral good and evil, but seems to refer to the fact merely without any thought of a hypothesis to account for the phenomenon of moral approbation. It was enough, in his apprehension, that the distinction of moral excellence is real, and that we are by our nature well qualified to perceive it. In this, also, the sects of ancient philosophy seem to have acquiesced, without requiring any other account of the matter.

If it be understood, therefore, that difficulties arising on the question of theory, relating to the explanation of the phenomenon of moral approbation, do not amount to any degree of uncertainty in the fact, and if it be admitted that moral right and wrong are of the most serious consequence to mankind, [then] the faculty, by which we perceive the opposite conditions of men in this particular, may be known by any name that does not tend to confound the subject with others of a different nature.

If *moral sense,* therefore, be no more than a figurative expression, by which to distinguish the discernment of right and wrong, admitting this to be an ultimate fact in the constitution of our nature, it may appear nugatory to dispute about words, or to require any other form of expression than is fit to point out the fact in question. And if this fact, though no way susceptible of explanation or proof, being uniform to a great extent in the operations or nature, is itself a law, not a phenomenon, it may no doubt serve as a principle of science, to account for appearances that result from itself, and to direct the practice of arts throughout the departments in which it prevails.

Thus the laws of motion, gravitation, cohesion, magnetism, electricity, fluidity, elasticity, and so forth, which are not explicable upon any principle previously known in nature, are nevertheless received as unquestionable facts, and with great advantage pursued, to their consequences in the order of things. In this pursuit they furnish at once a secure direction to the practice of arts, and the most satisfactory account of appearances in the terrestrial and solar systems.

Men of speculation were sometimes amused with conjectures, respecting the cause of *gravitation,* and the intimate nature of other *physical laws;* but science made little progress, while these were considered as phenomena to be explained, and not as principles of science applicable to explain their diversified effects throughout the physical system.

Such, also, we may suppose to be the fate of theory, when employed to explain the law of estimation in the mind of man. The existence of this law is known, as the existence of mind itself is known, without anything previously understood, from which to infer or explain it, or on which to rest our belief of its truth. Its applications, in our judgment of manners, are no less proper than the application of any physical law in accounting for its own specific appearances. They enable the moralist, in particular instances, to ascertain what is good for mankind, and to form a regular system of moral estimation and precept, throughout all the subdivisions of *law*, of *manners*, or political *institutions*.

We may, or may not, conceive the power of discerning between excellence and defect, as a faculty inherent to intelligent being. To such being, indeed, it appears essential to be conscious of himself; and in his attainments, whether actually varied, or only conceived to be variable, it may be essential that he consider unequal degrees of *excellence* and *defect*, as measures of the *good* or the *evil* of which he himself is susceptible. Created intelligence may advance in the use of this discerning faculty, and have a continued approach to the model of divine wisdom, a termination from which its distance may diminish, but at which it never can arrive.

The essence of almighty God we must conceive to be most *simple*, being that which necessarily exists from eternity. Of his supreme intelligence, we have full evidence in the system of nature; and of his distinguishing the opposite conditions of moral good and evil, there is equally irresistible proof.

The distinction of excellence and defect originates in the unequal conditions of mind, and the discernment of such condition is not only peculiar, but necessary also to the course which created beings of this order are destined to run. Hunger and thirst, or any other incitement to self preservation, is not more essential to the animal frame, than the preference of what is perfect, to what is defective, is to the constitution of mind: It is a preservative of reason, a main spring of exertion, and a principle of advancement, in the track of intelligent nature.

Hence it is that numbers of men, who are far from conceiving virtue as the constituent of happiness, nevertheless consider it as the constituent of excellence and perfection, which they behold with respect and esteem.

Man alone in this animal kingdom, for ought we know, apprehends the gradation of excellence in the scale of being; and, though all men are agreed upon the reality of a comparative eminence, in the ascending steps of this scale, it may be difficult to assign the principle of estimation, so as to justify the preference which is given to one order of being above another. Mr. [Georges, Comte de] Buffon ascribes this preference to the greater number of relations, which certain orders of being bear to the system of nature around them:

In the multitude of things presented on this globe; in the infinite number of different productions, with which its surface is covered or peopled, the animals,

he observes,

occupy the first or the highest rank, whether by their resemblance to us, or by the superiority which we perceive in them, to the vegetable or inanimate natures. The animals, by their make and by their sensitive and moving powers, have many more relations to the subjects around than the vegetables have. These, in their turn, by the unfolding of their parts; by their figure, their organization, and growth, have many more relations than the minerals, or any mere lifeless mass of matter. And it is by virtue of this greater number of relations, that the animal is superior to the vegetable; and the vegetable is superior [to] the mineral. Even we ourselves, considered in respect to the material part of our frame, are not otherwise superior to the animals, than by a few relations more, such as accrue to us from the use of the hand and the tongue; and, though all the works of God are in themselves equally perfect, yet, in our own way of conceiving them, the animal is most complete; and man the master-piece of all.

This is, perhaps, the first attempt that ever was made to give a reason why animals are reckoned of a higher order than plants, and these of a higher order than minerals or unorganized matter of any sort. And though no one disputes this order of things, yet this attempt to explain it will scarcely appear satisfactory. Many will be ready to ask, why estimation should keep pace with the number of relations, which a subject bears to other parts of the world around. One relation, completely and beneficently adjusted, may be preferable to many. And, if a beneficent purpose can be obtained by one relation, however simple, the multiplication must appear rather a defect than a beauty. It appears, indeed, that where a number and variety of expedients or relations are wanting to obtain a purpose, the disposition and ability to combine such a variety to one common beneficent end, is a great perfection in the power by whom such arrangement is made. When man has formed to himself any number of relations to the subjects around him, such as he bears to the field he has cultivated, the city he has built, the work of any kind he has performed, the law or institution he has adopted, in such relations, indeed, the superiority of his own nature appears. But, in what his Maker has done for him, or for the other animals; in what is done for plants and minerals, it is the majesty of God that we revere; and the relations of things merely inanimate serve only as the steps, by which we are led to contemplate the wisdom and goodness of the first cause.

In this sense, we already observed, beauty and excellence are ascribed to material subjects. And the inequality of rank which appears so real in the system of things, is a mere gradation of the luster or effect, with which intelligence, or its principal features of goodness and wisdom, are made to appear in the different orders of being. The eloquent naturalist, cited above, seems to drop his arithmetic of relations, when he considers the pre-eminence of intelligent forms in the system of nature. For he applies it only to the material part of man, and, in reality, mere number of relations could ill account for the superiority of any nature whatever, as the relation between any two species of being must be mutual, and in point of number at least the same. For so many relations as man has to the system of nature around him so many precisely must the system of nature have to him. But no one ever questioned the pre-eminence of intelligent being, ever required an account to be given of it, or desired to know by what faculty it is perceived. Dimensions are measured by some standard quantity of the same dimension: length, by some standard measure of length; and solid content, by some standard measure of solid dimension; and why not intelligence, also, by some standard conception of intelligent nature. The degrees to be estimated consist in variable measures of wisdom and goodness; and whoever has an idea of these, will judge accordingly of the specimens that approach to the standard, or of the defects that come short of it.

Some who have carried the analogy of animal sense and perception into this subject, have started a question, whether moral excellence be not a secondary quality — that is, like the perception of smell, sound, or taste, if it may not proceed from a cause in nature very different from that we conceive?[6] But in the esteem of wisdom and goodness, there is not any danger that the quality we conceive is different from the quality that exists, as our conception of sound is different from a tremor in the particles of air: for it is the very existing thing itself of which we have a conception, taken indeed from feeble, occasional, and passing specimens, but easily abstracted by us from their defects and imperfections, to serve as a standard of estimation for what we propose as the model of excellence, wherever our judgment applies of wherever a choice is to be made.

If we are asked, therefore, what is the principle of moral approbation in the human mind, we may answer: It is the *idea* of *perfection* or excellence, which the intelligent and associated being forms to himself, and to which he refers in every sentiment of esteem or contempt, and in every expression of commendation or censure.

Nay, but mankind are not agreed on this subject; they differ no less in what they admire, than in what they enjoy. The idea of perfection no doubt may be associated with subjects divested of merit. But notwithstanding the effect of such association in warping the judgment, virtue is approved as the specific perfection or excellence of man's nature. And as no one ever inquired why perfection should be esteemed; it is difficult to conceive why they should look for any other account of moral approbation than this.

---

[6]   See Lord Kames' Moral Essays [*Essays on the Principles of Morality and Natural Religion*, 1751].

From the predilections of birth and fortune, few, if any, are altogether blind to the distinctions of wisdom and folly, of benevolence and malice, of sobriety and debauchery, of courage and cowardice. And if these characters of mind could be perceived without any intervention of external signs, the difference of judgment on the subjects of moral good and evil would, in a great measure disappear — or there would not be so much diversity of opinion as we observe amongst men, concerning the forms or description of virtue. But the external actions which may result from any given disposition of mind being different in different instances, may occasion a difference of judgment, or a variety of custom and manners, and suggest the necessity of a principle or standard estimation, on which their rate of merit or demerit may be sagely established. We accordingly proceed to the consideration of these particulars.

## Part II, Chapter III
## Of Jurisprudence of Compulsory Law

### Section I: Of the Principle of Compulsory Law

It is a well known fact that mankind sometimes employ force to obtain the observance of moral laws, and that the right to compel the performance of a duty, though not universal in every case, is, at least, in some instances fully acknowledged.

We are now to investigate and to state the principle from which this right in any case can be derived.

It may be observed, that in all the instances in which the right of one man to compel another is acknowledged, compulsion, either in its immediate operation, or in its final effect, is an act of defense.

The sovereign employs force to defend his country against foreign enemies, or to make reprisals for a wrong that is done to his subjects. The magistrate employs force to repress crimes, the citizen to defend his dwelling or his person. And even in exacting the payment of a debt, or in requiring the performance of a contract, there is no more than an exaction of what is justly due; or, as we shall have occasion to evince, no more than an act of defense on the part of the exactor, maintaining a right of which he is already in possession.

The great principle of morality extends to beneficence, as well as innocence; but from this account of the circumstances in which compulsion is applicable, the principle of compulsory law is limited to the repulsion of wrongs, and to that part in the object of the moral precept above cited, which forbids one person to be the author of harm to another.

In search of this or any other principle in nature, by whatever steps we proceed, we must arrive at last at something that is self-evident. And such we may say is the maxim, *that every innocent person may defend himself,* to which we may join what is equally evident, that *everyone having power, may employ it in defense of any other innocent person.*

To the purpose of defense a sufficient measure of *force* is required, and in many instances is the only means that can be successfully employed. A person disposed to commit an injury may not be persuaded to desist from his purpose, nor can he be eluded perhaps by any artifice or stratagem; it remains therefore that a *force* superior to his may be the only means sufficient to restrain him.

In every case of defense, force is employed to secure the innocent, rather than to obtain, from those who would injure him, the discharge of a duty. And the specific end of compulsory law being to reply a wrong, the means are adequate and just.

But if any one, instead of disputing the legality of *force* in a case of defense, should contend, that it is not peculiar merely to such cases, but may be employed, not only in defending a right, but in obtaining any other end beneficial to mankind, [and] that as religion and virtue are confessedly of the highest value, every effectual means, and force no less than any other, may be employed to obtain them, whether by propagating faith towards God or charity towards men.

These no doubt are blessings, in obtaining of which no effectual means are to be spared, but if we wish to promote the cause of religion and virtue, means are to be employed which inform the mind, conciliate the affections, and gain the will. To these purposes force is inadequate. Its effects, on the contrary, are to render the understanding less docile, and to alienate the mind. And it must be rejected as an instrument of instruction or moral improvement, because it would be irrational to employ means which have a tendency adverse to the purpose for which they are employed.

Nay, but force is competent to obtain, even from those against whom it is employed, the external fruits of faith and charity! To this it may be answered, that if these fruits be required as a moral good in those who are made to yield them, the reality of any such good may be questioned; or rather it is evident, that a forced performance of supposed good works does not constitute any good in him who is compelled to perform them. Virtue cannot be forced. It is voluntary, or it does not exist. Faith is sincere; or its profession is a mere hypocrisy.

If the fruit of good works be required in one man for the benefit of another, it is evident that force cannot be justly employed for this purpose. Benefits extorted by *force* are robberies, not acts of beneficence.

We may conclude, therefore, that the use of force, which is admissible in the case of defense, whether immediate or remote, is also limited to such cases; and that although men are bound, under every other sanction of duty, to avoid being authors of harm, yet, that they are, in this duty of abstaining from harm, peculiarly repressible by force also. And from this we may safely assume, that the *right of defense is the specific principle of compulsory law.*

In treating of this subject, accordingly, we are not so much to consider the obligation under which every person lies to be innocent, as to consider the right which every person has to defend himself, and his fellow creature, by every effectual means in his power.

This right amounts to a permission of whatever may be necessary to safety, but does not contain any positive injunction to do all that may be wanted for this purpose. A person attacked in his person may kill the aggressor, but is not required to do so much.

In the application of our principle, therefore, we endeavor to point out how far the right of defense extends, but do not, in any case whatever, pretend to lay the person who defends himself or his neighbor, under any tie of necessity to go to the utmost extent. The citizen, it is admitted, may kill the housebreaker who alarms his dwelling in the night, but is not required to proceed so far. Nay, on the supposition that he may defend himself and his dwelling, without having recourse to this extremity, he is by the law of nature actually restrained from it.

In conceiving a just and complete act of defense, we must suppose some thing that is to be defended or maintained, and specify the means that may be lawfully employed for this purpose.

That which a person may lawfully defend or maintain is termed his *right*. The circumstances under which a right is exposed or invaded may point out the means which are adequate and necessary to its preservation; and the subject of jurisprudence or compulsory law, so conceived, admits of being divided into two principal parts, of which one relates to the *rights* of men, the other to the *means of defense*.

### Section IV: Of the general Titles under which the Rights of Men may be classed

In a subject familiar and obvious to every person there is more danger that we overlook what is evident, than what may require investigation and research.

After having assumed as a self-evident maxim, that a person may defend himself, it appears unnecessary to subjoin, or it is rather a repetition of the same thing in other words, to say, that he may defend his person, the limbs and organs of his body, and exercise the faculties of his mind. Yet these, in pursuing our subject methodically, we shall have occasion to cite; and much depends on their being kept in view, when we would discuss certain questions relating to the origin as well as progress of justice in the affairs of men.

These are original appurtenances of human nature or inseparable from it, and the maxims of justice relating to these subjects must have been coeval with the subjects, and inseparable from human nature also.

There cannot therefore have been a time in which man had yet to acquire his right of defense in respect to the particulars mentioned, nor a time in which it was not just to respect the person of a man, as much or more than to respect his possession or his estate.

In this view of the matter, justice cannot be said to be an artificial virtue, any more than the person of a man to which it refers is artificial. And no time can be assigned for the commencement of a person's right to defend himself different from the time at which he began to exist. In every state of his existence, by whatever name we call it, whether the state of nature, the state of society or convention, as everyone had a right to defend himself, so in every one it would have been wrong to invade that right.

It is absurd therefore to allege, that in any state of mankind all men had equal rights to all things, or that the right of anyone to defend his own person took its rise from convention. It is indeed probable, that such a doctrine never would have been advanced, nor would justice in the most general and comprehensive terms have been supposed to be an artificial or adventitious virtue, if reasoners had not overlooked the self-evident rights of the person, and carried their view at once to matters of property in which the right is confessedly artificial or adventitious.

With respect to subjects of possession or property, it is admitted, that until they were possessed by some one, they were open to any one, and became matter of just possession to the first occupier.

To these only Mr. Hobbes seems to have adverted, when he says, that in the state of nature "all men had equal rights to all things", and the meaning must be, that no one had any right to any thing until he had occupied it. That occupancy was equally open to all men, but he ought to have subjoined, that after a subject was fairly possessed, no one had a right to disturb the first occupier in his use of the subject.

The undeniable evidence of obvious and uncontrived truths makes it absurd or impertinent to state them for information, or in the form of discovery; but to assume principles, or to adopt conclusions in direct contradiction to such obvious truths may indeed have the merit of novelty, or seem to proceed from profound observation, but is certainly in a much higher degree absurd than the repetition of any truth, however obvious and previously known.

To guard against the first of these errors we may be obliged to incur the second, and attempt the enumeration of rights even under titles to which the attention of all mankind might be taken for granted, without any mention of them.

On this account, then, we begin with observing, that the rights of men may be considered, either in respect to their subject, or in respect to their origin.

Considered in respect to their subject, they are by lawyers sometimes termed *personal* and *real*.[7]

Considered in respect to their origin, they may be termed *natural* and *artificial*, or, in terms perhaps less apt to be mistaken, *original* and *adventitious*.

---

[7]    See [William] Blackstone's *Commentaries on the Laws of England* [1765–9].

Personal rights subsist in the person, and relate to the constituents of his nature and frame. Such are the limbs and organs of the body, and the faculties of the mind, with the uses of both. Such is life itself, freedom of innocent action, and enjoyment of what, without injury to another, is fairly occupied.

*Persons* are distinguished in the terms of law under the names of persons *natural* and persons *artificial*. The individual is a person natural; corporations, states, or any plurality of men acting collectively, or under any common direction, are persons artificial.

In persons of the latter description, political forms, and the constituent members of the body politic, analogous to the frame and organic parts of the natural body, may be considered as matter of personal right to the community.

Rights *real* subsist in things separate from the person, provided they may become subjects of exclusive or incompatible use. Such is the right which a person obtains to the clothes with which he is covered, or to the ground or other subject which he has fairly possessed.

Real rights, or the right to things, may be referred to three principal heads: *Possession, Property,* and *Command.*

The right of *possession subsists* only so long as the thing is in actual use, and may therefore be transient or subject to intermission.

The right of *property* is exclusive, and continues even during the intermissions of actual use; it continues therefore until it has ceased with consent of the proprietor.

The right to *command* respects the services or the obedience supposed due from one person to another.

Rights considered in respect to their source, being *original* or *adventitious*, it is of moment with respect to the first to specify their subject, and with respect to the second, to ascertain the titles on which they are founded.

## Section V: Of Rights Original

The subjects of original right, being coeval with man, must be limited to the constituents of his nature, or the common appurtenances of his kind.

Original rights are therefore personal, and express what every one from his birth is entitled to defend in himself, and what no one has a right to invade in another.

These rights may be modified by alienation or consent; but, prior to convention of any sort, remain entire, and in one person exactly correspond to those of another.

The existence of every such right is self-evident: It may be overlooked from inadvertency or design, but once stated cannot be controverted.

Mr. Hobbes in laying the foundation of his system appears to have overlooked the original rights of the person. But if they had been stated to him, or if he had been asked, whether every person in his supposed state of nature had not a right to preserve himself? Or whether any person had a right to destroy his innocent neighbor? It is difficult to conceive, that a person, who acknowledges the obligation of one man to keep faith with another, should not acknowledge also his obligation to abstain from any harm to his person.

## Section VI: Of Rights Adventitious

In the term *adventitious* is implied a preceding period of existence, however short, in which the thing adventitious was yet future, a time in which it began to be, and a subsequent period of its continuance.

In the first period of man's existence, he had his original rights; in a second period those rights may be modified by his own consent, or new rights accrue to him from some act of his own, or the voluntary deed of some other person concerned.

Original rights are recognized upon being merely stated; adventitious rights require to be supported by evidence, in which the manner of their acquisition is to be cited and considered.

When a person lays claim to the exclusive use of any subject, or requires the service and obedience of other men, he may be asked, whence his right is derived? Or by what evidence he is enabled to support his claim? Such right, however fairly constituted, is still matter of discussion, and the object of science, in every such discussion, is to ascertain by what means a subject, not originally matter of right to anyone, may become so to someone; or, in other words, if a claim should be laid to any such, it is material to know by what evidence it may be evinced or supported.

As rights personal, agreeably to the definition which hath been given of them, for the most part are original, or coeval with the existence of the person, so the rights real, such as *possession, property*, or *command*, are, for the most part adventitious, and may begin to exist at any period subsequent to the existence of the person and the thing to which they relate; and, as both the person and the thing might have continued to exist, without any apprehended relation of one to the other, we are in the following sections to enquire whence such relation may have arisen; how they are constituted, and how they are to be verified in any particular instance.

## Section VII: Of the different Sources of Adventitious Rights

Before we proceed to affirm whence an adventitious right may arise, it is proper to observe negatively, that it cannot arise from any act of injustice or wrong, nor be constituted where the thing is impossible or not real.

Injustice or wrong has reference to a person injured or wronged, who may defend himself; and to a person committing an injury or doing a wrong, who, instead of reaping benefit from his wrong, exposes himself to suffer whatever may be necessary to repel his injurious attempt; or whatever may be necessary to obtain reparation of the harm he may have done.

This negative proposition were too obvious to need being formally stated, if it were not necessary to correct a common solecism in language, by which we are told of the *right of conquest*, arising from a successful application of mere force, without regard to the justice or injustice of the cause in which that force was employed.

Where conquest is matter of right, there must be supposed a previous title to the subject conquered; and, if such title be verified, the conquest amounts to no more than a just possession obtained by force.

To this negative proposition, that right cannot arise to an injurious person from the wrong he has committed, we may subjoin what is equally evident, that no title can arise to what is not possible or not real.

Where either the thing or the person has no existence, there cannot be any relation. Upon this ground, we shall have occasion to observe, that although parties stipulating what is impossible may, by such proceeding, give rise to some claim in the one against the other, yet that there cannot be any obligation to the performance of any such article, however directly stipulated.

In treating the history of adventitious rights, there are two questions which may be separately discussed. The first question relates to things which, prior to the origin of the right in question, had not become matter of right to anyone; and the object of science is to ascertain by what means a thing till then open to the first occupier, may have become a matter of exclusive right to some particular person. The second question relates to the transfer or conveyance from one person to another of a right previously supposed to exist in the person by whom the conveyance is made.

To the first of these question we may answer in general, that things belonging to *no one* may become matter of right to *someone*, either by mere occupancy, or in consequence of labor employed to improve or accommodate the subject to use. To the second question, we may answer, in like general terms, that a right may be conveyed from one person to another by *convention* or *forfeiture*.

We are, therefore, in the following sections, to define the titles of *occupancy, labor, convention,* and *forfeiture,* and to apply the law of acquisition, founded in these several titles, to the specific rights originating in the law or determinable according to this rule.

### Section VIII:
*Of Occupancy, and the Species of Right that may result from it*

Occupancy is the relation of a person to a thing, such that no other person can use the same thing without molestation or detriment to the occupier.

In this manner a person may occupy the unappropriated ground on which he reposes himself, the spring at which he drinks, or the cover to which he has betaken himself as a shelter from the storm. In any of these instances, an attempt to use the same thing may harm or molest the occupier. He may therefore defend himself against any such attempt; or in other words, he has an exclusive right to the subject in question, so long as he continues to occupy it, or retains his possession.

This right, however, does not extend to the prohibition of any act by which the occupier is not any way disturbed or aggrieved: So that the occupier cannot justly resist another using the same thing with himself, if this may be done without any detriment to him. Everyone may breathe the air of the atmosphere, enjoy the light and heat of the sun, pass on the highway, and navigate the high sea with mutual freedom from harm or molestation.

The right that results from occupancy is no more than that of possession, beginning and ceasing with the act of occupying the subject to the extent described. So that, as this right does not extend to the prohibition of any act by which the occupier is not aggrieved, it evidently does not preclude anyone from resting on the same ground after the first occupier has removed from it; nor preclude a second person from drinking of the same spring, after the first has ceased drinking; or from having recourse to the same cover, after it has been abandoned by a former occupier.

As the effect of occupancy, therefore, ceases with the actual use, it does not amount to *property*, or to any right supposed to continue during the intermission of such actual use.

No right in one person to command the services of another can arise from any title of occupancy, supposed to take place without the consent of the person whose services are required. To occupy the service of another without his consent implies the use of force to obtain such service. Force so employed amounts to an injury, and, instead of constituting a right, may be resisted on the most evident principles of the law of self-defense.

It is justly held to be a public interest, that fair possession in every instance should be as little precarious as possible, and upon this account mankind willingly enter into conventions, by which fair possession of a certain duration is admitted as property.

The duration of such possession in the laws of different countries is termed prescription, and was unequal in the jurisprudence of different nations, and in respect to the occupancy of different subjects. By the ancient law of the Romans, respecting some subjects, a fair possession of three years amounted to prescription. In our law and respecting the subject of land estate, forty years fair possession is required to the same effect.

It is a maxim in the law of nature self-evident and uncontroverted, that all subjects unoccupied and unappropriated are open to the first occupier. If, therefore, by the state of nature, it be meant to design a state in which nothing is yet occupied or appropriated—or if we hold the negation of any right to be an equality of right, as if we should say, that the dead are all equally alive, or that such as have nothing are all equally rich—the maxim of Mr. Hobbes may be admitted, so far as it relates to matters of adventitious right: *"That in the state of nature all men had equal right to all things."*

There could be no rule by which to settle any rights which did not exist, but, with respect to the existing rights of the person coeval with human nature, there certainly was an existing rule, *that no one was entitled to injure or molest his neighbor.* To this rule mankind have at all times resorted; and by this rule they have generally been governed, notwithstanding the occasional eruptions of force and violence. When they are at any time in a state of war, this proceeds not from the want of an amicable rule, by which to decide their differences, but from the influence of passion or error, which inclines someone or more of the parties to infringe the rule.

Mr. Hobbes seems to make the state of war to consist, not so much in actual hostility, as in the want of any rule by which differences could be amicably terminated, and in the necessary reference of parties to the decision of force alone. But it is evident that the state of war thus defined did never actually exist, and that in the midst of hostilities seemingly the most implacable nations refer to a standard of right, according to which they plead that the quarrel should be amicably terminated in their own favor.

Mankind, in every state, not only had original rights of the person, but could not continue to exist without proceeding to occupy and possess the means of subsistence and accommodation, and without being engaged in transactions which amounted to some species of conversion or bargain. So that the supposition of a state, prior even to the origin of adventitious rights, must have been of so short a duration as to resemble an abstraction of the mind, in which coexistent circumstances are separately conceived, rather than a period of history, during which they actually existed apart.

## Section IX: Of Labor, and the Species of Right that results from it

Labor, considered as the origin of a right, is an effort, by which a person may, for his own use, fabricate, procure, or improve any unoccupied and unappropriated subject.

It is evident that, by that law of nature, a person is not permitted to labor on a subject occupied, because his labor may be detriment to the occupier; nor is he permitted to labor on a subject appropriated without the consent of the proprietor.

Under this title of labor is supposed an effort productive of some permanent effect, some fruit of invention, of skill, or of power any way applied; and the laborer having, by the law of nature, an original right to the use of his talents or powers, has, by evident consequence, a right to the effects produced by any of their applications.

As the right of possession continues during the continuance of occupancy, so the right acquired by labor continues together with the subject produced, and belongs to the producer, until he himself, shall consent to forego, or transfer it to another.

The right, therefore, which is thus acquired, comes up to the idea of property. It is a right, in the laborer, to the exclusive use of his powers, and of their lawful effects, even during the intermissions of that use.

The right acquired by labor does not determine with possession: This may be discontinued during any period, and may be resumed again. If the subject be moveable, and during any time mislaid, it may be recovered wherever it is found; if in the possession of another, that other may be lawfully forced to restore it.

It may be argued, however, that as the right of property thus originating in labor is limited to the actual effect which that labor has produced, and, as it is not in the power of man to produce any substance, he cannot by his labor acquire a property in any such subject whatever. Human labor may combine materials together, or give to a substance some new modification or form; and so far the right of the laborer extends. But, as the substance itself is not an effect of his labor, whenever he shall cease to use it, the substance shall be open to the first occupier.

If any difficulty be supposed to arise from such subtleties of argumentation, it may be removed by observing, that, although the right of a laborer may extend only to the form, modification, or improvement, he has made, not to the subject or substance which exists independent of his labor, yet, if no one can occupy that subject or substance, without encroaching upon his right to the modification or improvement, it is evident, that, in defending his right to the modification, he may exclude every person from occupying the substance of which the form or improvement is his property.

The savage who has wrought a piece of wood into the form of a bow, in maintaining his right to the form, necessarily excludes every other person from the use of the wood. The husbandman, who, in breaking up uncultivated land, has acquired a right to the fruits of his culture, must, in order to preserve his right, exclude every other person from occupying the earth or stone of the soil to which his culture has been applied, although he has not in reality produced those substances.

The plea of right resulting from labor is limited to the right of property alone. When applied to any other species of right, whether a right of possession, or a right to command, it is either not necessary, or not adequate. It is not necessary to constitute a right of possession; nor is it adequate to establish the claim of one person to a right in the services of another.

Possession is valid, because the occupier must not be disturbed, although he may not have bestowed any labor on the subject in possession. Labor, therefore, is not necessary to establish this species of right.

As to the second, or the right to *command*, if it be asked, whether this may not result from labor? we must answer in the negative. For, although one person may have taken pains to qualify another for the performance of some specific service, yet we must contend, that no right to his service can be founded on this plea. Labor employed by one on the person of another without his own consent, may be an injury, and cannot be the foundation of a right. If applied with his consent, but without any stipulated conditions, the person to whom any new art is thus communicated, retains all his personal rights, and cannot justly be forced to work for another. "If you taught me an art, might such a person plead with his instructor, without having stipulated that I should employ it for you, it must be understood that I am free to employ it for myself." Gratitude may incline him to make some return to a benefactor, but the demand of a return may cancel that obligation; and, in answer to such a demand, the apprentice may plead: "If you taught me an art that I might employ it for yourself, you cannot plead a benefit intended to me, nor lay claim to my gratitude; or, if you intended a benefit to me, you must leave me to enjoy its fruits."

A person may innocently labor upon the property of another without knowing it to be already appropriated. He may give a new form; he may compose a mixture, of which the materials either entirely, or in part, belong to some other person. In all these instances, the decision of the law of nature is clear and peremptory, that no one is bound to suffer a diminution of his right from the act of another, however free from guile or sinister intention.

As the party, acting however without guile or malice, cannot be charged with injustice, the law of nature awards, that the right of any other party concerned should be preserved or restored, with the least possible detriment to the fair and innocent dealer. And this is wisely provided for, in the conventional law of every well-ordered community. But the rule that is adopted, in adjusting the relative claims of parties, on such occasions, may vary at the discretion of those on whom the practice of law depends. According to the law of the Romans, property thus brought into dispute, was sometimes made to follow the original subject, and sometimes the specification or form bestowed upon it. When the materials, as in the case of bullion wrought into plate, could be restored to their pristine form, the property was awarded to him to whom the bullion belonged. Where the specification, or new form, was of a certain value compared to the subject on which a work was performed, as in the case of a picture, compared to the canvas on which it is painted, or in the case of a writing compared to the paper or vellum on which it is executed, there the material, from favor to the art which was practiced upon it, was adjudged to be the property of the artist. Where subjects, belonging to two or more different persons, were unwarily mixed by either of them, and could not be again separated, it was awarded, that the mixture should be divided among the parties concerned, in proportion to the share of materials which each had in the composition or mixture; and the least inconvenient manner of terminating a dispute was, in this manner, intended, or provided for in these different instances.

Labor constitutes a right to property in the effect, which that labor has produced. Although there may have been labor, therefore, in any particular case, if there be no permanent effect, there is no subject of property. Mariners may have navigated the sea, they may have traversed new and unappropriated islands, but, if the land is no way changed by their labor, the earth, no more than the trackless ocean, can become a subject of property to the person by whom it is merely traversed.

It is nevertheless a custom of some standing, among the nations of Europe, to claim the dominion of newly discovered lands or islands, as founded in prior discovery, and confirmed alone by symbolical forms or acts of possession, such as the erecting of columns, with dates and inscriptions recording the claim of the sovereign, in whose behalf it is made.

So far as any number of nations have been in practice of claiming an acknowledging rights, founded in such forms as these, they must be understood to have entered into a fair convention respecting such subjects. A mere symbolical occupancy is valid against those who have repeatedly availed themselves of the same plea, and who are therefore come under an obligation to give way to it in their turn. It is a plea sufficient to exclude those who have agreed to be excluded by it, but not to exclude any stranger who is not a party to any convention in the case, whether express or tacit, much less a plea sufficient to deprive the native, however rude or barbarous, of the inheritance or possession to which he is born.

The right of the claimant, therefore, among the nations of Europe, upon the ground of discovery or symbolical possessions, is matter of convention merely among such nations, and cannot be derived, either from the principle of occupancy, or the principle of labor, at least, until the subject is actually occupied, or, from the labor bestowed upon it, has received some actual change or improvement.

Such are the ways in which a subject, the right of *no one*, may become the right of *someone*, either while he occupies it, or in consequence of the effect he has produced in it by his labor.

It remains that we consider by what means the right of one person may be transferred to another, as in convention or forfeiture.

# Manuscript Essay

## Of the Principle of Moral Estimation: A Discourse between David Hume, Robert Clerk, and Adam Smith[1]

When Mr. Hume was at London about to publish some volume of *The History of England*, General Clerk called in a morning and soon after Mr. Smith came in also.

Mr. Clerk & Mr. Hume had been talking of the *History* and Mr. Clerk, after some compliments on Mr. Hume's style and politeness in writing, said he was glad he had taken to history in which he could not avoid being instructive and agreeable too.

HUME. I certainly shall not endeavor to avoid either of these effects, but I hope you don't think I have endeavored to avoid them in any of my other writings.

CLERK. If you endeavored, you have not succeeded. You are very much in fashion, and I do not mean for your doctrines. For I think you rather try to pull down other people's doctrines than establish any of your own.

HUME. Pardon me, did I not set out with a complete theory of human nature, which was so ill received that I determined to refrain from system making?[2]

CLERK. That was rash. The world's a system and the best we can do is to assist one another in perceiving and communicating its parts and their connections.

HUME. I don't know what a man of letters is to get by that — to be writing what everybody knows or may hear from every coffee house acquaintance.

---

1    This text is based on the manuscript edited by E.C. Mossner, " 'Of the Principle of Moral Estimation: A Discourse between David Hume, Robert Clerk, and Adam Smith': an Unpublished Manuscript of Adam Ferguson", *Journal of the History of Ideas* 21 (1960): 222–32. Unless otherwise indicated by brackets, all footnotes are from Mossner's edition.

2    [Hume is referring to his great work, *A Treatise of Human Nature* (1739–40), a work that Hume described as falling "dead-born from the Press." "My Own Life", reprinted in Mossner, *The Life of David Hume*, Oxford: Oxford University Press, 1970), 611–15.]

CLERK. That would be very idle, but I do not think Mr. Hume is in danger of that even if he should discard all paradox and take to the investigation of useful truths.

HUME. I own I am inclined to skepticism and would avoid the pedantry of dogmatism. But have [I] not declared opinions on commerce, politics, and morals?

CLERK. I like some of your thoughts on the subject of commerce. But for morals and politics you seem [rather] to play with them than to be serious.

HUME. You surely think I am serious in my essays on morality?[3]

CLERK. I do not doubt it. But it sounds odd to say that morality is founded on utility and that virtue is only a cow that gives milk of a particular sort, alms to the poor, and every man's due to himself. It is very true that these actions are useful. The good man performs them because they are useful and neighbors applaud them for the same reason; but is there any thing more useful than a good cornfield? People say there is a plentiful crop, but no one says there is a virtuous field.

HUME. No, for a good reason: Moral virtue is peculiar to mind and is the utility or usefulness that proceeds from mind, that is, from a benevolent or good intention.

CLERK. Do we not esteem a good intention although from any circumstance it be prevented of external effect, and do we not withhold moral approbation from mere utility that comes without intention? In short, mind is approved without external effect and external effect is not approved without mind. And it is the mind we approve not the utility.

HUME. Pardon me, it is both when they come together. A man's pretensions to virtue are very doubtful if it have no effect in his manners or behavior.

CLERK. Very doubtful indeed. The elasticity of a bow is very doubtful or rather incredible if an arrow drawn to the point is not made to fly from the string. Where benevolence is real it will be beneficent. But we are not talking of the evidence required to evince the reality of benevolence. We are supposing benevolence to be real and know how agreeable it is apart from its external effects.

HUME. That I own: But to me virtue is a course of life directed, if you will, by good intentions but realized in all the effects of innocence, beneficence, sobriety, and candor.

CLERK. I understand, and because you conceive a virtuous [life] and its external effects together you choose to ascribe the approbation of it to the external effect alone. For my part, I am inclined to consider [it] rather in respect to its value in the mind that possesses it, than in its effects towards those who are within reach of its external influence. To every man, his own happiness is the first and most important concern, and nature cannot require of a man what is not of any value to himself.

3   [*An Enquiry concerning the Principles of Morals* (1751).]

HUME. Yet virtue for the most part is admired as a principle of self-denial.

CLERK. That proceeds from the stupid notion that man is to estimate himself as he estimates a dead ox, from his belly and four quarters, so that whatever he does without a view to that self is said to be self-denial, and in this point of view but happiness itself may be a system of self-denial. We set out with supposing we know what virtue is without considering whether it be happy or miserable. For my part, I choose to refrain [from] all terms of praise, till I know what it is to be happy and this to every intelligent being is the first and highest praise. If a person be a wretch, praise him who will. He had better be a clod or a block of wood than a man without the requisites of a happy mind. In this consists the excellence of mind that it may be happy and, if it fail of this, existence is an evil.

HUME. Happiness is surely very different from mind: for every man thinks himself happy in being gratified, some with a dinner, some with money, and all with respect and a good name.

CLERK. When I talk of happiness I do not go to the rabble in the street for an account of it. If there be in nature affections and habits agreeable, others disagreeable — as benevolence is agreeable, malice the reverse; courage agreeable, cowardice in all its forms the reverse — I call that man happy who is habitually courageous and benevolent, whose actions and thoughts are pleasant, whose very existence is the tranquility of a mind undisturbed with the consequences of error and mistake, or sense of meanness, degradation, or wrong. If virtue is a term of peace and felicity, then I fix it on goodness and wisdom, on fortitude, temperance, and the occupations of a strenuous mind.

It is well known that there is distinction of good and evil in human life, and till we have ascertained that distinction and made our choice, all our inquiries and pretensions to philosophy are nugatory and absurd.

Here the conversation was about to terminate when the servant announced Mr. Adam Smith, who at the same time entered the room with a smile on his countenance and muttering somewhat to himself. After the first salutations Mr. Hume said, Smith, the General and I have been upon a subject in you are well versed and I should have been glad of your assistance.

SMITH. What was it?

HUME. No less than *The Theory of Moral Sentiments*.

SMITH. My Book. I am sorry to have been away. I should willingly profit by your remarks. General, he said then, observing him for the first time, I have long wished to know your opinion. I think I have removed all the difficulties and made the theory complete.[4]

---

4    [The *Theory of Moral Sentiments* was first published in 1759, but it is likely that Smith is referring here to the sixth and last edition of 1790.]

To this the General made no answer though Mr. Smith made some pause as expecting to hear what he would say. But [he] continued, people thought I should never be able to get over the difficulty of supposing a man to sympathize with himself or if he did not chance to take that trouble what means he had of being admonished of his faults. I have removed both these difficulties and I should be glad to know your opinion.

CLERK. I don't much like to trouble authors with my opinion of their works.

SMITH. Ah, do, you will oblige me!

CLERK. If you insist upon it. I must be plain and leave no doubts.

SMITH. Surely. Surely.

CLERK. Your book is to me a heap of absolute nonsense.

Smith seemed to be stunned and Clerk went on, You endeavor to explain away the distinction of right and wrong by telling us that all the difference is the sympathy or want of sympathy, that is, the assent or dissent of some two or more persons of whom someone acts and some other observes the action and agrees or does not agree in the same feeling with the actor. If the observer agree, sympathize, go along with him, or feel that he would have done the same himself, he cannot but approve of the action. If, on the contrary, he does not sympathize or agree with the actor, he dissents and cannot but disapprove of him. And you seem to mean that where there is neither assent nor dissent there is neither right nor wrong, and no one would ever suppose any such thing. Or if you don't deny the reality of the distinction, you at least furnish but a very inadequate means of discovering it. How can I believe that a person is in the right because I sympathize with him? May not I myself be in the wrong? Does the presence of any sympathy ascertain a good action, or the want, of a bad one?

SMITH. No! I have cleared up that point. Parties concerned in any transaction may be willing each to flatter himself or both mutually to flatter one another, but to the monitor may not fail to present himself. The well-informed and impartial observer will bring to view what the ignorant or prejudiced would overlook.

CLERK. That is convenient, to be able to bring virtue itself to your aid when actual sympathy fails. You began with calling sympathy to explain moral sentiment. You now call up moral sentiment to explain itself: What is a well-informed and impartial observer, but a virtuous person whose sympathy may be relied on as a test of virtue? If he be well informed, of what is he informed? Not of astronomy or geography, for these would be of little use to him in distinguishing the characters of men. For this purpose he must be informed of the distinction of right, how [it is] constituted and applied in particular instances. And to be impartial [he] must aim at a fair application without [bias] to any side. Such a person is not likely to mislead those who confide in him, and such a person everyone is concerned to become in himself, and instead of acquiescing in sympathy as the test of virtue, appeals to virtue as the test of just sympathy.

Here then ends your system. After beating round a circle of objections and answers, you return to the point from which you set the phenomena of moral distinctions, moral sentiments, to be explained. And let us try once more [to consider] how far sympathy is adequate to this purpose. You do not fail to tell us that moral sentiments are real and, we trust, familiar to all men. You inform us that they constitute satisfaction in some cases and distress in others. This [is] of great importance and the consequence is that we should be careful to obtain the satisfaction and avoid the distress.

I do not see how we can be aided in this by merely resolving these sentiments into some other affection of the mind, especially into any affection differing from themselves. What is this sympathy which you talk of? The word is not new, but the meaning probably is so. It is commonly synonymous with pity or a fellow feeling for the distresses of others. But who ever heard of sympathizing with a person who pays his debts? Or if this were said, it would be supposed that we pitied him for being obliged to part with his money; but you tell us of sympathizing with a hero on having gained a battle although he escaped unhurt. The word sympathy in this sense is generally unknown and to explain moral sentiment by sympathy is to explain the known by the unknown, the very reverse of what is required in theory.

But if sympathy in all the affections or passions were as well known as it is in commiseration or pity to the distressed, I do not see how it could explain moral sentiment: For when it is best known it does [not] produce any moral sentiment, either of approbation or blame. When we pity a beggar we do not admire him for begging nor think that a person has any merit in the toothache, even if the thoughts of it should set our teeth on edge or draw tears from our eyes. If sympathy means participation of any passion without distinction, I do not see how a passion participated should be any other than some shade or degree of the passion participated. If I participate in a person's anger, I am angry too; if in his joy, I too am glad. But neither one nor the other is moral approbation.

SMITH. I do not say it is, but that a man who participates in the passion of another cannot but approve of it. Every passion or strong motive urging a person to act justifies itself, and if others go along with it or sympathize, they too approve. If they do not go along with it, they disapprove or condemn his conduct and so he does himself if, when the occasion is past, he cannot go along with the passion which actuated him.

CLERK. The whole amount then is that what others term conscience, you term sympathy or the want of sympathy. Everybody knows, that under the operation of any strong passion men are incapable of cool reflection. This you call justifying their passion; but when it [is] over and they come to reflect, a crime if committed stares them in the face and they become a prey to remorse or self-condemnation. I do not see that your account of the matter is any way more intelligible than this, or that we are any way nearer the ultimate in the one account than in the other. Most men repose on the fact that men are by nature endued with a principle of conscience. But you say the fact commonly called conscience is sympathy or the want of sympathy, and the supposed theory is a mere change of words or at best an attempt to confound two distinct principles of nature.

This practice is too common and, when substituted for theory, is insufferable. One great object of study certainly is to distinguish what is different, as well as to bring things of a kind together. In morals, especially, the judgment is badly confounded by substituting one thing for another. A fashionable philosopher has told us of late that judgments are but sensations, that integrity or elevation of mind is no more than pride; he owns indeed that it is enlightened pride, *orgueil éclairé*.[5] Others have told us that benevolence is mere self-love or tends alike to personal gratification whether in his own welfare or that of his neighbor.[6]

And in both these hopeful theories, we are cautioned not to be imposed upon by the specious appearances of magnanimity or benevolence, for the one is mere pride, the other mere selfishness. Thus to bespeak our animosity to a friend by announcing him under the name of our enemy. At the same time the gentleman undertakes great merit to himself for his penetration and knowledge of persons.

I confess I was afraid that your sympathy might have some such effects as this or that the difference of right and wrong might vanish into an assent or dissent of two or more persons who may agree in the wrong as well [as] in the right. But you relieve us at last by telling us you do not mean any assent or dissent at random but that of a well-informed and impartial observer, who we would say in common language is a virtuous man or competent judge. And the preference due to such a person is what no one doubts, though it is the phenomenon which you set out with a purpose to explain in your theory, and so have it at last as others do as a self-evident truth which needs no explanation.

I do not find that moralists of old ever went into this question. They observed that human life was happy or miserable and they were curious to know how one or the other was brought about, or in other words, what was the good on which men might rely for happiness or avoid as misery. This was certainly the first or most important question to be settled in human life, and it was certainly wise to go into it even if they should mistake the solution.

Let the solution, however, be what it may, if a chief good was acknowledged there could no longer be any doubt of the choice to be

---

5    Presumably David Hartley, *Observations on Man, his frame, his duty, and his expectations* (1749).
6    [Bernard Mandeville, *The Fable of the Bees, or Private Vices, Publick Benefits* (1714).]

made; or if it were found that conscience concurred with experience in recommending the same thing, could there be any question of the grounds on which conscience proceeded. I have sometimes been puzzled to guess how this question came to be started in modern times, or how it came to hold such a place in modern philosophy.

HUME. You may believe I do not doubt its importance as I have treated it myself. Yet I believe the introduction of it was in a great measure accidental. A performance which made some noise, *The Fable of the Bees*,[7] calling virtue the offspring of flattery begot upon pride and pretending that private vices were public benefits, gave a general alarm to the friends of morality. And some of them set about refuting this sophism. One contended that the distinction of virtue and vice was founded in the nature and fitness of things.[8] Another that it was founded in truth.[9] Another that it was founded in the natural principle of benevolence.[10] Another, in a specific sense, inspired [by] nature, and which to distinguish it from mere corporeal sensation was called the moral sense.[11]

They were all perhaps in the right, and the author of *The Fable of the Bees* betrayed himself when he maintained that private vice was public benefit: for as virtue consists in public utility or good, how can that which is a public good be a vice? Moral sense is a mere figurative expression taken from the analogy of our corporeal organs in distinguishing their respective objects, but it appears trifling to me to be inquiring for reasons to approve what is so useful as all the virtues of men are in society or human life, and I hoped to silence the question forever by pointing out this very real and important ground of approbation or preference in behalf of virtue.[12]

CLERK. Well done, but while you considered what virtue was in its communications and external effects, which are the objects of law and in part the recommendation of good manners, you forgot or overlooked what is the real recommendation of it to the person who is to embrace it in his own mind without whose will it is not to exist. If it be happiness to him, as wisdom, goodness, fortitude, and temperance certainly are, it is

---

7   [Mandeville's work was first published as a poem, 1705, under the title, "The Grumbling Hive: or, Knaves Turned Honest." With the addition of Mandeville's prose commentary, it was reissued, in 1714, as *The Fable of the Bees*. Subsequent editions, in particular that of 1723, brought forth controversy and denunciation.]

8   Presumably William Law, *Remarks upon a late Book, entitled The Fable of the Bees* (1724).

9   Presumably George Berkeley, *Alciphron: or, The Minute Philosopher* (1732), second dialogue.

10  Presumably Joseph Butler, *Fifteen Sermons Preached at the Rolls Chapel* (1726)…[In his first sermon, he states, "There is a natural principle of *benevolence* in man."]

11  Presumably Francis Hutcheson, *An Inquiry in the Original of our Ideas of Beauty and Virtue* (1725); *An Essay on the Nature and Conduct of the Passions and Affections. With Illustrations on the Moral Sense* (1728).

12  [In his essay, "Of Refinement in the Arts" (1752) Hume offers a response to Mandeville. See Hume's *Essays Moral, Political, and Literary*].

certainly a thing good in itself, not a thing recommended merely by its utility in procuring something else. We are apt to laugh now at the old distinctions, divisions, and definitions of the schools, but it were well sometimes to mind them. Some things are coveted as means to an end, others as ends valuable in themselves. And if these were not sometimes such an end, the whole fabric of successive means would fall to the ground. Hence the important and genuine question of moral philosophy [is] *de finibus*, or what is the end? And I believe that the utility which you point out are not ends but means concurring to the preservation of society, and thus as means to furnish the wise with the proper scene and object of his enjoyment, in the condition of his happy mind whom no false allurements can mislead or dangers deter.

# *Bibliography*

## Source of this Edition

*An Essay on the History of Civil Society*, Duncan Forbes, ed. (Edinburgh: Edinburgh University Press, 1966). Forbes' edition, like that of Oz-Salzberger and Schneider, is based on the first (1767) edition.

*Institutes of Moral Philosophy: For the use of Students in the College of Edinburgh*, reprint of edition of 1769 (London: Routledge/Thoemmes Press, 1994).

*The History and Progress of the Roman Republic* (New York: J.C. Derby, 1856), as reprinted by The Scholarly Publishing Office, University of Michigan.

*Principles of Moral and Political Science*, reprint of edition of 1792 (New York: AMS Press, 1973). For this text, each word count assumes 300 words per page.

E.C. Mossner, "'Of the Principle of Moral Estimation: A Discourse between David Hume, Robert Clerk, and Adam Smith': an Unpublished MS by Adam Ferguson," *Journal of the History of Ideas* 21 (1960): 222–32.

## Primary Sources

With the exception of the *Essay on the History of Civil Society*, many of the Ferguson texts are not easily located. There are three versions of the *Essay*, that of Duncan Forbes (Edinburgh: University of Edinburgh, 1966), Louis Schneider (New Brunswick, N.J.: Transaction Publishers, 1980), and, most recently, Fania Oz-Salzberger (Cambridge: Cambridge University, 1995).

*Institutes of Moral Philosophy for the use of Students in the College of Edinburgh*. London: Routledge/Thoemmes Press, 1994. Another edition was published by Garland Press, New York, 1978.

*The History of the Progress and Termination of the Roman Republic*. Ann Arbor, Michigan: Scholarly Publishing Office, University of Michigan, n.d..

*Principles of Moral and Political Science*, introduction by Jean Hecht. Hildesheim: Georg Olms Verlag, 1995. Another edition, with a preface by Lawrence Castiglione, was published by AMS Press, New York, 1973.

*The Manuscripts of Adam Ferguson*, ed. Vincenzo Merolle. London: Pickering & Chatto, 2006 (along with the manuscript essays of Ferguson, this volume includes introductory essays by Merolle, "Ferguson's Political Philosophy", Eugene Heath, "Ferguson's Moral Philosophy", and Robin Dix, "Ferguson's Aesthetics"). The manuscript essays may also be found in Yasuo Amoh, ed., *Adam Ferguson: Collection of Essays*. Kyoto: Rinsen Book, 1996.

*The Correspondence of Adam Ferguson*, ed. Vincenzo Merolle, with a biographical introduction by Jane Fagg. 2 vols. London: Pickering & Chatto, 1995.

## Secondary Sources in English

The best biography is that of Jane Fagg, "Biographical Introduction", in Vincenzo Merolle, ed., *The Correspondence of Adam Ferguson, vol. 1, 1745–1780* (London: Pickering & Chatto, 1995), xx–cxxxvi. A biographical chapter is also available in David Kettler's book, listed below.

*Relevant scholarly studies include:*

Allan, David. *Adam Ferguson*. Aberdeen: Centre for Irish and Scottish Studies, University of Aberdeen, 2006.

Berry, Christopher J. *Social Theory of the Scottish Enlightenment*. Edinburgh: Edinburgh University, 1997.

Bryson, Gladys. *Man and Society: the Scottish Enquiry of the Eighteenth Century*. Princeton: Princeton University Press, 1945. (A reprint is published by Augustus M. Kelley, New York, 1968.)

Hamowy, Ronald. "Progress and Commerce in Anglo-American Thought: The Social Philosophy of Adam Ferguson", *Interpretation: A Journal of Political Philosophy* 14 (January 1986), 61–87. (This essay is also available in Hamowy, *The Political Sociology of Freedom: Adam Ferguson and F. A. Hayek*. Cheltenham, U.K.: Edward Elgar, 2005).

Hamowy, Ronald. *The Scottish Enlightenment and the Theory of Spontaneous Order*. Carbondale, Illinois: Southern Illinois University, 1987.

Heath, Eugene and Vincenzo Merolle, eds. *Adam Ferguson: History, Human Nature and Progress*. London: Pickering & Chatto, 2007.

Heath, Eugene and Vincenzo Merolle, eds. *Adam Ferguson: Philosophy, Politics and Society*. London: Pickering & Chatto, 2008.

Hill, Lisa. *The Passionate Society: The Social, Political and Moral Thought of Adam Ferguson*. Dordrecht: Springer, 2006.

Kettler, David. *The Social and Political Thought of Adam Ferguson*. Columbus: Ohio State University, 1965. (Republished as *Adam Ferguson: His Social and Political Thought*. New Brunswick: Transaction, 2005.)

Lehmann, William C. *Adam Ferguson and the Beginnings of Modern Sociology* New York: Columbia University, 1960.

Sher, Richard. *Church and University in the Scottish Enlightenment: The Moderate Literati of Edinburgh*. Princeton: Princeton University, 1985.

## Secondary Sources in Languages other than English

Amoh, Yasuo. *Ferguson and the Scottish Enlightenment*. Tokyo: Keiso, 1993 [Japanese].

Geuna, Marco. "Aspetti della critica di Adam Ferguson al contrattualismo", in M. Geuna and M. L. Pesante, eds., *Passioni, Interessi, Convenzioni. Discussioni Settecentesche su Virtù e Civiltà*. Milan: Franco Angeli, 1992, pp. 129–80.

Jogland, Herta Helena. *Ursprünge und Grundlagen der Soziologie bei Adam Ferguson*. Berlin: Duncker & Humboldt, 1959.

Merolle, Vincenzo. *Saggio su Ferguson, con un Saggio su Millar*. Rome: Gangemi, 1994.

Salvucci, Pasquale. *Adam Ferguson: Sociologia e Filosofia Politica*. Urbino: Argalía, 1972.

Wences Simon, María Isabel. *Sociedad civil y virtud cívica en Adam Ferguson*. Madrid: Centro de Estudios Políticos y Constitucionales, 2006.

# Index